Blackie's Diary

Also by Jerome Tonneson

Buttercup:
The Legendary Charm and Love
of a Domestic Short-Haired Tabby Cat

Blackie's Diary

The Daily Life of a
Former Rescue Cat

Jerome Tonneson

LBB

**BLB
PRESS**

Lenexa, Kansas

Published by BLB Press
blb-press.com

Photo credits:
Pages 1 and 3: J and L Schultz; Pages 44, 45, 47, and 48: Ron Tonneson; Pages 185, 186 and 187: Deanna Wenstrup; Pages 219 and 220: Natalie Patton. All other photos provided by the author.

The portrait on the cover and the drawing on page 5 were provided by Devin Araujo.

Paperback ISBN: 978-0-9891242-2-5

Library of Congress Control Number: 2020909971
Library of Congress subject headings:
Cats—Biography
Cats—Anecdotes
Human-animal relationships

1.0

To Buttercup, Lily, and Bubba,

*if even half the stories I've heard about you are true,
you were amazing cats.*

Foreword

Blackie and I first met at Purrfect Pets Cat Adoptions, a non-profit, no-kill, all-volunteer, all-feline animal rescue and adoption agency where I have volunteered for several years. She was a favorite among the volunteers. Everyone wanted to be the one to clean Blackie's living quarters. When she was in a small multi-level condo she would leap out into your arms or lap when you opened the door. Later, when she had a walk-in room, she would ask you to sit on the floor so she could use your lap. Whenever someone took care of Blackie's area, a little extra time was always set aside so she could enjoy a human's lap.

The odds were stacked against Blackie finding a home. People looking to adopt a cat are often interested in a colorful, playful kitten. At five years old, Blackie was already an adult. As her name suggested, she was also all black except for 13 individual white hairs (I counted them) on her chest. Of all the color markings, cats that are all black take the longest to find homes. This may be due to superstition, or it may just be that people prefer the various colors and patterns of tabbies, tortoiseshells, calicoes, and tuxedo kitties. That's a shame because a black cat typically has a very friendly personality and loving temperament. Blackie was no exception.

Blackie also had some medical conditions. She'd had surgery due to a bladder obstruction and was on a special (and not cheap) prescription food to help prevent a recurrence of bladder stones. To help cut down on stress and reduce the chances of a recurrence, she needed to be the only cat and in a quiet house.

The thought had crossed my mind to adopt Blackie, but the timing wasn't right. Living with me at the time was Lily, a senior cat who had her own medical issues. She had been diabetic for many years, and along with arthritis, had recently developed high blood pressure. She was also pretty demanding of food and attention. Being a tortoiseshell, she was quite vocal, especially around mealtime. Bringing another cat into the house wouldn't have been fair to either of them. Lily was over 17 years old—the oldest of any cat who had ever lived with me. With her advanced age and growing list of medical conditions, I knew she wouldn't be around much longer. In her final months, I spent as much time as I could with her.

Lily passed away in the autumn of 2018. Later that week, I inquired about Blackie's status. She had recently returned from "vacation" (a month at a foster home). Unfortunately, when she came back to the adoption center the only space available was a two-level floor-standing condo, one of the shelter's smaller accommodations. I was a bit torn. On one paw, it was too soon since I was still recovering from the loss of Lily, but on the other paw, the shelter was very full, plus Blackie had had a bit of a rough time. She had being adopted and returned twice, gone through surgery, recovered from surgery, and then forced to live in a tiny space.

She was such a sweet girl, though. By the end of the week, she was living with me.

Upon moving into my house, Blackie began a diary documenting life in her new home. The following pages contain 365 daily entries in her own words. As the year wrapped up and I helped her format her journal, I realized I had never told her my name. Apparently, no one at the shelter did either, or maybe someone had and she just didn't pay attention because throughout her journal she just referred to me as her human.

Jerome Tonneson, Blackie's human

Introduction

As far back as I could remember, I had lived at a shelter with a bunch of other cats. At first, I didn't have my own space. I had to share a condo with my sister. She picked on me a lot. I'm not sure why because I never did anything to her. Maybe it was because I was so small? I couldn't help it; I was sick, although at the time no one but me knew that.

It was a happy day when I thought my sister and I found our forever home. We were there for a few years, but things didn't work out. We found ourselves back at the shelter. Even worse, my sister continued to pick on me. Why did she have to be so mean? Our condo had multiple levels so I could at least attempt to stay away from her. When space opened up, my sister moved to a different kitty condo. That eliminated one stress from my life.

Then one day another human put an application in for me. I went home with him a few days later. I still wasn't feeling well. The human who adopted me took me to a doctor. The doctor decided to take some X-rays of me and found something bad. The human was irate and sent me back to the shelter. It turned out the reason I wasn't feeling well was due to some stones that had developed in my bladder. I needed surgery, and surgery wasn't cheap.

The nice humans at the shelter were able to arrange for my surgery. It went well. After the surgery, I went to live with one of them for a few months. I enjoyed being away from the shelter while I recovered. Soon, though, I was back at the shelter once again, looking for an appropriate human. Everyone there seemed to like me, and I liked all of them. By that time, I was fortunate to have an enclosure that was big enough for humans to enter. Any time someone came into my living space I would shower them with affection. I'd hop onto their lap and purr loudly. The humans seemed to enjoy their time with me. I certainly enjoyed being with them.

At one point the shelter became very crowded, mostly with a bunch of youngsters. Kittens. Lots of them. I went on vacation to a foster home for about a month. It was a nice break. When I returned to the shelter, I discovered a bunch of buff tabby kittens had taken over the space that had previously been mine. I had to settle for a small two-story condo, just like the one I originally had. It was okay, but I much preferred the larger space.

I didn't know it at the time, but I wouldn't have to live in that small space very long. Just a few weeks later, I went to live with one of the volunteers. I was told this new place was my "fur-ever" home— that this entire house was now my territory, and I wouldn't have to move around anymore or be confined to small quarters. As I began this new phase of my life, I decided to record my thoughts and activities in this journal.

Blackie's Diary

Day 1, Friday, October 26, 2018:
Wow, what a busy day it was. The shelter has been unusually full lately, and the place was practically crawling with adolescent kittens. A nasty, highly contagious upper respiratory illness has been making the rounds, and the group of six kittens next to me just came down with it. To top it off, I made a trip across the street to a cat doctor's office to get up to date on my FVRCP[1] and rabies vaccinations. Once back at shelter, I received additional preventative shots for fleas and various parasites. I didn't get any canned food this evening, even though everyone else did. I was told it was because I would soon be making another trip, this time to my "fur-ever" home.

Elaine removed me from my condo and placed me on the lap of one of the volunteers. I like sitting on laps, but something was different about this. I was a bit nervous. The volunteer put his arms around me to secure me. Elaine took a photo of us while some other volunteers stood around and watched. Everyone seemed happy. They said that I now have my very own human. After the photo session, I was placed in a travel pod that I hadn't seen before. It was much bigger than the one I had used to go to the doctor earlier in the day. I really liked the extra headroom. I still hunkered down, though, not knowing what was in store for me.

We left the shelter and entered the cool autumn night. We got into a car and went for a drive. The drive wasn't very long, but it wasn't nearly as short as the trip to the doctor's office earlier that day. When we arrived at our destination, we went into a house and down some steps. The volunteer set the travel pod down on the floor and opened the door. I looked out and saw that I was in a room that was much bigger than I was used to. I noticed a litter pan was prepared for

---

[1]Feline Viral Rhinotracheitis, Calicivirus, and Panleukopenia.

me. I cautiously stepped out of the travel pod. The floor was soft and mostly empty. There were tall things at the edges piled with various items. My new human left the room for a few minutes, mumbling something about unloading the car on his way out. I spied a small bench almost hidden behind a curtain and decided to duck under it while I assessed the situation.

A while later, my human brought a shiny set of bowls containing food and water and also provided a plate of my wet food. I eat a special food because a while back I developed bladder stones that made it difficult and painful for me to use a litter box. I've had surgery and have been doing well since then, but I stay on this special food to help prevent the stones from recurring.

My human seems nice. He gave me some pleasant neck rubs before leaving the room and going up the stairs we came down earlier. Since he volunteers at the shelter, I've known him for a while. We've even socialized together on several occasions, but since I was still getting used to this new environment, I decided to just hang out under the bench for a while. I must say, it's a lot quieter here than it was at the shelter with all those kittens.

After a few hours, I decided to take a brief unescorted tour of my new territory. There are three levels in this house. The first room I was in was the lowest. I found my human in a room at the highest part of the house. Despite enjoying his lap several times at the shelter, there was no time for that today; I had too much left to explore.

I'm really light on my paws, making it easy for me to sneak around this place. I was even able to sneak past my new human this evening. He left the room looking for me and even went all the way down to the first room I was in—twice—apparently looking for me. It took him several minutes to find me sitting behind a box right next to the chair where he had been sitting. My black fur helps me hide in the shadows. I think the only thing that gives me away are my bright-golden eyes.

Day 2, Saturday, October 27, 2018:
On the middle floor of this house, I found a place to hide. It's an enclosed, carpet-covered cubbyhole with walls that have multiple diamond-shaped windows. The enclosure provides protection, while the windows let me observe many parts of the house. It's also several feet up from the floor, providing even more protection.

I was hiding in this enclosure soon after sunrise today when I heard my human moving around. I watched from the shadows as he cleaned and filled my water and food dishes. He had moved them from the soft floor in that lower room to a slick floor on this level. I guess I wasn't hiding very well because he soon noticed me.

I did some more exploring of my new territory, but only when my human wasn't in the room. When I saw him, I retreated to my cozy cave. I also spent some time on top of the cave.

The perch above the cave gave me a great view of the house.

I stayed on guard because I sensed there was another cat in this house, or at least one had been here recently. The last time I lived with a cat she was mean to me, so I try to avoid other cats.

Just before sundown, my human was kind enough to prepare a plate of wet food for me. He presented the plate to me near one of the diamond-shaped windows but wouldn't let me eat it there. Rather, he placed it on the floor and went deeper into the kitchen to prepare his own food. Since he was preoccupied, I figured it was safe to climb down and have my meal.

A bit later, he walked by me. I was still a bit cautious, but I didn't run. I kept an eye on him since I was still trying to figure out the situation, but this house seems like a safe place for me.

Later this evening, I found him in the big room on the highest level of the house. He seems to spend a lot of time there. I'll call this the *upper room*, even though there are some other smaller rooms on this level.

I jumped onto his lap several times this evening. Each time I didn't stay very long, but I enjoyed stretching out on his warm legs and received plenty of neck scratches and back rubs. I even let him hold my paw briefly.

In this room there is a strange carpet-covered structure with multiple tiny flat areas. It reminds me of the stairs that I used to go between the different levels of the house, but it's much smaller and only contains three levels. It's set up next to a table. I wondered if it was safe to walk on it, but I didn't attempt to do that.

Day 3, Sunday, October 28, 2018:
My human left the house for several hours today to go help at the shelter. He was there for quite a while since there are a lot of cats living there right now.

While he was away, I explored more of my new home. In the upper room, there are some tables and a desk. Next to the desk is a tall metal box with drawers. I jumped onto the desk and investigated everything on it. Then I got on top of the metal box. On the other side of the box was a small, funny-looking shelf.[2] I tried stepping on it, but it wasn't secure. It slid partway down but somehow managed to stay stuck to the box. Hmm . . . I left a paw print in the dust of this shelf thingy. Oh well. He'll won't know who did it.

My human apparently went hunting on his way home, or whatever humans do to acquire sustenance, because he arrived with several bags of food. I watched him take the bags to the kitchen and empty them.

He took a nap on the sofa this afternoon while I went to the upper room. Later, he decided to also go to the upper room, so of course I went elsewhere. But just before dinnertime, I decided to go visit him and ended up taking a nap on his lap for nearly an hour. I also discovered a second chair nearby that has a soft blanket on it that seems like a perfect place for me to nap. I'll have to remember that.

Day 4, Monday, October 29, 2018:
My human was gone for most of the day today. He said he had to go

---

[2] A cable holder magnetically attached to the side of the file cabinet.

to work. This gave me plenty of time to further explore my new home. He'll never know all the places I've found.

He arrived home just before mealtime. He gave me some tasty wet food and then prepared his own meal. He took his food to the upper room and ate while sitting in his chair. Well, he *attempted* to eat. By the time he was ready to eat, I was already finished and decided it was lap time. He made some comment about it being hard to eat with such a wiggly kitty on his lap. Once he finished eating, I decided to stretch out and take a nap on his legs. After an hour and a half, he appeared to be in pain, but human discomfort is of no concern to a contented cat.

A while later, he moved the chair with the blanket closer, so I decided to rest there for a few minutes. We had an interesting conversation as he attempted to speak my language. He doesn't know what he's talking about.

Day 5, Tuesday, October 30, 2018:
I spent part of the night in the room adjacent to my human's bedroom. I'm not sure if it's all right to share a bed with him. I've seen him at the shelter, but I don't really know him all that well yet, and I'm just not sure if it's safe.

This morning I followed him to the kitchen and socialized with him while he cleaned my food and water dishes. I even rubbed the side of my body against his legs.

Today I enjoyed the perch in the living room some more. It is tall like a tree and has many levels that are covered in various shades of soft carpet. It provides many places to sit or lie down. From there, I can observe both this room and the kitchen. It almost seems like this was designed just for someone of my size since there's no way my human could fit in any of these spots.

I also discovered a big carpeted bench in the front room by the big window. It seemed like a good place to relax and look out the window, but I didn't have time for that tonight because I was too busy keeping an eye on my human.

This evening my human went back to the shelter to help with some projects. When he returned, he presented me with a gift: a new scratching post. He put it in the upper room. After several minutes on his lap, I decided to hop down and test the new post. It worked! It's tall, but almost not tall enough for my long body.

Day 6, Wednesday, October 31, 2018:
I think those kittens who were at the shelter just before I came here were kind enough to share their cold with me. I was sneezing on and off all evening. Fortunately, it didn't bother me too much.

My human has put all sorts of cat toys on the floor of both the front room and the upper room. I really enjoy batting the mice around and chasing them all over the house.

Tonight, he also opened the door to a small room he called a closet. When he was done in there, he was kind enough to leave the door open and leave the room so I could explore it on my own.

Day 7, Thursday, November 1, 2018:
Today started out really well. My human went off to work, so I spent the day napping and chasing toys around the house. The stuffed mice are my favorite, but I also discovered a bright-orange plastic ring about the size of my paw that is fun to fling around.

I was in the upper room when my human arrived home. It was just before dinnertime so I thought I was going to get a meal, but instead he brought my travel pod into the room. I tried to get away, but he closed the door. I was trapped! He seemed pretty calm and spent some time with me. I even purred for a bit. He pretended to go about his business, but I knew he was faking it, just waiting for me to let my guard down. I stayed under the table, where it was hard for him to reach me. After a few minutes, he picked me up and, despite my complaints, put me in the travel pod. I've been through this enough recently. I wasn't interested in any more traveling.

This trip was shorter than the last one. I arrived at a place where other cats and humans were coming and going. We spent a few minutes in a big room near the door before going down a hallway to a small room. Once in the small room, the door to my travel pod was opened. A young lady picked me up and placed me on a towel that was draped across a platform. She made me stay on the towel for a few seconds but then let me jump down from it. She spoke with my human a bit while I roamed around the small room. She left the room but returned a few minutes later with another lady. This one was wearing a white lab coat. Uh-oh. A doctor. I've gone through this before. She had nice things to say about me. She was also very gentle and polite. Well, at least until she decided to take my temperature. That was rather rude. I kept my composure and took it all like the lady that I am. I didn't give them the satisfaction of complaining.

Soon I was back in my travel pod, and we returned to the big room. Before we left the doctor's office, several more humans came by to greet me. It was nice to be the center of attention. They even gave me a present: a brand-new toy mouse!

Day 8, Friday, November 2, 2018:
Last night, I saw my human off to bed. I sat with him for a while but then left the room to sleep elsewhere. In the morning, I decided to go wake him up. I meowed from the side of the bed, but apparently he was in deep sleep because he didn't hear me. Surely he wouldn't have just ignored me, right?

Today, I got to explore a new part of the house. It was another room in the basement. I saw the door when I first arrived and have been wondering what was on the other side. The floor in there is hard and cold, unlike the floors in the rest of the house.[3] I shall call this the *cold floor room*. There are a lot of places someone my size could hide in there. Maybe that's why the door is always closed? I think the only reason the door was open tonight was because my human was in there. At one end of the room there are two large, squarish, white metal boxes. He tilted one of them up against the wall and reached underneath it with his paws. It looked like he was removing parts from it and then putting them back on. Humans are weird. I kept an eye on him as I explored the various nooks and crannies of this room.

Tonight I also discovered a water bowl just for me set out on the sink in the upper room. I wonder how long it has been there? Even better, there is a set of small steps up to the counter, which makes it very easy to get to the water.

Day 9, Saturday, November 3, 2018:
I saw my human off to bed again last night. I stayed a bit longer this time. I really wanted to be close to his paws, but he kept pulling them under the blankets. I didn't bother to try to wake him up this morning, even though he slept in longer than most days.

I played around the house and did more exploring since my human was gone most of the day. I tried stepping on that small shelf again, but like last time it started to slide down the side of the metal box. I don't get it—shouldn't a shelf be secure enough to walk on?

This evening I was able to get plenty of lap time. I also got to go into that big room in the basement again. My human was down there,

---

[3] An unfinished utility room and workshop.

too, again working with those white boxes. This time, though, he was placing his clothing in them. When he left the room, he was nice enough to leave the door open for me so I could look around a bit longer.

Later in the night, I was in the upper room enjoying more lap time with my human. The radio was on, and then something strange happened. I couldn't believe it, but they said my name on the radio! Now that I think about it, that voice sounded familiar.[4]

Day 10, Sunday, November 4, 2018:
My human and I cuddled on the sofa today. At first, I sat on his lap. Then I sat next to him. I got down briefly, but when I came back, he was entirely on the sofa under a blanket so I decided to lie down next to him. I leaned toward the edge a bit, but he put one of his paws out to keep me from falling off.

On the other side of the room is a short cat tree with a carpeted tube. This afternoon, I decided to check it out. I had to jump to get into it, but that was easy for me. It's really cozy for someone of my size. While I was in the tube, I kept an eye on my human over on the sofa.

Day 11, Monday, November 5, 2018:
This morning I discovered my human forgot to scoop my litter pan before he went to work. It was a bit unpleasant, but I managed to deal with it. Hopefully he'll do a better job in the future.

He provided me with a plate of nice wet food while he prepared his own meal. It always takes longer for him to make his meal than it does for him to make mine. In fact, mine is usually gone before he even starts to eat his. He decided to eat his food in the upper room, but I figured he needed a wiggly cat on his lap. It's fun to watch him try to eat while I rub my head all over his chest and lap and push my tail into his face.

Later this evening, he spent some time in that room in the basement with the cold, hard floor. He was doing things with wood and tools. I did my best to keep an eye on him, but I made sure to run away anytime he moved something big. I'm still not sure I trust him, at least when he's not sitting.

---

[4]The program was "Mind the Gap," which was aired on a community radio station and produced by J Zed, who provides shout-outs to her listeners in addition to being a volunteer at the shelter where Blackie once lived.

Day 12, Tuesday, November 6, 2018:
Once again, I saw my human off to bed last night. I even lay down next to him for more than an hour. Before he awoke in the morning, I jumped back onto his bed and rested at one of the corners until he decided to get up.

When he returned from work, he provided my evening meal, but he didn't prepare his own food. Instead, he went into the usually closed off room in the basement. For a couple of hours, a bunch of loud noises came from that room. I wanted to go in there and make sure he was safe, but the door was closed. Eventually, the loud sounds ceased, and he emerged from the room covered in some kind of dust.

It seemed whatever was going on in that room was over, so he changed into clothing that wasn't covered in dust. I really wanted him to sit down because I hadn't had any lap time yet today, but he was busy preparing his meal. I kept telling him it was lap time, and he kept telling me to be patient. He finally sat down to eat, which was my sign that I could jump onto his lap and spend the next 15 minutes getting comfortable. It sure takes him a long time to finish a meal.

Once he was done eating, I stood up on his lap. He grabbed me and held me in his arms like a human baby. I decided to humor him and didn't complain about this, but I turned my head and refused to look him in the eyes.

Day 13, Wednesday, November 7, 2018:
I'm getting more comfortable around my human. Last night, I spent the whole night with him. Well, most of the night. I got up about an hour before sunrise to do cat stuff. Once he was up, I followed him to the kitchen and supervised as he cleaned and filled my dishes.

In the kitchen, there is a tall but narrow door that is normally closed. My human opened it this morning. Behind that door is a tiny room with many shelves. On the floor under the shelves is a cardboard box. I hopped into that box because, well, it's a cat thing.

This evening, my human opened another door in the kitchen. It was a small door to the left of the sink. There was a single shelf behind that door, along with some small boxes. There was enough room, though, that I was able to get my whole body into it and even turn around.

I didn't get as much lap time as I would have liked tonight because my human was busy. He wasn't in the basement making loud noises this time, but rather in the room I first saw when I arrived here —the one where the car is kept. At least he was quiet this time.

Day 14, Thursday, November 8, 2018:
There's a short bench in the basement that I hid under when I first moved in here. Today, I decided to sit on top of it. It is in front of a large glass door. The bench is covered in carpet and is very soft and comfortable. It's a perfect place for me to sit and look out the window. My human calls it "cat television." On today's program, there was a bunch of white stuff slowly falling from the sky. The only problem with sitting here watching this is that it's a bit cold.

This evening, I talked to my human as he was preparing his meal. I convinced him to play with me for a bit. We batted some balls and mice around the front room.

I made sure to get plenty of lap time with my human today. He also gave my back a very satisfying scratching. After that, he brushed me, and that felt *really* good. It was kind of pointless, though, because every hair of my soft, silky coat was perfect just the way it was.

I protected my human from a plush green toy mouse tonight. I pounced on it while he was folding clothing. You should have seen it! It went flying clear across the room when I attacked it. I chased it down and batted it out of the room, down the hall, and even chased it down the stairs, all the way to the front door.

Day 15, Friday, November 9, 2018:
This morning, I noticed a door in the hallway was open. Behind it was a very small room with a lot of shelves, similar to the tiny room off the kitchen. I wanted to check it out, but my human went to the kitchen, and I needed to go see what he was doing. I'll have to investigate this tiny room at some later date.

When my human arrived home after work, things were rather chaotic. He was carrying some large pieces of wood when he came through the door. He took them to the basement. In fact, he made several trips from the car room to the cold floor room in the basement. I tried to see what was going on, but I didn't feel safe when he was moving those things so I kept my distance.

Once he was done moving things, I got to enjoy some lap time. He even put one of his front paws out for me to use as a chin rest. A bit later, I stretched out on his lap and put my chin on one of his knees. After a long while he made me get down because he said his legs ached. I don't know what his problem was—I was quite comfortable.

Later, I followed him to the kitchen, where he did something quite surprising. I was attempting to have a polite conversation with him when he reached down and picked me up! I meowed in shock and gave him a surprised look. It was nice to be close to him, though. Soon he knelt down and set me back on the floor, but rather than stay there, I jumped onto his lap.

Oh, I almost forgot. In the upper room, I found an empty paper bag on the floor. It'd be a nice place to hide if it didn't make so much noise when I walked into it.

Day 16, Saturday, November 10, 2018:
My human was home all day, so I had plenty of lap time today. After lunchtime, he lay down on the sofa. I joined him and leaned against one of his legs. He put one of his arms around me and gave me a gentle neck massage. I was really enjoying this when something caught my eye. I was looking toward the carpeted tube on the other side of the room. The tube is just below a window, and on top of the tube is a flat platform that is at the same level as the window. Something floated by outside the window.[5] I hopped down from the sofa and trotted over to the perch. With one well-calculated leap, I was sitting on the platform and able to look out the window. Whatever floated by was long gone. I kept watch out the window for a while longer, but it never came back.

That afternoon, my human opened another new door for me. It had yet another tiny room with a bunch of stuff in it. This door was near the front door and the steps that lead to the hallway. He pulled out a long hose and some other device with a long pole and a flat base with wheels. He put one end of the hose into the pole. He shoved the other end of the hose into the wall. Soon the thing with the wheels started to growl. It seemed like my human was fighting with the growling thing. It kept going away from him, but he kept pulling it back. This went on over several minutes as the growling thing rolled all over the carpet. I kept my distance since it was rather loud and a bit scary. My human won the fight. When the pole thing stopped growling, he put both it and the hose back into the closet and closed the door.

Every hour or so, my human took a metal can and shook it on the way to the cold floor room in the basement. Each time, he would spend only a few minutes in there. Since he kept the door closed I

---

[5]A leaf.

couldn't see what was going on. He repeated this activity several times throughout the day.

Later this evening, I found my human in the upper room. I wanted to lie on his lap. He was kind enough to put his hind legs up on a chair for me. I put my chin on his knees and stretched out to make optimal use of his entire lap, while he spent time either watching the television or reading a magazine. After a few hours, he got up to go do that basement thing again. He struggled and appeared to be in pain. I'm not sure why our evening together would make him sore; I was comfortable the entire time.

I followed him and his metal can to the basement, but yet again, he closed the door so I couldn't get in. I stood by the door and listened while waiting for him to return. While he was in there, I repeatedly heard something rattling, followed by a hissing sound.

This evening, I walked across the table in the upper room and discovered my human had left his dinner plate there. It still had some tasty crumbs on it, so I decided to help myself.

Day 17, Sunday, November 11, 2018:
It was warmer today, so I spent more time looking out the window from the short perch in the living room. I spent some time with my human on the sofa, too. He's still doing that funny thing with the metal rattling cans in the basement, but he also spent some time in the car room today. When he came back from there, he smelled kind of funny, but he changed his shirt and that helped.

Just before dinnertime, I crawled into that paper bag in the upper room. I was really quiet, but my fur brushing against the paper made a sound that startled my human. I froze when he jumped up and looked for the source of the sound. He didn't seem upset, though. He just sat back down when he saw it was me.

Later, I spent some time on that chair with the folded blanket while my human sat close by and occasionally got up to do things. As the evening wore on, I moved over to his lap. He put his arm out to support me, so I extended my front paws toward his shoulder and rested my chin on them.

Before we went to bed, I followed him into the kitchen, where he opened the cabinet directly below the sink. He left it open while he started to wash the dishes. I've seen him open this cabinet before and have wanted to check it out for some time, but I've been nervous about it because he always stood in front of it. I decided to go for it this time, but as I approached, I stopped and looked up at him. He looked down at me but didn't say anything, and then he went back to washing. With him preoccupied, I poked my head into the dark space. It's mostly full of smelly bottles and a bunch of pipes. It didn't look like there was very much room for me to move around, so I didn't go all the way in.

Day 18, Monday, November 12, 2018:
It was a cold day with more of that white stuff falling outside. I spent part of the day napping. I also chased various toys around the house.

My dinner was delayed tonight. Not only did my human arrive home later than normal, but once he was here he didn't come into the house right away. Rather, he stayed outside and pushed the white stuff around. I saw him from the big window in the front room. Once he came inside, I let him know that he should have fed me before playing outside.

I followed my human to the basement tonight. He went into the cold floor room. This time he left the door open so I could see what was going on. He picked up some plastic sheets and a bunch of messy newspapers that weren't there the last time I was in there. There was also a big wooden box that I hadn't seen before. Could this stuff have anything to do with those rattling cans and hissing noises? I explored this room a bit more as he moved the wooden box upstairs.

Tonight, he also took some bags out to the car room. I couldn't see what was going on out there, but I heard the big noisy door go up. I went to the front room and jumped onto the bench by the big window. From there, I watched my human push two large plastic bins down the driveway.

This evening, I played with a variety of balls on the upper room floor. At one point, my human also played with them, too. These toys aren't new. I understand that some other cats lived in this house before me. Perhaps they belonged to them? They're really nice. Some of them are very soft, like pom-poms, while others are hard. A few are shiny and make neat crinkly sounds when they're smacked. I like all of them.

I enjoyed some great cuddle time with my human tonight. He folded one of his arms across his chest, which created a wonderful spot for me to lie down. I wrapped my right front paw around his arm and rested my chin on his arm. It was really comfy. It's so nice having my very own human.

Day 19, Tuesday, November 13, 2018:
During the middle of the night, my human got up to use his litter box

contraption. I got up at the same time, but when he returned to bed, I went back and curled up on top of him for warmth.

I saw my human off to work this morning. It was dark when he left for work and dark when he came back home. I wish he didn't have to go to work so much.

This evening, I once again followed him into the cold floor room in the basement. I got scared when he started moving large pieces of wood around, so I ran out of the room. After I left, he closed the door, and then a bunch of loud noises came from that room. I was worried about him and stood guard on the other side of the door. After a while, it opened, and I saw he was fine. He was somewhat dirtier than he was before he went in.

We went back upstairs, where he cleaned up. Then he put his arms out to make a comfy space for me to nap. I leaned my left side against his chest and rested my chin on his left arm as he put his left front paw on my thigh. It was nice to be held.

Day 20, Wednesday, November 14, 2018:
My human opened the cabinet below the sink while he was in the bathroom this morning. I hadn't investigated that cabinet yet, so I approached it to see if he would let me take a look. Not only did he do that, but he removed two small rolls of white sheets and set them on the floor so that I could walk deep into the cabinet. That tiny space contained several of those white rolls, along with some aromatic bottles and bars. There wasn't much room to move around because there were some pipes in the way.

When my human arrived home from work, he spent more time than normal preparing his meal. That greatly annoyed me because it delayed my lap time. I made him aware of my displeasure.

After we both ate, I got to enjoy my first round of lap time. Then I followed him to the cold floor room in the basement, where he once again started moving pieces of wood around. I left the room, and he quickly closed the door. That was followed by all sorts of loud sounds. It wasn't very long, though, before things got quiet again and he opened the door. I was glad to see that he was safe, even if he was a bit dirty.

Later that evening, I followed him into the bathroom. He stepped into a big white basin and hid behind a curtain. Suddenly something horrible happened! Water started spraying out from above and got him very wet! Why didn't he try to escape? I would have run if that had happened to me. For several minutes I watched him through the translucent curtain as he moved around while being pummeled by water. Eventually, the water stopped, and he moved the curtain back. Fortunately, there was a large towel close by so he was able to dry himself. While he worked on drying himself, I stepped into the basin to check it out. It was still wet. I got out and dried my paws on the rug and then tried to exit the room. The door was closed, but it didn't look like it was latched. I touched the edge of the door but couldn't figure out how to open it. Thankfully, my human saw my predicament and pulled the door open enough that I could slip through.

Day 21, Thursday, November 15, 2018:
Before leaving for work this morning, my human went to the basement to scoop my litter pan. I expressed an interest in socializing with him. He knelt down, and I hopped onto his lap. I kept him home as long as I could. I wish he didn't have to leave.

This evening, he went back to the basement to do more work in the room with the cold floor. I followed him there to see what he was doing and asked him if I could sit on his lap. To my surprise, he sat down on a small stool and motioned for me to sit with him. He presented one of his front paws to me, creating a perfect place to rest my chin. I closed my eyes as he softly stroked the top of my head. It was quite relaxing. He even gave me a kiss on my head, which I wasn't expecting. We enjoyed quite a bit of time together. Once I had my fill of attention, I got down and walked out of the room. He got up and closed the door as I left. I went upstairs while he stayed down there and made loud noises.

Day 22, Friday, November 16, 2018:
Something strange happened today. I heard some commotion outside, so I went to the front room and hopped onto the bench by the big window. Invading my territory was a lady I'd never seen before. She was playing in the dirt, digging holes and stuffing round things into them. I sat and watched her for some time. She eventually spotted me, but I held my ground. In fact, I didn't leave until I saw my human arrive in the car. I went over to wait for him at the top of the staircase, but he didn't come into the house. After a while, I heard tapping on the window where the dirt lady was playing, so I went back over there. My human was outside with her. Why was he out there instead of in here feeding me? Did he forget that it's time for wet food? As the sun set, the dirt lady finally left, and my human came into the house. I let

him know how disappointed I was with his lack of speed in providing my evening meal. To get him back, I waited for him to start his own meal and then I hopped on his lap and swooshed my tail in his face as he tried to eat.

Day 23, Saturday, November 17, 2018:
My human was very busy all day today. He left home around the normal time but came back later in the morning only to leave again for a while. When he was here, he was busy in the car room but finally came back into the house for a late lunch. I made sure to get on his lap at that time.

When I jumped off his lap, he went outside to push leaves around and brush the lawn. I wonder if the lawn enjoys being brushed as much as I do. It certainly needs it more than I do.

After he was done outside, he went to the basement to make more loud noises. He wasn't there very long, though, before he came upstairs to serve dinner. I was excited! I really enjoy the food I get every evening. It comes from a small can. It smells and tastes great.

After dinner, I requested and received more lap time. However, something rather shocking happened while I sat on his lap. I was enjoying his lap, purring contentedly and minding my own business, when he tried to kiss the top of my head again. What's up with that? I immediately stopped purring while I thought about what to do next. He seemed to get the message, at least for a while. Later that evening, when I was on his lap again, he gently gave me a couple of kisses on the top of my head. It was kind of annoying, but I guess it's all right.

Day 24, Sunday, November 18, 2018:
I enjoyed plenty of lap time this afternoon and evening. While watching the television, my human once again positioned his arms to create a perfect cradle for me. I put my front paws around his arm and even gave him a hug when I stretched.

When I got up from my nap, I discovered a surprise in one of my toys. It was a plastic ball composed of two parts, but the two pieces had become separated. It turned out the ball wasn't solid but had a cavity inside it. Even better, that cavity wasn't empty but was full of catnip! Since the ball was now in two parts, the tasty treat had spilled onto the floor. It was kind of stale, though. I wonder if there's any good, fresh stuff around here.

Tonight, while my human was making some hot apple cider, a small stack of napkins leapt off the microwave and onto the floor. I was in the front room but saw it happen, so I ran into the kitchen and pounced on them before they could move. My human knelt next to me and petted me. He seemed appreciative of my work at protecting him.

Once again this evening, I followed my human into the bathroom, where he subjected himself to falling water. Like last time, the door was closed but not latched. Unlike last time, I figured out how to pull the door open and get away so I didn't have to witness that horrendous situation.

Day 25, Monday, November 19, 2018:
My internal clock told me my human should have gone to work today, but he didn't. That's fine with me because it meant more lap time! Extra lap time is especially nice on cold autumn mornings.

In the evening, my human once again put his arm on his chest in such a way that it created the perfect spot for me to nap. I really like it when he does that. I get so relaxed that some of my paws end up hanging down. At one point, I gave his arm another hug with my front paws while I stretched.

I also tried using that small cat-sized staircase in the upper room. Those steps made it really easy to get onto the tables. I didn't even have to jump. There are three tables in a U-shape. From one table I can get to the next and then to the third. I wasn't sure if I should be on the tables, but my human has seen me do it and hasn't said anything to me about it, so I guess it's okay with him.

Day 26, Tuesday, November 20, 2018:
Today my human left home at the normal time, but not with his normal stuff. Instead, he loaded a cooler and a large box with a variety of things and then left in the truck instead of the car. He arrived home earlier than normal, too, which was great for me because it meant I got my delicious wet food sooner.

In the evening, he worked in the basement some more. He wasn't making any loud noises, so he left the door open for me. I explored the room a bit and investigated a device that wasn't there before. It's a tall metal thing with a handle, a flat platform, and two wheels.[6]

I went over to my human, who was busy making pencil marks on a piece of wood. I asked if I could sit on his lap, and much to my surprise, he went all the way upstairs and sat on the chair in the upper

---

[6]A hand truck.

room. I enjoyed his lap for a while. When I got down, he went back to the basement and resumed making pencil marks. Later, I asked to sit on his lap again, but this time he sat on the small stool in the basement. I sat on his lap, but not for very long.

I also did a lot of playing today. There are several toys in the upper room, including a shiny, crinkly ball that makes a neat sound whenever I touch it. I enjoy batting it around.

Tonight I also got some exercise by running around the house. There's a sharp turn at the bottom of the short staircase by the front door. There's also a rug near that door. It turns out that rug can go flying when a high-speed cat attempts to make the turn without slowing down. Oops!

Later that evening, I decided to rest on the chair with the blanket in the upper room. My human had one of his hind paws on it but was kind enough to only use the edge, which left enough room for me to lie down.

Day 27, Wednesday, November 21, 2018:
This seemed like a normal day for my human since he left for work and came home at the normal times. I spent the day napping and getting exercise by chasing balls and other toys all over the house. Some of them ended up in the basement. A few even got stuck under some shelves.

In the evening, my human came to the kitchen after working downstairs. He found me curiously looking around the tall curtain that covers the glass door in the kitchen. Something there had caught my attention, but I didn't tell him what it was. He prepared a snack and went upstairs. I followed him and decided to rest on his arm and chest, like I had done previously. We watched an animated show on the television about a funny-looking dog that prepared a meal of toast, pretzel sticks, popcorn, and jelly beans for some humans. I wasn't impressed, but my human seemed to enjoy it.

Later this evening, I decided to lie down on my human's lap again. This time, he gave me the most amazing chin and neck massage I'd ever had. After that, I gave myself a bath.

Day 28, Thursday, November 22, 2018:
Today my human arrived home early. He smelled like he had been at the shelter. I guess he didn't go to his normal job today. He spent the afternoon making loud noises in the basement, while I spent most of the day napping. Late in the afternoon, a bell rang, but my human

didn't hear it. Then there was pounding at the door. He heard that and turned off the noisy machines. I was on the blanket chair in the upper room when I heard the front door open and the sounds of a stranger. Seconds later, much to my horror, he led the stranger into the upper room. They sat on the floor and looked at me.

It turns out the stranger was the same lady I saw the other day playing in the dirt outside my front window. She and my human sat and talked about me for several minutes. She mentioned my big, beautiful eyes. At one point, she came a bit closer and politely extended one of her front paws toward me. I appreciated being able to sniff it, but when she attempted to touch me, I backed away since I didn't know what she was planning to do.

Closer to bedtime, I decided to sharpen my claws on the textured wall in the front room. My human saw me from the kitchen. He asked me not to do that, so I stopped.

Day 29, Friday, November 23, 2018:
It was another strange day for my human. He left around the normal time but came home early. While he was gone, I chased toy mice around the house. One of them ended up on the staircase.

I was sick this evening, but I'm not sure why. I threw up twice right after I ate my wet food. I offered to clean it up, but my human said he would take care of it. I appreciated that he took the time to do that, especially since I interrupted his own dinner. To pay him back, I lay quietly on his lap and let him massage my neck and the top of my head.

Tonight, while my human was sitting in his chair in the upper room, he put his hind paws up on the table. This created a nicely sloped lap for me to stretch out on for a brief nap. I extended one of my front paws down his calves while I rested my chin on his knees. When I did this, he gently stroked my back. Two massages in one evening!

Day 30, Saturday, November 24, 2018:
My human left the house for a while this morning. When he returned, I found him in the basement where my litter pan was located. I was on the staircase looking down at him, and he was in the basement looking up at me. And then he closed the door! How was I supposed to get to my litter pan? Fortunately, I didn't need to use it at that moment.

I sat and listened, since I couldn't see what was happening. I heard some commotion and then heard the sliding glass door open. For a few moments, there was silence. I think he went out the door. He soon returned, and I heard more commotion. It sounded like he was moving something.[7] Next, it sounded like he was in the cold floor room, but he didn't stay there very long. Right after that, he came back and opened the door so I could enter the room. Everything looked normal, but the curtain that usually covered the big window and sliding glass door had been pulled back. That was nice because it made it easier to get on the bench where I could look outside.

Today I also spent some time on the bench on the main level in the front room. Outside that window, there is a big tree where a bunch of squirrels live. I sat and watched the squirrels for a while.

While lying on my human's lap this afternoon, he looked at my left front paw. He acted like he was going to trim my nails, but he didn't. I got up and explored the closet in this room. I go in there fre-quently, even though nothing in there ever changes. After that, I decided to lie down on the floor between the closet and my human. That's when he decided to take several photos of me.

Resting near the upper room closet.

Later that afternoon, I was upstairs when I heard my human open the front door. I ran to check it out, but by the time I got there, he was already outside. That's when I discovered there is a second door on the other side of the front door, but it's thinner and made almost en-tirely of glass. I sat and watched my human dump the contents of a large metal can into a large plastic bin. When he brought the metal can back up to the front door, I ran to get out of the way.

Boy, he was busy today. My human briefly closed off access to my litter pan yet again and moved even more stuff from outside into

---

[7]More lumber.

the basement. When the door to my litter pan room opened again, I went to investigate. Before the loud noises started, I managed to sneak into the forbidden cold floor room to see what was going on. Stuff had moved around a lot from the last time I was there, and there were some large pieces of wood that hadn't been there before. It really annoyed me that he's spending so much time in there because that is time that he could have provided a lap for me. Late in the evening, he came upstairs, bathed himself that terrifying way that humans do, and finally sat down for some lap time.

Day 31, Sunday, November 25, 2018:
Today, my human left home early to go to the shelter. I spent the morning chasing toy mice while he was gone. When he came home, I lay down with him on the sofa while he ate lunch. After he was done eating, he gave me a fabulous two-pawed neck massage while I lifted my butt toward his face.

My position on the sofa gives me a great vantage point over the whole room, including the window to the backyard. There was stuff in the air outside, so I hopped off the sofa, trotted over to the perch near the window, and jumped onto the ledge. It was more of that white stuff, but this time there was a lot of it. In fact, I couldn't see much because it was mostly white outside.

A bit later, I walked across the room. My human was still on the sofa, watching the television. As I walked by, I turned and watched the screen for a bit. It wasn't very exciting.

I decided to check up on my human while he used his litter box device. He opened the doors under the sink, like he had done before, and once again removed a couple of white paper rolls so I could walk into the tiny room under the sink. I explored it some more, but there wasn't anything new to see. That didn't stop me from going into it twice, though.

In addition to my usual evening lap time, I explored the closet in the upper room a bit more. There are many levels in the closet, but most of them are occupied, leaving very narrow ledges for me to walk on. I haven't tried to get very high on these levels.

Day 32, Monday, November 26, 2018:
It was pretty cold last night, so I slept close to my human. A few times I moved closer to him for more warmth. He did the same with me once when he rolled over.

My human didn't go to work today. That was nice since it meant more lap time for me. During the afternoon, I took a nap on his lap while he was at the computer. He put one of his front paws on his lap, which let me rest my chin on his arm. I let my front paws dangle from his arm. I've become quite comfortable with my human. I slept really well. It was great. When I awoke, I let him know I appreciated his lap and arm by purring loudly. After my nap, I jumped down and gave myself a bath near his hind paws while he continued working on the computer.

This afternoon, I got to peek into the car room. My human had taken some plastic bags out there and had left the door ajar. I poked my head into the room, but before I could explore too far, he saw me and walked toward me. I decided to back away into the house, at which point he closed the door.

Day 33, Tuesday, November 27, 2018:
When my human arrived home from work today, he gave me my wet food and then had his own dinner. I sat on his lap as he ate. As soon as I got down from his lap, he took off for the basement. I followed him. He let me watch him work for a while. He worked quietly until I stepped out of the room. Then he closed the door, and the loud noises started. At least I got some good exploration time in tonight.

While he worked in the basement, I batted some balls and mice around the main level of the house. Some of them end up on the stair-case down to the basement. When my human found them, he returned them back to the floor on the main level.

Later this evening, while my human watched the television, I hopped onto his lap. He folded his arms in front of him and created the perfect place for me to rest. I put my chin on one of his arms and stretched, extending one of my hind paws over his other arm. He couldn't use his front paws when we sat like that, but that didn't bother me because it was *so* comfy. I got to lie like that twice tonight.

I decided to get off his lap and explore the room a bit more since this territory is still rather new to me. There are shelves next to his computer. The lowest shelf was half empty. The next one up was com-pletely full of books. The third one was a little over half full. There appeared to be enough room for me so I leapt up there. There wasn't much exciting there, although it did permit me to get a closer look at the next shelf up. That one was pretty full and also didn't have nearly enough vertical clearance, so I'm not sure I could safely jump up there.

After my time on the shelf, I went back to the closet and put my front paws on one of the shelves in there. They are all full, but there is a narrow clear area in front of one of them. Maybe I could get up there? Perhaps I should wait until my human isn't around.

With my need to explore satisfied for the evening, I went back to my human, who had put his hind paws up on the table. I hopped onto his lap and stretched out on his upward-sloping legs for some well-deserved relaxation.

Day 34, Wednesday, November 28, 2018:
Humans can be such a pain. Take tonight, for example. First, my human was late from work, so my evening meal of delicious wet food was delayed. Then, he spent way too much time working in the cold floor room with the door closed. And I mean *way* too much. It ate into my lap time! It was practically bedtime before he emerged from there. Once he did, I met him at the top of the steps and made him aware of my displeasure. At least he listened to me, and after he got a drink, he provided a lap for me.

Before he sat down, he produced a long springy thing from a big red box that sat on one of the tables in the upper room. While I was on his lap, he used it to grab items on the table that he couldn't reach with his front paws. I found this quite entertaining and even decided to chase the end of the tool as it bounced around.

On another note, remember that shelf in the closet that had just enough open space on the front that I thought I might be able to jump up there? This evening I discovered that I could make it. Doing so let me get a much closer look at what was up there. Sadly, there wasn't anything particularly interesting, so I didn't spend much time there.

Day 35, Thursday, November 29, 2018:
My human arrived home at his normal time, more or less. We went through what has become our normal routine of me eating dinner while he prepared his own food, followed by me on his lap while he attempted to eat his dinner. As soon as I got down, he was out of his chair and left the house again. He wasn't gone very long. I heard him return and decided to meet him at the door.

I almost got into the car room, but he was carrying some large, flat pieces of wood. I wasn't sure if he could handle them very well, so I ran down to the basement. I watched from the bottom of the staircase as he brought in several wood pieces and leaned them against the wall near the door. At that point, I lost interest in the car room and instead decided to check out these new materials. They smelled a lot like the stuff he has been working with in the basement. He took them all to the cold floor room. When he disappeared behind the door, I went up-stairs and chased a large toy mouse into the kitchen.

All of his work in the basement once again meant less lap time for me. Later in the evening, I decided to go down there and wait. Once the door opened, I told him he should stop working and go up-stairs to spend time with me. He obliged, but not before grabbing a snack from the kitchen. I led him to the upper room and waited for him to sit. I thought he was ready, but apparently he wasn't, so I stopped almost in mid-jump. We exchanged surprised looks. Then he motioned that he was ready for me, so I leapt to his awaiting lap. I rubbed my head on his arm and used my hind legs to lift my butt to-ward his face.

Later, while he worked nearby on the computer, I sat on the blanket chair and took a bath.

Day 36, Friday, November 30, 2018:
This evening, my human came home earlier than normal, so I got to enjoy my wet food sooner than I expected. What surprised me, though, was that he took my food to the upper room along with his own meal. That was nice because it meant I could eat my dinner but still be close to him. I cleaned my plate before jumping onto his awaiting lap.

I didn't get as much lap time tonight as I would have liked be-cause my human spent too much time in the cold floor room with the door closed making all of those loud noises. When he finally came up-stairs and provided a lap, I took full advantage of it. He held me with his left front paw while I hugged his arm. I pushed the back of my head against his chest and looked up at him. He gave me a great neck massage with his other front paw.

While he worked on the computer, I hopped back onto his lap. I watched as he typed on the keyboard. After a while, I decided I needed some exercise, so I got back on the floor and chased a soft purple pom-pom ball all over the room. I didn't reach for it when it landed near one of my human's hind paws, but when he rolled it back toward me, I continued my exercise routine. Later, I switched to one of those neat-sounding shiny, crinkly balls.

Day 37, Saturday, December 1, 2018:
My human slept in today, so I had to go wake him up. I don't have to jump onto the bed because there is a small, cat-sized staircase at the

foot of the bed. I walked up to the top of it and called to him. He was already awake, but he didn't get out of the bed until I told him to.

The great thing about a day like today (when my human stays home) is that I get more lap time. He worked on the computer this morning while I purred softly on his legs. After that, I got down to take a bath. Once I was clean, I sat on the floor near him but close to a small grated opening that was blowing some warm air.

Later this morning, I followed my human back to the basement. He sure has been spending a lot of time down there lately. This time he put a bunch of his clothing in one of those big white boxes. Then something horrible happened—I got trapped! When my human left the cold floor room, he closed the door. I could hear him in the other room, so I scratched at the door to let him know I wanted out. He quickly came to the door and opened it. He seemed surprised to see me, but I was just glad to get out.

Also this morning, I followed my human into a small room on the upper floor, across the hall from his litter box device. I've explored this room before on my own. My human doesn't go in there very often. He didn't spend very much time there today, but I decided to stick around after he left. There is a window in that room that looks the same direction as the big window in the front room, but this one is higher up. Unlike the front room, there isn't a bench at this window, but there is a small wooden table near the window that provides the perfect place for me to sit and observe the view. I sat there for a while to survey my territory from this higher location.

My human ate his lunch on the sofa today. I was lying next to him, so while he ate, he also gave me a massage. Normally, I face away from him, but I tend to move around a lot. At one point, we were nearly face-to-face. He grabbed me, pulled me toward his chest, and gave me a big hug. I tolerated this, but preferred greater control of my interaction with him.

Most of the day I napped on the blanket chair while my human made loud, irritating sounds in the basement. Late in the evening, some strange things happened. I heard a lot of commotion, so I went to check it out. I found the door to the basement closed. I also heard sound from some other human. Then things were quiet for a bit but were soon followed by sounds from the car room. While this was going on, I sat on the bench at the front window. Soon I saw a human walk by. It was the one who tried to touch me in the big upper room that one time—the dirt lady.[8] She saw me. I was protected by the window, so I didn't run. Rather, I watched her cross the yard and exit my territory. Soon I heard the car room door go down, followed by my own human entering the house.

Day 38, Sunday, December 2, 2018:
My human spent most of the morning at the shelter helping the home-less cats. I'm so glad I'm no longer homeless. What's more, not only did I find a human to live with, but today when he arrived home, he brought two new pieces of furniture into the house just for me. One was a scratching post, just like my others. The other was a curved, horizontal scratching pad that also provides a great place to relax. He put both of them in the front room. I really like the horizontal pad.

My new scratching pad.

After he set those up, I reminded him that I was overdue for some lap time. I rubbed the side of my head and body along his legs while he was in the kitchen. Once his food was ready, we sat on the sofa together. The last time we did this, he lay on his side and I stretched out in front of him. That's what I did at first today, but later I tried curling up in the space between his knees and the back of the

---

[8]She had helped move a bookcase from the basement to the garage.

sofa. It was rather comfortable. He gave me a belly rub, which I really enjoyed.

This afternoon, my human spent too much time in the car room. It was about two hours past my normal dinnertime before he came back into the house. The first thing he did was change clothes, but then he prepared my wet food. After I ate, I enjoyed his lap for a while before moving over to the blanket chair.

This evening, I lounged on my new scratching structure in the front room while my human worked in the kitchen. He then took a bunch of photos of me, I guess because I'm so cute.

Later, I checked out another cat structure in the upper room. It has a low tube and a higher elevated platform. The tube is so short I can't even get all of my tail into it before my head pops out the other side, but it's wide enough that I can turn around inside it. I'm really flexible, so that helped.

After that, I went into the paper bag right next to the structure with the tube. It makes a neat sound when I walk into it. I like to go all the way in and then turn around so I can see out into the room. While I was in there, I found a blue pom-pom ball within easy reach, so I took a swipe at it. That was fun, so I chased it all over the room. I stopped briefly when got it stuck near one of my human's hind paws, but after he batted it back toward me, I resumed the chase.

Day 39, Monday, December 3, 2018:
As usual, I got out of bed about an hour before my human to do some cat stuff. After that, I sat like a sphinx at the end of the hallway and waited for him to get up. From that location, I can not only see the hallway, but I can also look down toward the front door and into the front room. I can also see part of the room with my cat trees and part of the kitchen from there. It's a great vantage point for observing things in this house.

Tonight, my human once again spent way too much time in the basement with the door closed. There were loud noises coming from that area until he emerged just before bedtime. I managed to get some lap time before we went to bed. While on his lap, he decided to give me a manicure. Or at least he tried. He's not very good at it. This time he managed to take care of the claws on my left front paw and about half of those on my right front paw. It was okay, though, because he was cautious and didn't hurt me.

Day 40, Tuesday, December 4, 2018:
Today, my human spent some time in the cold floor room with the door closed and then spent a lot of time in the car room. I wanted to go out there and see what he was doing, but he wouldn't let me. After a couple of hours, he came back into the house and changed clothing. I let him know my displeasure at him spending too much time out there and not enough time providing a lap for me. He listened and finally sat down with his arms in front of him. I climbed onto his arms, rested my chin on one of them, and stretched one of my hind legs over the other.

Tonight, my human was playing with a small, squarish, yellow thing.[9] He pulled a long, thin, yellow metallic part from it and held it near the staircase and by the front door. I wasn't sure if he was trying to get me to play with it or not. I chased it as he moved it around, but he seemed to ignore me and instead kept his attention focused on the metal thing. This went on for a few minutes until the metal piece quickly disappeared back into the square part. I've said it before: humans are weird.

Later this evening, I got onto the table in the upper room while he was typing at the computer. I started to push his stuff on the table. He looked at me every time I touched something, but I stopped whenever he looked. He eventually got onto the floor and started to play with my toys, so I hopped off the table and started to play with them, too. Sometimes my human is a bit slow at understanding what I want.

My human also spent some time brushing me tonight. That felt *really* good. He used a brush with lots of little metallic tines. It not only extracts loose fur but also gives me a fantastic back scratching.

Day 41, Wednesday, December 5, 2018:
This evening, my human took the plate containing my wet food up to the upper room so we could have dinner together. I liked that. It annoyed me when he would leave my plate in the kitchen and then take his food upstairs because I was torn. I wanted to eat, but I also wanted to be near him. After I ate, I hopped onto his lap. He wasn't done eating yet but that didn't really concern me. As long as he put his arm out for me to rest on, I was happy.

He once again spent too much time in the car room and in the cold floor room of the basement. In both locations, he kept the door closed so I couldn't be near him. As before, once he emerged and went upstairs, he sat and let me stretch out on him. This time, I put my chin

---

[9]A tape measure, checking clearances for an upcoming furniture move.

on his knees and stretched one of my hind paws back so far that it hit him in his chest. I was quite comfortable until he grabbed that paw and attempted to trim my nails. That's when I got down and left the room to let him know I disapproved.

Later, I sat on the floor near his hind paws while I cleaned my right front paw. I spent more time on it than a cat should. There was a claw sheath on it that was ready to be shed.

Day 42, Thursday, December 6, 2018:
In the morning, I visited my human as he sat in the bathroom. When I sniffed at the cabinet under the sink, he opened one of the doors for me. He did that yesterday, too. I was able to walk inside the cabinet without him removing anything from it this time. I wondered if he'd keep it this way for me. Walking in there has kind of become a morning routine for me.

When he got home, he once again took both his food and my food to the upper room. We ate together while he watched TV. As usual, I enjoyed some lap time after my meal.

After he was done eating, and after I jumped off his lap, he left the room. I followed him to the basement, but he wouldn't let me into the cold floor room. I waited outside the door while he spent time in there with the things that make loud noises. When he came out, I told him he needed to go sit down for me. And would you believe he actually listened to me? We went to the upper room, where I stretched out in his arms for several minutes. But as soon as I got down, he left to go back downstairs. This time he went to work in the car room, so I went to the front room and chased toy mice.

Later, I enjoyed some more lap time while he once again watched TV. When I hopped off his lap, he turned to work at the computer. I hadn't checked the closet in a few days, so I inspected it briefly before lying down on the floor between him and the closet. I don't always need to sit on his lap. Sometimes I just like to be near him.

Day 43, Friday, December 7, 2018:
It was a cool night, so I slept close to my human until I got up to go on my early morning prowl. After that, I waited on my curved scratching pad for him to get up to do his normal routine.

As usual, I had to spend the day alone since he had to go to work. When he arrived home, he put my full dinner plate on the kitchen floor while he prepared his own food. This time, though, he didn't have a chance to take my food to the upper room because I had cleaned my plate before he even had his ready to go. As soon as he sat down in the upper room, I was on his lap. I was up there so fast, I think I surprised him, but he kindly folded his arms in front of him and cradled me for a while.

Later in the evening, I followed him to the basement. I was still there when he left the cold floor room. I happened to be near the door as he left the room when what did I find but a stray toy mouse in his path! I batted it and chased it clear across the room, away from my human. No fluffy toy mouse is going to attack *my* human. I think he appreciated it. And I appreciated him stopping to scoop out my litter pan on his way through the basement.

We went back upstairs, where I climbed onto his lap again. This time, I faced away from him and wrapped my tail around one of his arms. He extended both of his front paws up to simultaneously massage the top of my head and my neck. It felt great! I just lay there with my eyes closed and purred softly while I enjoyed his gentle touch. His paws really know how to make a girl feel good.

Day 44, Saturday, December 8, 2018:
This morning, I found a sunbeam while my human did his normal routine. I enjoyed the sunbeam on the bench in the front room and looked out the window. There were a lot of birds in the big tree. They were all talking to each other. I wonder what they were saying. I don't speak bird.

My human was home most of the day but spent a lot of time in the car room and basement. When he came up for lunch, he lay down on the sofa under the blanket to watch TV and eat. I spent some time with him but also went over to the perch with the tube near the window and looked outside. About the time he was going to get up, I figured I needed to do something to keep him from going back to the car room. After all, he should really spend more time with me on the days he doesn't leave the house. I trotted over to the sofa, hopped up to join him, and took a nap on the blanket behind his knees. It was actually a bunch of naps. Between naps, I pushed my back against his legs and stretched my paws out along the soft back of the sofa. I also turned my head to look at him to let him know I've got him. He didn't get up until it was time for my evening meal.

I noticed my human didn't prepare any food for himself but instead went back to work in the car room. While he was there, I chased balls, toy mice, and one of my plastic jacks. I left some of the toys on the steps near the car room, in case he wanted to play with them, too.

We didn't do our normal routine this evening. When my human finally got done in the car room, he came upstairs and cleaned himself. Normally, we would go to bed after that, but tonight I watched him go to the kitchen. I guess he decided to eat after all. I lay down next to him when he sat on the sofa. He gave me a nice massage while he consumed his late meal.

Day 45, Sunday, December 9, 2018:
While my human was busy at the cat shelter this morning, I chased a small plastic springy toy all the way down the stairs. My human found it when he came home and took it back to the front room.

This afternoon, I watched as my human put his clothing away. I've seen him do that before, but this time he showed me something new. It turns out there are drawers under the bed that I hadn't seen before. I watched him put some of his clothing in one of them. I wondered if I could walk into the drawer, but he closed it before I had a chance.

Tonight, something strange happened when I jumped onto my human's lap. As soon as I landed, he made a quick movement and let out a sound I hadn't heard before. I got scared, so I immediately jumped back down and put some distance between myself and him before looking back at him. He looked at me and appeared to be unharmed. Maybe he didn't see me coming and I just surprised him when I landed on his lap. I cautiously walked over to him. I wanted to go back on his lap, but I wasn't sure about it. He looked at me and made the motion that he does when he invites me to his lap, so I made the leap and everything was good.

I tried something new with my human tonight. While he was sitting in his chair in the upper room, he folded his arms for me, like he frequently did, but instead of lying with my left side against his chest as I normally did, I turned around and put my chin on his right arm. I liked it so much that later in the evening I did it again. He even brought his left front paw up to stroke the back of my head.

A bit before bedtime, I climbed the steps to the sink in the upper room to get a drink of water. Then I got down and crawled into the paper bag near my short cat tree.

Day 46, Monday, December 10, 2018:
I didn't stick around while my human cleaned my food and water

dishes this morning. Instead, I went to the basement and sat behind the curtain on the bench by the big glass door. I like looking out that door. It provides a similar view as the window upstairs next to my perch with the tube but is closer to ground level.

This morning, my human came down to the basement, too. I heard him scoop my litter pan. Once he was done with that, he poked his head behind the curtain and greeted me. Before he left for work, we exchanged a few kind words. He also rubbed the side of my head with his paw.

This evening, my human provided my meal on time but didn't make one for himself. While I ate, he disappeared downstairs. After I finished eating, I went down to find him and happily discovered he had left the door open for me. I sat on the cold, hard floor and watched as he cleaned up the room.

Later in the evening, he finally went back upstairs to prepare his food. I was happy because I knew what that meant: lap time! I eagerly followed him as he took his meal to the upper room. Well, at first I followed him. I was so excited and running so fast that I passed him halfway there. Once he sat down, I was finally able to enjoy some lap time for the first time today. I stretched out on his arm for a long time. This time I decided to go back to resting my left side against him. Between bites of his meal, he gave me a nice massage with his one (mostly) free front paw.

Before we went to bed, my human and I got some exercise in the front room where we batted various toys back and forth.

Day 47, Tuesday, December 11, 2018:
This morning, I once again went to the basement as my human got ready for work. When he came down to scoop my litter pan, I went over to talk to him. He knelt down near me and talked back to me, at which point I made my way onto his legs. It was as close to getting on his lap as I could get. We spent several minutes together before he went to work. I even let him kiss me on the head several times. I wish he could have stayed here with me.

In the evening, we went back to more or less our normal routine. I ate my meal while he prepared his own, only this time I finished before he was even ready to eat. He took his food to the upper room. I followed him and sat on his lap while he attempted to eat. Actually, I climbed onto his arm as he folded it against his chest. I think it was harder for him to eat with me on his arm, but that didn't really concern me.

Later, he opened a narrow door in the upper room that had been closed the entire time I've lived here. I saw another human-type litter device in there.

Just like last night, we spent some time in the front room playing with my toys. He batted them toward me, and I chased them. I enjoyed spending time with him like that.

Before bedtime, my human watched TV while I once again stretched out on his arm and leaned against his chest. I wasn't there very long, though, because I got scared when he made a sudden move-ment and some loud sound.[10] When that happened, I tried to get away, but he held me tightly. He stopped making the loud sounds and re-leased his grip, but I still crawled out of his grasp and made my way to the floor as soon as I could, not knowing if he would do it again. Loud, sudden sounds frighten me.

Day 48, Wednesday, December 12, 2018:
This morning, I waited in the front room on my curved scratching pad while my human cleaned my food and water dishes. I knew what he was going to do next, so I went to the basement to wait for him. Hu-mans are creatures of habit. When he arrived down there, I watched him as he scooped my litter pan. I talked to him, too. When he was done, he came over to me. I thought he just wanted to socialize with me, but then he picked me up! I tried to squirm away as he held me tightly, but then he loosened his grip and I was able to jump down to the floor. He was still kneeling on the floor when I turned and gave him a nasty look. I couldn't stay mad at him, though, and immediately crawled up onto his lap under my own power. I like being on his lap and in his arms, but it has to be *my* idea. He stroked my back and gave me kisses before he left for work.

When he arrived home this evening, he immediately scooped my wet food onto a plate, but he didn't put it on the floor like he nor-mally did. Instead, he took the plate upstairs and set it on the floor of the upper room before quickly returning to the hallway. I didn't notice right away because I was too distracted by my food, but he had closed the door on his way out, trapping me in the room.

As I ate my meal, I heard some commotion and the sound of a second human. When the door opened, I saw a tall wooden object in

---

[10]A cough.

the hallway that wasn't there just moments before.[11] I also saw that the second voice belonged to the dirt lady. Together, they pushed this tall wooden object into the room. They left that thing in the upper room and went back to the front room. I followed them and jumped onto the curved scratching pad. I lay down on it while I watched and listened to them. I also wanted her to know that this was *my* pad. I think she got the message because she quickly left.

Day 49, Thursday, December 13, 2018:
Finally! An evening where I had his complete attention! When my human arrived home from work tonight, he gave me some wet food while he fixed his own meal, and then he took both of our plates to the upper room. I finished my dinner and immediately hopped onto his lap. Before he could even finish his meal, I climbed up onto his arms and plopped down for the evening. I made sure he wasn't going to spend time in the basement or car room tonight. I stretched out on his arms and took a wonderful nap while he gently massaged me. I stayed there for a long time. It was great.

Oh, I almost forgot about my new toy. When my human came into the house tonight, before dinner and our evening-long snuggle session, he presented me with a gift. It was a string similar to the ones on his shoes. I already had one string, but it was shorter and black and in kind of rough shape. This string is white and looks newer than my other string. It's also longer. I got excited when he dragged it along the ground. I chased it as it moved and bounced. I pounced on it and man-aged to get it loose from his grip. He picked it up and walked upstairs with the string trailing behind him. Once again, I stalked and grabbed it. I like this game. He left the string on the floor for me. I can play with it by myself, but it's a lot more fun when we play with it together.

Day 50, Friday, December 14, 2018:
This morning, my human found the tiny toy mice I had chased under a door in the kitchen. It was the door that hid the tiny room with the shelves. I don't know what all is in that little room other than my wet and dry food. For a few hours, a couple of my little toy mice had been in there, too. While I was playing with them and chasing them on the slippery kitchen floor, I managed to lose them under that door. My human picked them up and tossed them back into the front room

---

[11]A bookcase that had been built in the basement and finished in the garage.

where a lot of my other toys are kept. My human is pretty useful for recovering stuck toys.

My human returned from work rather strangely tonight. I normally hear him before he gets into the house. I'll usually wait by the door to the car room when I hear the big door open. This time, I didn't hear the big door. Instead, he just appeared at the front door. Thankfully, though, when he came in the first thing he did was give me some tasty wet food.

He didn't prepare his own meal, though. Instead, he went to the car room, and I didn't see him again for quite a while. When I did, I let him know that I was displeased with him spending too much time out there and not enough time making a lap for me. I told him it was time to sit and make a lap, but he was too busy and returned to the car room. It wasn't until very late that he came back into the house to eat and provide a lap for me. I was annoyed that it took so long, but I was happy to finally have some time with him. I crawled onto his left arm and rested my chin on it while letting my right front paw dangle over his arm.

Day 51, Saturday, December 15, 2018:
Today was similar to last night in that my human spent *way* too much time in the car room. During the brief periods while he was in the house, he moved a bunch of things around in the upper room. It was quite a mess. I explored the shelf of a bookcase as he emptied it. He put most of my toys in a metal can while all of that was going on. That was okay because I didn't have time to play with them anyway. I was too fascinated watching him work. That was until he brought that beast with the long hose into the room. When that thing started to growl, I ran down the hallway to the other side of the house.

At least I got to spend some quality time with him during lunch. He ate while lying on the sofa, so I snuggled up in the little triangle between his knees and the back cushions. Later in the day, we spent some more time together in the upper room. It was going well until he tried to give me another manicure. I let him do a couple of nails on my left front paw, but that was it.

Day 52, Sunday, December 16, 2018:
The upper room is still a mess.[12] I wonder when he'll put it back to normal.

---

[12]Emptying and rearranging bookcases.

My human was at the shelter this morning but spent the rest of the day at home. The nice thing about having him home nearly all day is that my litter pan always stays clean. I enjoy having a human who takes care of that promptly.

Investigating the old bookcase as my human emptied it.

Day 53, Monday, December 17, 2018:
I've settled into a morning routine where I get up about an hour before my human, do cat things for a while, and then wait for him in the basement. My human is pretty predictable, so I know he'll show up there to scoop my litter pan before he goes to work. I also know that if I make a fuss and socialize with him, I can almost always work my way onto his lap. I've observed that he can't leave if I'm on his lap.

That, at least, was my plan. This morning, he surprised me. After he scooped my litter pan, instead of kneeling down to give me some attention, he picked me up! Not only that, but he held me so tightly I couldn't squirm away! After several seconds of suffering through this indignity, he knelt down, at which point I made my way onto his lap of my own free will. I forgave him for grabbing me, and we shared a nice moment together before he encouraged me to hop down so he could go to work.

This evening he showed me a new toy: a mouse on a string attached to a stick. It's a two-player toy. He held the stick and moved it around while I chased the mouse. Actually, I preferred to attack the string.

Day 54, Tuesday, December 18, 2018:
I really like being held as long as it is done under my control. Like tonight, for example. When my human arrived home, he did his normal routine of politely serving my food first before serving himself. After I ate and he went to sit down, I hopped on his lap and then immediately made my way up to his chest when he folded his left arm in front of himself. That created a nice place for me to lie down. I rested my chin on his arm and stretched my right front paw in front of him while he caressed me gently with his left front paw. Occasionally, I pushed my hind legs such that my back ended up near his face. He called this my "elevator butt." Other times, I extend one of my hind paws out over his arm. He didn't have a name for that. When he was done eating, he stroked my back with his right front paw. He basically held me like he did yesterday morning, except this was entirely my decision, unlike yesterday, when he just grabbed me.

I also spent some time this evening curling up and purring on his lap while he typed at the computer.

Day 55, Wednesday, December 19, 2018:
Tonight, my human fought with that loud thing with the long hose again. This time, they were all over the house. It kept trying to get away from him, but he kept pulling it back. I sought shelter at the top of the big cat tree in the living room. They came into that room, too, but since that monster appeared to stay on the floor, I felt safe since I was much higher than the floor.

Day 56, Thursday, December 20, 2018:
As usual, this morning I waited in the basement for my human to arrive. I talked to him as he scooped my litter pan. After he finished, I snuggled on his lap for a bit before he went to work.

While my human prepared his evening meal, I played with that shoestring he had given me a few days ago. He saw that one end of it was loose and frayed. He trimmed it and tied a knot at the end of the string so more of it wouldn't unravel.

Tonight, my human moved the big wood thingy that he and the dirt lady had taken to the upper room several days ago. I explored it a bit before he put all of the horizontal pieces in it. It had been blocking my access to the closet. After he moved it, I was able to inspect the closet again.

Several times this evening, I lay on my human's chest and arm. At one point, he held my left front paw with his right front paw. He gently squeezed my paw several times. I think he likes me.

Day 57, Friday, December 21, 2018:
I really like my shoestring. This morning, I dragged it to the kitchen while my human cleaned my food and water dishes. During the day, I took it all over the house. This evening, I played with it in the upper room in between naps on my human's arms. My human played with it tonight, too, which was really fun. I got excited as he made the string flop all over the place. It was good exercise.

Day 58, Saturday, December 22, 2018:
Today was a very interesting day. It started out like a normal weekend, with my human working both inside and outside the house. I sat on the bench in the front room and watched him push leaves around using a long stick that was really wide on one end. When he came inside, I napped on his arms for a while. As he ate lunch on the sofa, I curled up on the blanket near his legs. Then something unusual happened.

Two humans I had never met before appeared at the front door. My human had told me my adopted grandparents would be showing up, so I figured they must have been them. They brought several boxes and bags into the house. I wasn't sure about them, so I kept my distance for a while. I even hid in the upper room for an hour or so while they stayed in the living room.

After the commotion died down, I decided to go find my human. He was sitting on the floor in the living room near my original scratching post. The other humans were there, too, but sitting on the sofa. I walked across my human's lap before retreating to the safety of the carpeted tube below the window. I lay there and kept a close watch on the new humans. They seemed to be making the same observations of me. After a while, one of them came over and held a paw out for me to sniff.

I felt a bit more comfortable, so I got down onto the floor. My human brought my white string into the room, and we played with it some, but I never let my guard down about the new humans.

They were very nice to me, though. They even gave me some new toys. One is a round structure with three captive balls that I can bat around in a circle. They also gave me four springy balls. We all played with these for a while. It was entertaining to watch them play with these toys.

During the afternoon, all of the humans left for a couple of hours. That gave me some time to recover from the stress of meeting new people. When they returned, I sat at the top of the tall cat tree and carefully watched them. I felt comfortable enough with them that I was even able to give myself a complete bath.

Around my normal dinnertime, my human provided a plate of my wet food. After I ate, I went over and briefly joined the new humans on the sofa. I walked across them and sat between them while they stroked my back. They seemed nice.

They left the house again, leaving me alone with my own human. We went to the upper room. He worked on the computer, but I slept on his arm. It was exhausting meeting new people.

Day 59, Sunday, December 23, 2018:
Grandma and Grandpa returned today but didn't stay long. All three of the humans left for a while. When they returned, I could tell they had been at the cat shelter. They sat on the sofa while I sat on the small cat tree and looked out the window.

While Grandma prepared the midday meal for the humans, my human set a toy I had never seen down on the smooth kitchen floor. It looked like a big gray rat. He did something to it, and it suddenly started to make a noise and run all over the room! It was a pretty stupid rat because it kept running into the walls. At one point, it left the kitchen and went into the front room and stopped on the carpet. My human picked it up and set it back down on the kitchen floor, where it took off running again. This time it turned and ran directly at me! I quickly moved to get out of its way. After a while, my human picked it up, tickled its belly, and set it back down again. It didn't move after that, even when I tried to push it.

After that excitement, I spent a good part of the afternoon watching all of the humans while they sat on the sofa and floor. Grandpa played with his tiny computer and took a nap while Grandma and my human dumped a bunch of small, flat, oddly shaped, colorful pieces onto the table in front of the sofa. They spent a long time pushing the pieces together. I kept an eye on them between naps in the short tube of the big cat tree. When they were done, the pieces made a picture of kittens.

That evening, all three of the humans were on the sofa watching TV. There was a spot between my human and Grandma, so I jumped onto my human's lap and walked across him over to that spot. I lay down to watch TV with them while Grandma put a paw on me and stroked my head and back.

Day 60, Monday, December 24, 2018:
This morning, I watched from the front window as Grandma and Grandpa arrived again. For a while, all three of the humans sat on the sofa. My human sat at the end closest to my scratching post. At one point he, left the sofa, so I jumped up there and took his spot. I curled up there while Grandma petted me. My human came back and sat on the small table in front of me. He didn't try to take his space back.

On the big cat tree in front of Bubba's photo.

I didn't bother the humans while they ate lunch. Instead, I watched the birds at the front window before I joined the humans in the kitchen. I ate some dry food while they finished their meals.

Grandpa took some photos of me today, including one where I was at the top of the big cat tree in front of the photo of Bubba. He was one of the previous feline residents of this house. He was quite handsome. Grandpa also took a photo of me curled up on the sofa.

Curled up on the sofa.

Later in the day, I sat on the sofa between Grandma and my human. Once again, Grandma petted me and even gave me a nice neck massage. She also told me how pretty I was, but I already knew that because my human has been telling me that ever since we met.

Grandma also held my tail a lot. She seemed to like to do that. I didn't know why she did that, but I didn't mind.

Day 61, Tuesday, December 25, 2018:
Grandma and Grandpa were back today! I've been getting more comfortable with them. I even rubbed against Grandpa's legs and talked to him when he worked in the kitchen.

I spent a lot of time watching my big screen cat TV (the front window). A lot of leaves fell from the big tree today. Grandpa took a photo of me as I lay on the bench in front of the window. Grandma then came over to me and gave me a wonderful belly rub. My human also came over to the bench and gave me attention. It was great!

Later in the morning, all of the humans were on the sofa when I walked into the room and looked at them. I watched my human get up and go to the front room. He quickly returned with a small container. He opened the container and removed a soft, puffy pom-pom ball that looked just like some of my other toys. He gave this one to me. There was something different about it. It had a fascinating aroma. I flopped down with this ball, grasped it with my front paws, while kicking at it with both of my hind paws. It was loads of fun!

Grandma and Grandpa sitting on the sofa with me.

Grandma gives great back rubs.

Inspecting a new toy from Grandma and Grandpa.

I made it work!

On the front bench.

He also took that container and poured some of the contents out on the base of my scratching post. I went over to investigate. Raw catnip! I sniffed and licked it for several minutes. What a great morning!

Grandpa took more photos of me today and also recorded a video of me playing with the three-ball toy that he and Grandma had given me.

My human took photos of me, too, including a few while I was socializing with Grandma and Grandpa on the sofa. He even took photos as Grandma gave me the most amazing back rub that caused my hind legs to pop my butt and tail way up into the air.

While my human and Grandma played cards at the kitchen table, I took naps in the big cat tree, alternating between the small tube and the top tray below Bubba's photo. Once, though, I decided to play in the kitchen. I figured if they could play there, it was all right for me to play there, too. I took my white string from the front room and dropped it on the smooth kitchen floor. I pushed it around for a while. All of that activity can make a kitty hungry, so I trotted over to my food dish and ate a few bites. After that, I picked up my string and took it back to the front room.

Grandma and Grandpa said goodbye, since they were going back home. I enjoyed having them visit because all of those extra human paws meant more massages and belly rubs for me. After they left, I followed my human to the upper room. Exhausted from all the activity, I took a nap on his lap.

Day 62, Wednesday, December 26, 2018:
My human disappeared for a while this morning. I guess he went to

help at the shelter. I stayed home and watched water fall outside the big window in the front room. Later in the afternoon, more water fell from the sky. The water drops and light from outside combined to create captivating patterns on the window. It was fun to bat at them. Sometimes leaves fell from the tree and stuck to the window. I batted at them, too.

With Grandma and Grandpa gone, the house was quieter and less chaotic than the last few days. I spent more time on my human's lap and on his arms. It is nice to have him all to myself again.

Day 63, Thursday, December 27, 2018:
My human stayed home all day today. During the morning, I sat on his lap a few times while he worked on the computer. In the afternoon, we lay down on the sofa together. At first, I was at the end of the sofa near his hind paws. Later, while he slept, I curled up in my favorite spot: that triangular area behind his knees. After his nap, he sat up, so I moved to lie down next to him. He lovingly put his right front paw around me and gave me a neck rub. I dozed off and on with my front paws sometimes on top of his paw and sometimes underneath it. We spent a long time like that. In fact, we didn't get up until it was time for wet food.

Investigating the stacks of books.

Tonight, my human took both his food and my wet food to the upper room. After dinner, I spent most of the evening either on his lap or on his left arm.

Just before bedtime, I stepped off his lap and onto the table. He had a bunch of plastic books with metal rings stacked up on this table. The books were moved here during the chaos that happened in this room before Grandma and Grandpa's visit. I started to dig at a toy mouse that had found its way between a couple of the books. My human noticed me playing with it and joined in. He pulled the mouse out from between the books and set it on top of one of them. I pushed it so it fell between the books again. Then I dug it out myself and tossed it onto the floor, where I jumped down and chased it throughout the room.

Day 64, Friday, December 28, 2018:
Lap time! Since my human went back to work today, I spent most of the day alone. But when he returned home, he got an armful of kitty. Well, first I was excited to get some wonderfully tasty wet food. After that, he invited me onto his lap, and that's an invitation I could never decline. Throughout the evening, I was on his lap or on his arms several times.

I got a little annoyed when he tried to trim my nails, but later in the evening I relented and let him cut a couple on my left front paw. He still couldn't figure out how to get to my right front paw.

All of that napping on a human's arms can wear a kitty out. I wanted to go to bed tonight, but my human stayed up a lot later than normal, so I just went to bed without him. I figured he'd show up eventually.

Day 65, Saturday, December 29, 2018:
I'm so sneaky! Today, I managed to slip into the car room! My human stepped out there but was preoccupied with a plastic bag of trash. I let out a "meow" because I couldn't contain my excitement, but that gave away my location. My human called to me, but I ignored him. I walked around the car and explored under the truck. My human went into the house but came back a few moments later with my white shoestring. He dragged it along the ground. Knowing my weakness for strings, he took one end of the string into the house and down the stairs. I followed the string and caught it, at which point he closed the door to the car room. That terminated my exploration of that room— for a while, anyway.

While my human was preparing lunch, he opened the door to a small cabinet below and to the left of the sink. I had previously shown some interest in this cabinet, so he left the door open for me. I went inside the cabinet and explored its entire depth. Why was it okay for me to check out this tiny room but not the big car room?

My human had lunch on the sofa today. I curled up next to and at times on top of him while he ate. After that, we went to the upper room, where he raised the window blind so I could look out the window. That window was pretty high off the ground and provided a great view of the backyard. I spent part of the afternoon sleeping on the floor near my human's hind paws. At one point, I heard an animal outside, so I jumped onto the table to look out that window. I couldn't spot the animal that made the noise.

Later in the afternoon, I took a nap on the blanket chair while my human worked on the computer. After my nap, I convinced my human that I should have my wet food early. He agreed and also fixed his own food early. He took both of our plates to the upper room so we could have our meals together.

This evening, I jumped onto the smaller table in the upper room —the one next to the big metal cabinet. I found that he had put both of our empty dinner plates on that table. Mine was clean, but his had some crumbs on it that I sniffed and sampled. After that, I hopped onto the metal cabinet. I approached the edge that had that flimsy shelf. I remembered that it slid down the last time I stepped on it, so I didn't attempt to walk on it. The door of the closet adjacent to the cabinet was open. I spied the shelves in there but decided not to jump over to any of them. Instead, I turned around and walked onto the shelf on top of the small table.

I also checked out the big table where my human was working. That was a bit frightening because a pad of paper I stepped on wasn't very secure. It slipped when I walked on it, and I almost fell off the table. I saved myself and jumped over to the small steps that go between the table and floor. I sat on the top tread for a while to collect myself after that harrowing event.

My human was still working at the computer later in the evening when I went in to talk with him. I thought about jumping onto his lap, but I couldn't make up my mind. He turned his back on me, so I walked over in front of him. That was a mistake. He grabbed me! He pulled me up and held me close to his chest. I gave him a stare for a minute but then turned away and refused to look at him. I pushed my head back onto his arm while he caressed my neck and the side of my head. I'll tell you a secret: I kind of liked it. After a few minutes, I closed my eyes and began to relax as I enjoyed the massage. I'm glad no one else saw that. Several minutes later, I decided I'd had enough and wiggled my way onto his lap.

Day 66, Sunday, December 30, 2018:
Except for going to the shelter in the morning, my human spent the whole day home with me. Unlike most days, I didn't partake in much lap time, although I spent the whole day close to him. I snuggled with him on the sofa for a little bit around lunchtime, but most of the time I was on my blanket chair.

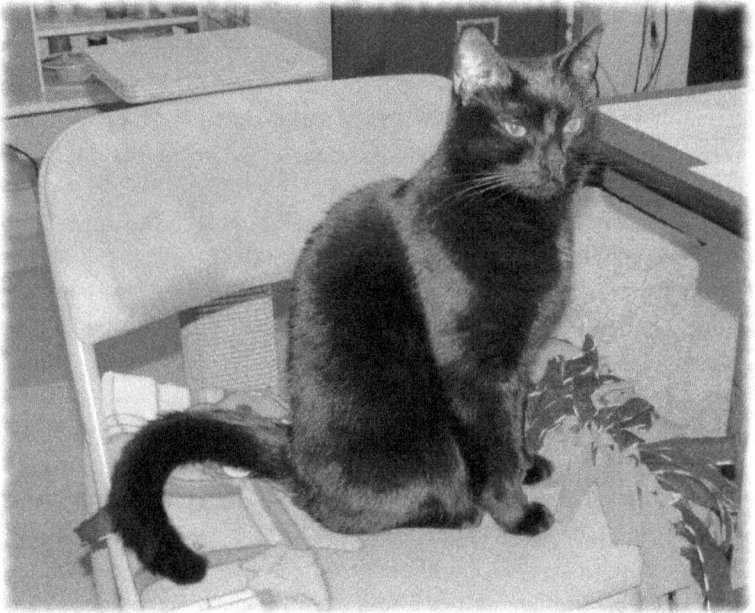

My blanket chair.

Day 67, Monday, December 31, 2018:
My human left me alone once again while he spent the day at work. I wish he didn't have to do that.

   This evening, I spent a long time on his lap and on his arms while he watched TV. After a few hours, he squirmed a bit and appeared to be in pain, but human discomfort doesn't really concern me. I was quite comfortable.

Later in the evening, he picked me up and held me close to his chest. Just like the last time, I refused to look at him. Doesn't he understand that he's only supposed to hold me when I crawl into his arms?

In between cuddle times (by choice or forced), I chased a toy mouse around the hallway.

Asleep on my blanket chair.

Day 68, Tuesday, January 1, 2019:
My human stayed home today for some reason. It was nice, and once again I stayed close to him most of the day. While he worked on the computer in the upper room, I spent time in my paper bag. He turned to look at me when I crawled into it, probably because I made too much noise. I was really quiet when I exited the bag a few minutes later and left the room. He never saw me leave.

When he ate his meal, I decided to change things up. Instead of climbing into his arms, I politely sat on his lap. That was easy to do because he had put his hind paws up on my blanket chair. Later, after he removed his paws from the blanket chair, I got onto the blanket. I kneaded it for a while before taking a nap.

My human provided some nice entertainment today. He removed a small gray box from the closet.[13] It had some buttons and a big knob. He played with the knob and buttons a bit, and when he pressed one of the buttons, the box started to make an interesting sound. It was like a soft growl. At that same time, it started to spit out

---

[13]A label maker.

a long, thin, flat thing. It was kind of like paper but was black and shiny on one side and white on the other. He spent some time pressing more buttons, and soon the box resumed taunting me with that string-like paper thing. This went on for quite a while. He never offered the paper to me, so I figured this was his toy and not mine. I just watched, wide-eyed, from a few feet away to make sure everything was okay. I batted at the paper a few times, but it didn't fight back.

After the gray box stopped spewing paper, my human took the long thread of paper and cut it into smaller pieces. I tried to play with the other end of the long paper string, but he pulled it away from me and put it on his lap.

At dinnertime, I decided I needed to make up for being ultra po-lite at lunch, so I jumped onto his lap and crawled onto his arms while he attempted to finish his meal. I liked being held. Well, as long as it was my idea.

Just before bedtime, I spent some time on his lap while he worked on the computer. I was doing a bit of shedding, and when I got down, he had to clean some fur from himself. He made some funny sounds as he used his front paws to pull fur from his mouth. I'm not even sure how it got up there. I don't know why he has a problem with it. I clean my fur with my tongue all the time.

Day 69, Wednesday, January 2, 2019:
This evening, I climbed onto my human's lap and brushed my right side against his chest rather than my left side, as I usually did. He ex-tended his right arm around me and let me climb onto it. He then put his left arm around me and caressed me with his left front paw. That was only the second time I'd sat like that on him. It was nice for some-thing different, but I still preferred to face the other direction.

Day 70, Thursday, January 3, 2019:
After taking care of my litter pan before going to work, my human knelt down so I could climb onto his lap. As I walked onto his angled legs, he pulled me up with one of his front paws. We spent about a minute socializing and being close before I hopped down and went to look out the window. I wanted him to stay, but I knew he had to leave. While he was gone, I played with my white string near his chair in the upper room.

My human was home a bit late today. As soon as he walked through the door, I let him know that my dinner was late. He immedi-ately set his stuff down and fed me. At least I have trained him well.

Later, while he was in the kitchen, he had the door to the room with all the shelves open. I jumped into a cardboard box that always sits on the floor in that tiny room. The last time I explored that box, it was empty, but this time there were some empty cans and a large piece of cardboard in it.[14] I landed on the cardboard, and it made a sound as my weight pushed it down. That got my human's attention, and he came over to see what I was doing. He didn't seem too alarmed and quickly left to resume his activity.

While we were in the upper room tonight, I didn't curl up on his lap or climb onto his arms for any long periods of time but instead made several short trips to those spots. Later, I took a nap next to him on my blanket chair. At one point, I tried to get a drink from the water dish in this room, but it was empty. Fortunately, once my human saw that, he cleaned and refilled the dish.

Day 71, Friday, January 4, 2019:
This day started out normal, but it soon got weird. My human left the house a bit later than normal, and he didn't take the bag that he normally took to work. About an hour later, I heard the big door in the car room move. I went to the front room to see what was going on, but I didn't see him outside. Soon, he came into the house from the car room with a small plastic bag.[15] He greeted me as he passed through the room on his way up the stairs. A few minutes later, he returned with his normal bag (and without the plastic bag) and told me he had to go to work. I thought that's where he went in the first place. I was once again left to run the house alone.

His schedule was really messed up. Not only did he leave late this morning, but he arrived home much later than normal, even later than last night. At least he fed me right as soon as he arrived.

After my dinner, we went to the upper room. That's where he found both my white and black strings. I had left them under his chair when I got done playing with them earlier today. He moved them out of the way before he sat down to eat with a kitty on his lap.

Day 72, Saturday, January 5, 2019:
It was cold this morning. After I awoke and got out of bed to do my morning cat stuff, I returned to the bedroom and curled up next to my human for warmth.

---

[14] The box is used to collect recyclable materials.
[15] Supplies from a dental checkup.

He left the house briefly a few times but was home most of the day. I was entertained watching him clean a kitchen cabinet. He took everything out of it, moving some things around and then putting almost everything back.

He entertained me again this afternoon, but this time in the upper room. He moved a bunch of books that had been sitting on the tables onto the bookcase that he and the dirt lady had moved to that room. Once he was done, I checked out his work by sniffing around the base of the bookcase. He took a picture of me while I did that, so I walked away and acted like I was uninterested.

After that, I went to the small room on the upper floor—the one with the window that overlooks the driveway—and looked out that window for a while. There were still some leaves falling from the big tree.

I spent a good part of the evening napping on my blanket chair in the upper room while my human sat close by listening to the radio and typing on the computer.

Day 73, Sunday, January 6, 2019:
My human arrived back from the shelter earlier than normal today. Hopefully, it was because more kitties had found homes, making it less crowded there. When he arrived home, he prepared lunch and took his meal to the sofa. He lay with his hind paws on the sofa, so I curled up behind his knees for a while before moving to the other end of the sofa.

This afternoon, I followed him to the upper room. I acted like I was going to jump onto his lap, but I didn't. As I sat there, a tiny intruder appeared in the room: a bright red dot. My attention was split between this dot and my human's lap. The dot wandered around and even approached me once before it went to the other side of the room. I didn't really get too excited about it until I saw it climb the closet door and walk across the ceiling. It came back down, went under the table, and then went up the short wall near the sink and my small cat tree. At that point, I ran across the room and leapt onto the V-shaped top of the cat tree, just inches away from the dot on the wall. I cautiously watched as the dot walked down the tree and onto the floor. It looked around my paper bag for a bit, but passed it up. It proceeded toward the hallway and disappeared behind the door. I jumped down to look for it, but couldn't spot it. I went back to the top of the cat tree and searched for it, but it never returned.

Inspecting the new bookcase.

I spent a lot of time today sitting on the bench in the front room, looking out the window. There wasn't much sunlight today. The branches on the big tree flailed about all afternoon, throwing leaves all over the lawn. Some water also fell from the sky.

Later in the afternoon, I followed my human back to the sofa. He looked like he didn't feel well. He crawled under the blankets and fell asleep. I decided I should take care of him, so I climbed onto the blanket and stretched out on his hind paws. A couple of hours later, I shifted to a new position. His paws were in the way of my normal spot, so instead, I leaned against his legs. I stayed there for a couple more hours.

Sometime after the sun set, he reached out to open one of the small doors under the table in front of the sofa. I knew these doors opened because I had seen them when I first moved in, but I hadn't explored behind them very much. It was time to change that. I hopped down and slunk into the dark cavity. It was basically a big, dark box. There were some small boxes in there and some games for humans. There was enough room that I could easily turn around to make my way back out.

After my exploration of that box, my human got off the sofa and went back to the upper room. I went after him and asked to jump onto his lap. He seemed to be doing much better, so I didn't spend much time with him. I stepped from his legs to the table, walked across the table, and jumped down. I left the room and went to the main level of the house. I kept an eye on things outside the front room for a while.

Before we went to bed, my human went to the basement and scooped my litter pan. Rather than kneel, he squatted down and balanced on his hind paws. That looked like a lap to me, so I jumped onto him. He held me for a while but then moved to sit on the floor with his back against the wall. We sat together for a long time while he gently massaged the top and sides of my head. He also stroked my back. It was the perfect end to the weekend.

Day 74, Monday, January 7, 2019:
Today my human scooped my litter pan first thing when he awoke. That totally threw off my morning routine. I much prefer when scooping my pan is the last thing he does before leaving for work. Normally, he'd kneel down to pet me, and I'd climb on his lap, which would delay his departure. Today, he scooped and then immediately

went upstairs to use his own litter device before I had a chance to use his lap.

This evening, he annoyed me some more. He grabbed me when I was on the table in the upper room. He told me he could clean some cobwebs from my whiskers. Doesn't he know I'm perfectly capable of cleaning myself when I want to? I just didn't see the need at that particular time.

I didn't spend much time on his lap tonight, but instead took a nap on my blanket chair while he scribbled on some papers on the nearby table.

Day 75, Tuesday, January 8, 2019:
Tonight, my human arrived home, fed me, and then almost immediately left again. He came back a few hours later. His absence really cut into my lap time, but I did my best to make up for it as he sat and watched TV.

Later in the evening, I followed him into the kitchen. He had the door to the shelf room open, so I jumped into the cardboard box again. It was empty this time. With nothing in my way, my landing was really quiet. Apparently, too quiet. I guess he didn't see me or hear me go in there because he closed the door and then left the kitchen! Some time elapsed before I decided to call him. He didn't respond. Several minutes later, he came back into the kitchen, so I yelled at him. This time, he heard me and quickly opened the door. He seemed surprised to see me and was very apologetic. That didn't stop me from giving him an earful about my displeasure at being trapped. It was all good, though, and we resumed our normal evening routine.

Day 76, Wednesday, January 9, 2019:
Once again, my human was home late. I'm really getting tired of that. He knows I don't have the thumbs needed to open my canned food. He's supposed to be here before sundown to open a can for me. Even worse, he didn't feed me right away when he arrived tonight. Instead, he brought a bunch of wood into the house and took it all down to the basement before providing dinner. I guessed that meant there would be more loud noises coming from the basement soon.

While he was in the basement, he scooped my litter pan. I had slightly missed the pan earlier today and ended up with a little bit of a wet mess outside the box. He folded up the disposable pad that was under the box and cleaned up the small spot that didn't get caught by the pad. He then put two new pads down that covered a greater area than the old single pad. I was so embarrassed, but he didn't say a word and took care of everything for me. I rubbed the top of my head against him as he worked to let him know how much I appreciated it.

This evening, I enjoyed a lot of time on his arms. I wrapped my front paws around his left arm as I rested on it. The cuddling didn't stop there. It was a bit of a cool night, so I curled up close to him after he crawled under the blankets on his bed.

Day 77, Thursday, January 10, 2019:
Unbelievable. He was late. Again. At least this time it wasn't as bad as some of the prior days. And even better, he came home with two cases of my yummy canned food! That will be enough to last for three months or more. He fed me pretty quickly once he arrived.

I was on and off his lap and his arms many times tonight. Later in the evening, I sat and looked longingly at my blanket chair. I wanted to lie on it, but his hind paws were in my way. He saw me and moved his paws, which made room for me to jump up there. Once there, I gave myself a bath before settling in for a nap.

Day 78, Friday, January 11, 2019:
Finally, a day where my human came home when he should! It was excellent to get my wet food meal at the appropriate time.

I didn't spend a lot of time on his lap tonight. That was because I was too fascinated with what was happening outside. White stuff was falling from the sky again. This time, there was a lot of it. For a while, I sat at the big window in the front room and watched it. Later, when my human went into the smaller front room on the upper level, I went and sat on the perch at that window and looked at the white stuff.

Day 79, Saturday, January 12, 2019:
It was kind of a strange, bright night. There was so much of that white stuff outside that it never really got dark. It was also eerily quiet. I spent the whole night next to my human on his bed. In the morning, my human got up later than normal. That was okay with me because while he stayed in bed he gave me a long, relaxing massage.

When we finally got out of bed, I went to the front room. Outside, everything was pure white! It was all over the grass, the dirt, and the trees. My human came over to the perch at the big window and looked outside with me. He seemed more interested in the big tree, but something farther away caught my attention. Two houses away there was a lady pushing the white stuff around. It wasn't the dirt lady, but someone else.

My human stayed home today. We played with some toy mice and some balls. And when I say "we," I mean mostly him. He flicked them with one of his claws and watched them go flying. I'd usually chase after them, but today I just watched him.

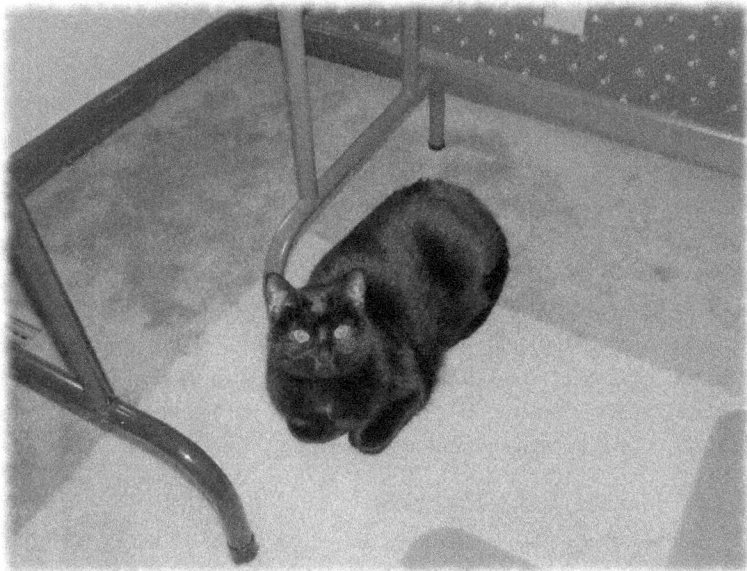

On the floor in the upper room.

Today, my human had one of his weird streaks. He chased me around the house! We like to play chase sometimes. He never catches me, though, because I'm too fast for him. We started in the big upper room, then went through the hallway, down the stairs, past my scratching post in the front room, where I stopped to let him catch up. Before he got to me, I took off again toward the kitchen. It can be hard to turn at full speed in the kitchen because it has a slick floor, but I'm pretty good at it and hastily made my way into the living room and to the scratching post near the sofa. I stopped to wait for him again. He followed me all the way, but I could tell he was about to give up, so I waited for him at the post. He extended a paw and gave me a nice neck rub before going back to the upper room. I went up there, too, and relaxed on the floor under one of the tables.

He spent part of the day in the cold floor room with the door closed making loud noises again. I wondered what he's up to. While he was busy in the basement, I alternated between napping and looking out various windows.

Day 80, Sunday, January 13, 2019:
This morning started out like yesterday, with a massage in bed. My human tried to put his paw around me and pull me close to him, but I didn't care for that. I like the petting, but I wanted to have some distance.

He spent some time at the shelter today but was home fairly early. He had an early lunch on the sofa, so I decided to stretch out between his legs and the back of the sofa. I rested my front paws on his hind paws. We each took a brief nap, although I think mine was longer than his. After that, he went back to the basement to make more noises. It wasn't too long, though, before he came back and went to the upper room to watch TV. I sat on his lap for a while. I also crawled up his arm and raised my back toward his face, brushing my tail alongside his head. I did that several times, actually. When he was done with the TV, he returned to the basement, so I disappeared to a place a human couldn't find me, as cats are wont to do. I didn't emerge until he returned from the basement and said it was time for food.

Day 81, Monday, January 14, 2019:
My human returned to work today, so I spent most of the day relaxing. Tonight, I had a good amount of lap time before bed. Actually, it was more like "climb-on-my-human's-arms" time. It was nice.

Day 82, Tuesday, January 15, 2019:
This morning, I got out of bed before my human. I played with my black shoestring while he took care of my food and water dishes.

He was home late, which really annoyed me. He also brought a lot of stuff into the house before feeding me. While he moved the stuff into the house, I tried to sneak out into the car room. He stopped me the first few times, but I eventually got past him. It was much colder out there than inside the house. He called me to come into the house, but I wanted to explore the car room. He even brought my white shoestring to the car room and tried to lure me back into the house. It almost worked, but I didn't fall for that a second time.

He closed the door between the car room and the staircase and left me out there for a minute or so. When he returned, he grabbed a long metal rod and took it to one side of the big door. He touched one end of the rod to a small wood and metal thing on the floor. When he did that, the thing jumped into the air and made a loud snapping sound that startled me. He did this several times on either side of the door and once along the back wall. A few times the wood and metal things grabbed the rod and he had to push them off.[16] Once he was done with that, he turned the lights off and went back into the house, leaving me alone in the cold, dark car room.

About ten minutes later, he returned and called me again. He brought my white shoestring back with him. Once again, he tried to get me to follow him into the house, but I wasn't going to go in on his command. He came back out and slowly approached from behind. I started to make my way toward the door. He followed me, and I walked faster. I went back into the house, but only because I wanted to.

I followed him very closely the rest of the evening. He went back to the car room for a bit but closed the door before I could get out there. I called for him, though, and clawed at the door. He got the message and didn't stay out there very long.

Soon after that, I followed him to the cold floor room in the basement, where he has been spending a lot of time. He didn't close the door this time, so I went in after him. I talked to him quite a bit as he worked at the bench. He then sat on a stool and had his front paws inside a box on the table. With his arms up like that, I had an opportunity to jump onto his lap. I took it. He immediately stopped what he was doing and started caressing my back. He suggested we go upstairs to cuddle, so I hopped down and followed him to the upper room.

On the way there, he stopped by the kitchen. While he fixed a snack, I played with balls and mice on the floor of the front room. I chased a hard pink ball into the kitchen, where it made a wonderful sound against the slick floor. Apparently, my human thought so, too, because he knelt down and started to play with it. He bounced it around with his front paws a couple of times and then flicked it back toward me in the front room. I sat and watched him, waiting to see what he'd do next, which happened to be grabbing my black shoestring and dragging it across the floor. When he let it go, I ran over and grabbed it.

After that, we went to the upper room, where he ate his snack with me stretched out on his lap. It was a good evening, although I would have liked more time to investigate the car room, preferably with the light on.

---

[16]Tripping mouse traps to eliminate the danger to a cat paw or tail.

Day 83, Wednesday, January 16, 2019:
When I returned to the bed this morning after doing my usual morning cat routine, I found my human was still there but facing the wrong way. I liked to be on the side of the bed closest to the window, and he should face the same way so I can curl up by his stomach. Today, he was facing the closet. I let him know that he messed up. I meowed enough that he rolled over to face the correct direction. It can be rather challenging living with a human.

This evening, I followed my human to the basement. After he scooped my litter pan, we spent some time playing with the various toys down there, including one of the plastic springy balls that Grandma and Grandpa gave me when they were here. I wondered when they'd come back. We also played with a soft purple ball. After that, he disappeared into the cold floor room. I went upstairs to get away from the loud noises that I knew would happen.

Later in the evening, I batted some toys around the upper room while he worked on the computer. One was a soft green pom-pom and another was a hard pink ball. I stopped batting at the green one when it got close to one of my human's hind paws. He saw it and batted it back to me, so I resumed play. I also attacked one of his big toes. He must have been surprised because he quickly pulled his paw away.

After playtime, I lay down on my blanket chair and rested while my human cleaned up in the small room farther down the hallway.

Day 84, Thursday, January 17, 2019:
Before my human left for work today, we spent a lot of time cuddling in the basement. I brushed against him as he cleaned my litter pan, and when he was done, I climbed onto his lap. It was a little uncomfortable because he had knelt down so his legs were at an angle, but at least I got to be close to him before he spent all day away from me. He held me closely and rubbed my head, back, and belly. I really liked having my belly rubbed.

This evening, I spent a lot of time on his lap. I faced away from him, which is my preferred position when sitting on his lap. He gave me a fantastic two-pawed neck massage.

During one of our lap sessions, he gave my right front paw a manicure. I didn't really want that, but he held me tightly until he had done all of the claws on that paw. It was the first time I had let him do that entire paw. I had to admit it was necessary. Lately, my claws have been sticking to things like blankets and my human's shirts.

I followed him to the basement tonight. After he scooped my litter pan, he went into the cold floor room with those noisy machines. He invited me into the room, but I declined. He left the door open for a while, but I still stayed on the soft and slightly warmer carpet. After a bit, he closed the door between the two rooms. I figured the noises would start soon, so I went back upstairs to wait for him.

Day 85, Friday, January 18, 2019:
My human spent a lot of time with me before he got out of his bed this morning. He started with a full head-to-tail massage, then moved on to scratching my neck and chin, and then finished with a belly rub. Some cats don't like having their bellies rubbed because it's kind of a sensitive area, but I really enjoyed it. It was nice to spend some extra time with him this morning.

That wasn't the only extra bit of attention I received in the morning. For some reason, he sat down and used the computer before leaving for work, so I hopped onto his lap. I faced away from him, like I almost always do, and lay on his lap to receive some attention. He operated the computer with his right front paw, but that still left his left front paw free to pet me.

There's more. Before he left for work, he went down to the basement to scoop my litter pan. When he finished, he knelt down and gave me access to his lap. I made my way onto it and received more affection from him. I knew he had to leave, so I hopped down after a while and watched him go toward the door to the car room. I watched as he put shoes on his hind paws and then ran past him up the stairs.

In the evening, I played with some of my toys in the front room while he worked in the kitchen. Tonight, he seemed to spend more time in the kitchen than normal. I stopped by a few times to check up on him, but he seemed rather busy, so I left to entertain myself.

At one point, while he was in the kitchen, I climbed onto the back of the sofa. I must have made a sound he wasn't expecting because he quickly showed up and seemed surprised to see me up there. He didn't say anything, though, and went back to the kitchen.

Before bedtime, my human spent time standing in that small rectangular room where water fell on him. While he did that, I sat on the bench by the big window in the front room. There was more of that white stuff falling from the sky. It was kind of windy, too, because the leaves on the tree were moving. That tree had lost a lot of its leaves, but there were still many on the lower branches.

Day 86, Saturday, January 19, 2019:

Today, my human and I both slept in. He gave me another fantastic massage before we got up. We spent quite a bit of time together before I got off the bed. He got up soon after me. After taking care of my food and water, he went to the basement, where I supervised as he took care of my litter pan. I rubbed my head against his left leg to let him know how much I appreciated him keeping my litter pan clean. Then I climbed onto his lap. When I hopped down from his lap, I was glad to see that he didn't go to work today.

Things were kind of strange, though. After washing his paws, he went back to the kitchen. He was preparing some kind of food, but it was too early for lunch so I don't know what he was doing. He was making a bit of a mess, though. At one point, I jumped onto a chair by the table to get a better look at what was going on. The table was pretty crowded, and he was getting white powder everywhere.[17] I didn't get close to it because I'm a very clean kitty and this looked rather messy. I left the room soon after because I didn't want to get my fur dirty. I popped into the kitchen a few more times to keep tabs on him but mostly spent time in the living room, the front room, and the basement while he made a mess of the kitchen.

Later in the day, I followed my human to the basement. I stayed on the soft carpet and watched him go into the cold floor room. I went back upstairs. He spent most of the day down there making lots of loud sounds.

When he finally reappeared from the cold floor room, it was past my normal dinnertime. He must have noticed his mistake because he quickly fixed meals for both me and himself. After we ate, he worked on the computer for a bit while I rested on the floor near his hind paws. I stretched my front paws out in front of me and put my chin on the soft carpet. My human mentioned that he had never seen a cat lie down like that, but it seemed perfectly normal to me.

After that, he went back to the basement to make more noises. Later in the evening, he came back upstairs. I enjoyed some lap time while he worked on the computer and listened to the radio. They said my name on the radio again! How do they do that?

Day 87, Sunday, January 20, 2019:

When my human returned from the shelter today, he didn't look very good. After having something to eat, he lay down on the sofa. I curled

---

[17]Flour.

up at his hind paws for a while before moving to the center of the sofa to be closer to him. He put his right arm around me and caressed my chin with his paw. That was okay, but I didn't want to be surrounded, so I moved to the other side of his arm. We spent most of the day like that.

After having our evening meals, I followed my human to the basement. He closed the door, but I could hear him working in the cold floor room. He didn't make the loud sounds this time. He also wasn't there very long. When he emerged from the room, he went upstairs. I ran after him and passed him on the staircase. I ran all the way to the kitchen, but I misjudged his intentions because he turned the corner and went up more stairs and all the way to the upper room. He picked up a few things and returned to the basement. The loud noises started, so I stayed upstairs.

Later in the evening, I napped on my blanket chair while he watched TV and typed on the computer. I was pleased to see that he seemed to feel better.

Day 88, Monday, January 21, 2019:
When my human arrived home from work, he made several trips between the house and the car room. I tried multiple times to enter the car room, but he stopped me on every attempt.

Later, we went to the basement. I had been playing with several of my toys there the last few days. Some of them had gone out of my reach under the bottom shelf of a bookcase. He extracted them and placed them back in the center of the room. Most of them were soft pom-pom balls, but there was also a mouse and one of those springy plastic balls from Grandma and Grandpa. We played with them as he pulled them out. Sometimes he'd toss them toward me; other times he'd roll them.

We also went into the cold floor room. He sat on a stool and worked at the bench, while I explored various nooks and crannies. I also sat on his lap for a while as he attempted to work. For some reason, he doesn't seem to get much work done when I sit on his lap. It was nice to get my chin and head scratched, though. When I'd had enough attention, I hopped down and left the room. He closed the door behind me and began making loud noises. I went upstairs and looked out the front window while I waited for him.

Day 89, Tuesday, January 22, 2019:
After my early morning prowl, I returned to the bedroom and climbed

up next to my human. Instead of the side by the window, like I'd done in the past, I went to the side by the closet. I stretched out alongside him and waited for him to wake up. When he did, he gave me a full head-to-tail back rub. I lapped up all the attention I could. It had to end, though, because he said he had to go to work.

This evening, I spent a lot of time on my human's arm while he sat on his chair. Instead of one long cuddle session, I made many trips to his arms.

Day 90, Wednesday, January 23, 2019:
Today, my human slept in.[18] That worked to my advantage because it meant an extended back rub and chin scratching. Like yesterday, I stretched out on his right side, while he caressed my soft fur with his right front paw.

When we finally got out of bed and went downstairs, I sat on the bench at the front window while he prepared my food and water in the kitchen. The ground outside was covered in more of that white stuff. It was really bright because the sun was shining. I sat in a sunbeam as my human headed off to work.

This evening, I watched as my human made several trips between the cold floor room and the car room. He was carrying a lot of wooden things. I tried multiple times to go into the car room to see what was going on, but he kept getting in the way. I think he's on to me and my attempts to explore the car room because he seems to always block my path. After he moved that stuff, he spent quite a bit of time out there.[19] I called him from the other side of the door, but he refused to let me out there. I finally gave up and entertained myself in the house.

He eventually came back in and went to the upper room. I followed him there and then spent a lot of time on his arms.

Day 91, Thursday, January 24, 2019:
This morning, I once again stretched out along my human's right side. That has kind of become my thing now. He stroked my back, which instantly caused my legs to extend and my rear end to pop into the air. I flopped down with my left side on my human and draped my tail over his stomach. I really enjoyed the attention. Sadly, it didn't last very long. Unlike yesterday, my human decided to get out of bed at his normal time.

---

[18]A delayed commute due to a snow and ice storm.
[19]Applying stain to the latest project.

In the evening, my human once again made several trips between the car room and the cold floor room, only this time he moved the pieces of wood back to the basement. The wood was a darker color than before. He set them up on little stands in the basement, on top of sheets of plastic. I didn't pay too much attention to them, though. I was too fascinated exploring behind one of those big metallic white boxes. My human tried to find me and spotted me right away. I guess he saw my tail sticking out from behind the white box.

We went upstairs for dinner. While my human prepared our meals, I chased a ball in the front room. He didn't set my food down on the kitchen floor. Instead, he took both his meal and mine to the upper room. It was nice to have dinner together.

After eating, I jumped on his lap, climbed onto his left arm, and rested my head on his arm. Instead of stretching either of my hind paws out over his other arm, I tucked both of them up under me and sat on his left front paw. I enjoyed spending time with my human after he had been gone all day.

Before bedtime, I played with my white string in the upper room while my human occupied himself with the computer.

Day 92, Friday, January 25, 2019:
Last night, my human went to bed before me. I was resting on my blanket chair when I heard him call me from the bedroom. He was on the bed but had more pillows than normal and was lying with his head elevated. I think he wasn't feeling well again. I spent the whole night next to him near his right front paw. Before he went to sleep, he spent some time petting me, which I greatly enjoyed. When he awoke this morning, he gave me even more attention.

After seeing him off to work, I spent the day playing with some toy mice and keeping an eye on my territory. I also took a nap.

In the evening, my human went to the cold floor room, where those wood things were still perched on their little stands. I tried to follow him, but he wouldn't let me into that room. Soon I heard a rattling noise followed by a hissing sound.[20] I left him to his weird noises and went back upstairs.

When he came upstairs, he washed up and then prepared our meals. After I ate, I hopped onto his lap, where I lay down while he watched TV. He spent a lot of time scratching the right side of my

---

[20]Spraying polyurethane.

head. It was fantastic. I felt lucky to have found a human who knew how to make me feel so good.

He made a few more trips into the basement this evening, but I stayed upstairs where it was warm. I took a nap on my blanket chair while he alternated between basement trips and typing on the computer.

Day 93, Saturday, January 26, 2019:
Today my human stayed home but was very busy. He kept going down to the closed-off room in the basement every few hours. From the other side of the door, I could hear the now familiar rattling and hissing sounds. He still refused to let me in to see what was going on.

I spent some time on the top shelf of the big cat tree today. While up there, my human came by a few times to talk to me and lightly rub the top of my head.

I got plenty of exercise today chasing all sorts of balls around the house. While I played with one of the soft purple ones in the upper room, I heard my human doing something in the kitchen. I stopped what I was doing and went to the hallway with the ball securely held in my mouth. He came over to the staircase and looked down the hall at me. He seemed to be entertained by me but let me be. I dropped the ball and batted it around the hallway.

After exercising, I returned to the upper room and took a long nap on the blanket chair. My human worked nearby on the computer, except for his periodic trips to the basement.

When my human finished his dinner, he left his big plate on the table. There wasn't much left on the plate. I stood on it and rubbed my neck on it. That was interesting because the plate curved up at the edges, and when I shifted my front paws toward the curve, the plate tilted up and I just about lost my balance! It also made a sound that drew my human's attention.

Day 94, Sunday, January 27, 2019:
My human came home from the shelter smellier than normal today. He put his shirts and pants in one of those big white boxes and then left the house again.

I spent a lot of time looking out the front window this afternoon. Most of the white stuff was gone, but some of it was still piled up at the edges of the road and driveway.

Once my human returned, I climbed onto his lap and arms multiple times. I purred and enjoyed his attention. Later in the evening, while I was on his lap, he tried to give my right front paw a manicure, but I wasn't having any of that. I stopped purring and jumped off his lap.

At one point this evening, I found my human in the bedroom messing with a big wooden box. It sits across the room from the bed and has many drawers in it. He had completely removed one of the drawers from the box. That left a rectangular hole in the front of the box. I had to stand on my hind legs and secure myself with my front paws to get a closer look. It looked like the drawer below the opening held some of his clothing.

Later, I found him in the upper room with a long metal part he had removed from the wooden box. He played with it and tried to get it to move. I watched as he grabbed a small metal can with one of his paws. The can hissed and spit on the long metal part. I followed him to the bedroom and watched him put the metal part and drawer back in the box.

Day 95, Monday, January 28, 2019:
My human got up a bit early today. In fact, I wasn't even done with my morning cat routine before he was up. By the time I got to the bed-room, he was already getting dressed.

Before he left for work, my human scooped my litter pan, just as he normally did. When he knelt down, I walked across the backs of his legs. I didn't stay there long because he had to get up to put the scoop and waste away. After that, he knelt down again, and I climbed onto his lap. We cuddled for several minutes. I got down because I knew he had to go to work. I went upstairs and sat at the front window, where I watched him drive away.

I spent a lot of time at the front window today. This evening, I sat on the bench and looked out the window while my human prepared my wet food. I also spent time there later in the evening while my human was in the upper room.

Tonight, I played with my white string in the upper room while my human played with some of the wood parts he had brought up from the basement.

Day 96, Tuesday, January 29, 2019:
My human got out of bed very early today, but only briefly. He mum-bled something about pipes freezing. I heard him go to the kitchen.[21] I

---

[21]Opened the cabinet below the sink for better air circulation.

stayed on the warm bed. For some reason the bed always seems warm, even when other parts of the house (especially places near the windows) are cold.[22] When my human came back upstairs, I heard him use his litter box thingy and wash up before he came back to bed. I made room for him. He crawled under the blankets, after which I curled up near his chest.

When he got up for real, I sat on the bench at the front window and watched the outside world while I waited for him to clean my food and water dishes. A lady walked by on the sidewalk. She was all bundled up. I've seen her walk by many mornings. She isn't the dirt lady but the one I saw pushing the white stuff some time ago.

This evening, my human brought his and my food to the upper room. I ate on the floor by his hind paws, while he sat on his chair. When I was done, I spent time on his lap. He continued to eat. I wish he would eat faster because then he could fully concentrate on petting me.

Tonight, I jumped on a shelf in the upper room. There were some books and papers on that shelf. I've been up there before, but this time there were more papers. They weren't very interesting. After that, I took a long nap on my blanket chair, while my human worked at the table.

Day 97, Wednesday, January 30, 2019:
It was really cold close to the windows today, so I spent most of the day finding warmer places in the house.

I had my evening meal in the upper room along with my human. After we finished eating, we went to the basement. He didn't let me into the cold floor room. Soon, he started making those loud sounds. Thankfully, the sounds didn't last very long, and soon we went back upstairs.

I wasn't feeling very well today, so I spent a lot of time napping. My eyes were doing a strange thing today. They do that sometimes. One of the pupils got really big, and the other got really small. It makes me look kind of funny. It normally lasts for a few days. The doctor said not to worry about it, but it can be a bit irritating. Sometimes when it happens, I just want to sleep it off.

Like last night, I slept on the blanket chair while my human worked in the upper room. In between naps, I explored the closet in the upper room. Nothing much had changed in it.

---

[22]A heated waterbed.

Day 98, Thursday, January 31, 2019:
I stretched out alongside my human before he got out of bed today and received a nice back rub. I wanted him to stay, but he got up and did his morning routine before going off to work.

When he arrived home, he made several trips from the car room to the house carrying bags of food. He must have gone hunting on his way home. I waited by the door and tried to enter the car room, but he stopped me every time. He also piled things up next to the door, which made it even harder for me to sneak out.

He put a few things away and then fed me my delicious wet food. I ate in the kitchen while he continued to put his own food and supplies away.

He didn't spend any time in the basement today. Instead, he worked at the table in the upper room. I slept on the blanket chair next to him. Between naps, we socialized a bit. He leaned toward me, and we sniffed each other's noses.

Later in the evening, while he was typing on the computer, I asked for and received lap time. He offered me his left arm. I climbed onto it and rested my head on his upper arm. Any time he reached over with his right front paw to pet me, my legs involuntarily extended, pushing my back up toward his face. I have no control over that; I just love the feel of his paw caressing my back.

Today, my eyes started returning to normal. I look kind of funny when they're not.

While my human cleaned up before going to bed, I batted and chased balls around the hallway.

Day 99, Friday, February 1, 2019:
This morning, I received a fantastic belly rub from my human before he got out of bed. Once he got up, I went down to the basement and waited for him while he did his morning routine.

While my human was at work, I kept tabs on things around the house, interrupted only to nibble on my dry food and nap on the warm bed.

Tonight, when my human returned home, he made a few trips to the cold floor room. On his first trip, I followed him to see what he was doing. He was moving wooden boxes and placing them on little stands again. Later, after I left the room, I heard those familiar rattle and hissing sounds again.

I ate my wet food during his first trip to the basement. That trip was longer than the others, and I was able to finish my meal before he came up to make his own meal. Tonight, I let him finish eating before I got on his lap.

I spent most of the evening sleeping on the blanket chair next to my human. I'd get up occasionally when I'd hear him leave the room, but since he usually returned pretty quickly, I would just sit on the blanket and wait for him.

My eyes finally returned to normal today. I feel and look much better now.

Day 100, Saturday, February 2, 2019:
Before going to sleep last night, my human gave me another incredible belly rub. I think he likes touching me because I'm so soft. He has said my fur is as soft as a bunny's.

He stayed home today, which meant I got plenty of lap time. I also spent some time looking out the big front window. My human even sat and looked out the window with me for a while. The white stuff is almost all gone now. The big tree outside this window still has a few of its leaves, but most of them have gone.

This afternoon, my human took a nap on the sofa with his head covered.[23] I think he wasn't feeling well again. I sat with him briefly but then went to the tube high up on the big cat tree, where I could watch over the whole room. When he awoke a while later, I lay down with him again. At first, I faced away from him, but then I switched directions and faced him. I changed directions again as he dozed off and on. He extended an arm out and put his paw around me. We stayed there until well after my normal dinnertime. Before we got up, he gave me a magnificent belly rub.

He suggested we have dinner, so I hopped down from the sofa and followed him to the kitchen. I had half of my meal in the kitchen and finished it after he took it to the upper room along with his own meal.

This evening, I took a nap on the blanket chair while he worked on the computer and table.

Day 101, Sunday, February 3, 2019:
I spent a lot of time looking out the front window today. All of the

---

[23]Human's frequent headaches.

white stuff has disappeared. It wasn't nearly as cold when I sat on the bench as it had been the last few days.

My human was at the shelter for a couple of hours this morning. When he returned, we played with the white string on the kitchen floor. I also spent time on his lap and on his arm enjoying a nice neck massage.

I lay down near his hind paws as he sat and worked on the computer this afternoon. He took a photo of me because he said he had never seen a cat lie down the way I did. He called it my platypus pose. I rested my chin on the carpet, tucked my hind paws under myself, folded my front paws under my front legs, and pushed my front legs and paws out to the sides. I don't know what's so special or weird about it; I just did what was comfortable for me.

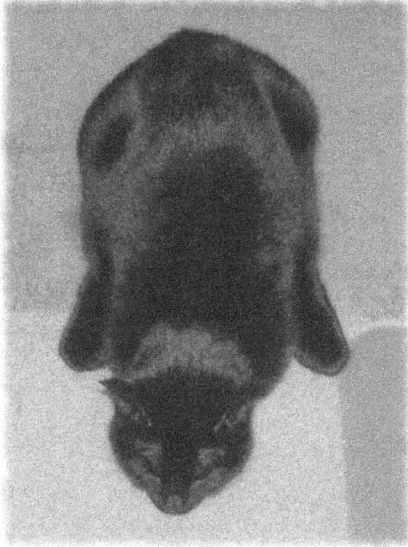

My platypus pose.

Day 102, Monday, February 4, 2019:
My human did his normal morning routine today, but I didn't. I looked out the front window for a bit, but when he went down to the basement to scoop my litter pan, I stayed in the front room.

When he arrived home, he prepared my food, but I didn't eat it right away. Instead, I waited for him to get his own food ready and then take both of our plates to the upper room so we could eat together. As usual, I only ate part of my meal at that time and saved the rest for later in the evening.

While he worked in the upper room, I got some exercise chasing balls around that room and down the hallway. At one point, he got onto the floor with me and flicked a few balls toward me, but I didn't chase them. Instead, I decided to just sit and watch him. He can be kind of entertaining.

Later in the evening, I played with a soft doughnut-shaped toy while my human worked on the computer.

Day 103, Tuesday, February 5, 2019:

This evening, I followed my human to the cold floor room. I think he tried to stop me, but I was able to quickly slip past him. I explored the room while he worked at a table. I found a dead bug on the floor. My human saw me investigating it and came over to clean it up.

After a while, my human suggested I leave the room, but I didn't. Suddenly, a big red machine started to roar! Two large cream-colored bags attached to the machine began to expand.[24] I stood there in shock, not knowing what that beast was going to do. My human approached, but I decided I'd had enough and took off toward the safety of the other room. The door closed behind me, and then I heard another loud sound. I turned around and watched the door since I was concerned for the safety of my human on the other side. The noises didn't last very long. When all was quiet and the door opened again, I was relieved to see my human survived his encounter with the loud machines.

After that ordeal, we spent some time in the upper room. On one of the tables, I found the plate that held his meal. When he was done with it, I sniffed and licked it a little bit. After that, I took a nap while my human worked at the table.

Checking out my human's plate.

Just before bedtime, my human went into the bathroom. I could see into the room through a crack since the door was not closed all the

---

[24]A dust collector.

way. The door wasn't open far enough for me to enter the room, though. I know it should open farther, but I'm not sure how to do it. I got close to the door and stretched my right front paw as far into the crack as I could, nearly reaching the cabinet. That caused the door to move enough that I could squeeze my head into the room. After that, it was easier to get the rest of my body in there. I walked around on the floor near my human's hind paws while he stood at the sink and pushed a white stick back and forth in his mouth with one of his front paws. Yeah, he was being weird again.

My human's plate had a nice aroma.

Day 104, Wednesday, February 6, 2019:
This evening, my human prepared my food and then spent a lot more time making his own meal. While he was doing that, he opened a cabinet in the kitchen that I have never explored. He left the door open and even asked if I wanted to take a look in there. While he was busy opening a box and pouring its contents into a pan, I crept toward the cabinet door for a closer look. There was a shelf in the cabinet. The space below the shelf was occupied, but the front of the shelf was empty, so I hopped onto it. There was enough room that I could fit my entire body in there. It really wasn't all that interesting, though, so I didn't spend too much time in there.

Later in the evening, I saw my human working at the table in the upper room. He had wood pieces and metal pieces and was connecting them to each other. Since he was playing with his toys, I got onto the floor to play with my toys. I tossed my black string around for a bit. I also chased a yellow mouse until it got stuck under a bookcase. I tried really hard to reach it, but it was too far away. My human saw me frantically reaching for it and came over to see what was going on. He held a little blue cylinder with one of his paws. When he pushed a button on the cylinder, the other end of it lit up. He used the cylinder to make the space under the bookcase much brighter. I could see the dark space under the bookcase very well, but I guess humans aren't nearly as evolved as us cats and need extra help to see in dark spaces.

He got up and went over to the table with the big red box. He opened the box and pulled out a long and kind of floppy stick. It was the same one he had used several days ago to reach things on the table while I sat on his lap. He returned to the bookcase and used the long stick to grab the tail of my toy mouse. He extracted the mouse from under the bookcase and placed it on the floor in front of me. Humans may not be very smart or advanced, but they are useful to have around.

Day 105, Thursday, February 7, 2019:
My human stayed home today for some reason. That was really nice because I got to be near him all day. Well, it wasn't very nice when he tried to give me a manicure, but other than that, it was a great day.

This morning, I looked out the front window and saw that the white stuff was back. It completely covered the ground.

I slept most of the day, usually on the blanket chair because it was close to where my human was seated. He spent most of his time in the upper room, except for some trips into the basement to do that rattle-and-hiss thing.

I played a bit between naps. I took my white string down to the basement for a while but later brought it back upstairs and played with it in the kitchen.

Day 106, Friday, February 8, 2019:
Today, I took my white string to the upper room and played with it there. Later in the evening, I took it back to the kitchen. I really like that string, so I take it all over the house.

Tonight, my human went out to the car room briefly. I waited by the door to see if I could sneak out there, but he saw me and prevented yet another exploration of that room.

I also followed my human to the basement. He left the door open, so I was able to get into the cold floor room. He didn't stay long.

Fortunately, when he left that room, he didn't close the door, so I was still able to get out.

Several minutes later, I went to the upper room. That is where I found my human doing something I hadn't seen him do before. There was a big white blanket in the middle of the room. I also saw him move a lamp into the room that was normally in the storage room across the hall. He set a big box down on the blanket. It was the wood and metal thing he had played with a few days ago. I walked onto the blanket to investigate this thing while he got a camera and began taking photos of me and the box.

Later in the evening, while my human was watching TV, I walked onto the table and discovered a plastic bottle that had a very appealing aroma. It smelled like really tasty fish.[25] I tried to open it, but my human took it away from me.

Inspecting the new wooden thing.

---

[25]Omega-3 fish oil capsules.

That wooden thing was boring.

Day 107, Saturday, February 9, 2019:
Overnight, I moved my white string to the front room. I played with it there while my human prepared his lunch. I tossed it around and jumped after it so much that I drew his attention. He looked at me through the doorway while I sat on my string and swished my tail back and forth. Satisfied, he went back to working in the kitchen, and I resumed play.

This afternoon, my human moved the small set of steps in the upper room that lead to my water dish. That was okay because I didn't need a drink at the time. Besides, I was too distracted because he also opened a small door below my water dish. I had never seen this door opened since it was usually blocked by the steps. The door led to a small cabinet under the sink. It contained a shelf. He removed several things from the shelf. The area below the shelf was still blocked, but I was able to climb onto the shelf. It was rather dark in there. There wasn't really anything exciting to see, so I didn't spend much time in there. As soon as I emerged, my human closed the door and put the steps back in their appropriate place.

Later, I found my human working in the upper room. I climbed the steps and walked along the table when I picked up an exciting scent. It was the fishes again! I sniffed around for it. One of the tables had some tall but shallow boxes with many plastic drawers. I stood on my hind paws and stretched as far as I could, using the plastic drawers to support myself with my front paws. There it was! On top of the plastic bins, but out of my reach, sat the jar emitting that wonderful fishy smell! I guess my human liked it, too, because he took the jar and left the room with it. I don't know where he put it.

This evening, my human once more attempted to give me a manicure while I sat on his lap. It didn't happen.

Day 108, Sunday, February 10, 2019:
This morning, I went to the basement to wait for my human. He came down after he cleaned himself and fixed my food and water dishes. When he arrived to take care of my litter pan, I greeted him and rubbed my head against his legs. Then I left the room and went halfway up the stairs to wait for him at the door to the car room. That's when he appeared at the bottom of the staircase with a large box.[26] I got scared and retreated to the top of the staircase. He set the box by the car room door and then went back for another box. He took the boxes when he left for the shelter. He was gone for a few hours.

This afternoon, I walked by my human as he sat in the chair in the upper room. Suddenly, he grabbed me and put me on his lap! I fought him a little bit, but I really liked the way he caressed me. I lay down, wrap my front paws around his left leg, and just enjoyed the attention. He used both of his front paws to give me a long back and neck massage. I like when he does that because it helps work out loose fur when I shed.

I got lots of exercise today. Early in the day, I played with my white shoestring, and things got pretty wild. During the melee, the rug by the front door turned into a piled-up mess with my string buried underneath it. My human pulled the string out from under the rug and set it by the staircase. He also neatly put the rug back in its normal place.

In the evening, my exercise routine switched to chasing my yellow toy mouse all over the upper room. It ended with me running into the paper bag between the bookcase and the small cat tree.

Day 109, Monday, February 11, 2019:
My human went back to work today, leaving me in charge of the house. Before he left, I waited for him in the basement. When he ar-

---

[26]Food for the shelter.

rived to take care of my litter pan, I emerged from behind the curtain at the glass door and asked him to kneel down. He did, and I sat on the floor with my front paws on his lap. I hoped he wouldn't leave.

In the evening, I received a lot of lap time. Well, actually, more like arm time. I climbed onto his left arm and received a massage.

Later in the evening, I sat on the table behind him while he watched TV. I groomed the fur on top of his head for a while before I, too, turned my attention to the TV. I went over to the small three-step staircase in the middle of the room and sat on the top step. From there, I could get a better look at the screen. It was the show with the guys in uniforms who have a tunnel under the bunk bed in their house. There was also a guy who wore half a pair of glasses.[27]

Day 110, Tuesday, February 12, 2019:
As usual, this morning I waited in the basement until my human came down to scoop my litter pan. He knelt down, like he frequently did. I started to climb onto his lap but changed my mind when he tried to scoop me up.

I played with my white string in the upper room today. It was in a pile between my paper bag and the steps that led up to the table. I leaped into the air and pounced on it with all four paws before grabbing it and tossing it into the air. It was fun!

After getting my exercise, I settled down for some lap time with my human. I keep calling it "lap time," but these days it's usually "arm time." Tonight, I climbed onto his left arm when he folded it against his chest. Naturally, he gave me a massage. We did that twice. After my massages, I took a nap on the blanket chair while he worked on the computer.

I got to explore behind another small door this evening. It's just like the one under my water dish in the upper room that I got to climb into the other day but on the other side of the sink. My human moved the steps that led up to the sink and opened not only that new door but the bigger one next to it. I poked my head into the space behind the smaller door. It had a shelf in it, just like the one on the other side, only there are boxes piled on top of and below the shelf, blocking me from entering the space. I was able to put my front paws up on the shelf and poke my head in far enough to see my human through the other open door. Apparently, the small doors all go to the same cozy space under the sink. My human grabbed a few plastic bags from a

---

[27]*Hogan's Heroes.*

box under the sink and then closed the door. Once I stepped back, he closed the other door and returned the steps to their appropriate place.

Day 111, Wednesday, February 13, 2019:
Last night, I went to bed with my human. I curled up on the blanket in front of his belly. For some reason, that part of the blanket has a lot of black fur on it. Anyway, as I was drifting off to sleep, I suddenly got spooked by a loud noise. The bed shook, too. It was my human! What did I do? What happened?[28] I didn't wait to find out but bolted out of the room. He called me a couple of times after that, but I waited until he was asleep before going back into the room. Once he was asleep and had been quiet for some time, I hopped back up onto the bed and curled up next to him again.

I got up before him, like I normally did. After my morning prowl, I didn't return to bed. Instead, I sat on the bench in the basement and looked out the big glass door. I knew my human would come into the basement soon. He did and, just like yesterday, when he knelt down, I climbed onto his lap. For a while I sat with my front paws and chest on his legs. I extended my front legs and pushed my head into his armpit. Then I started to climb onto his lap. Just like yesterday, he put his right front paw under my hind paws and scooped me onto his lap, only this time I let him. We cuddled for a while before I hopped down and returned to the bench. When I did that, he got up and left for work.

While he was at work, I played with my white string on the upper room floor. When I was done, I left it piled up on the plastic mat below my human's chair. I thought he might like to play with it once he returned. He didn't find it until late in the evening because he didn't go into that room when he arrived home. In fact, it was kind of strange. He surprised me when he came home earlier than normal. He fed me my wet food and then took a nap on the sofa. I cuddled with him briefly but then got down to play. I found a multicolored ball close to my scratching post and whacked it as hard as I could. It went flying across the room toward the small cat tree near the window. I chased it into the corner and then back out to the center of the room. I didn't play very long, though, and soon left the room to let my human nap.

A few hours later, my human awoke and got up. I followed him for a bit. Soon, he sat back down on the sofa and rested his hind paws

---

[28] A cough.

on the table. I lay down near him and leaned against his right arm. We stayed like that for a long time while he turned slightly and massaged my belly with his other front paw.

Later in the evening, I followed him to the upper room. While he sat and worked on the computer, I tried to get my white string. Part of it was stuck under one of his hind paws. He saw me reach for it and kindly moved his paw so I could get my string. I took the string and moved it so it wouldn't be under his paw anymore. Then I finished the evening with a nap on my blanket chair.

Day 112, Thursday, February 14, 2019:
When I woke up this morning, I received a full head-to-tail back rub from my human. He used both of his front paws. It felt amazing! Unfortunately, it didn't last long because he had to get up and go to work.

Before he left, we spent more time together in the basement. After we cuddled for a while, he got up and approached a table. A few of my toys, mostly balls, had ended up against the wall under the table. One by one, he pulled them out and put them in the middle of the room for me. After he left, I went upstairs and played with my strings in the kitchen.

When my human got home, he spent a lot of time working on the computer and playing with lots of papers. He was very busy and seemed a bit agitated.[29] I stayed close to him and took a nap on the blanket chair.

Later in the evening, I walked by him as he sat on his chair. I purred and talked to him for a bit. He scooped me up and held me close to his chest. Ugh. I stopped purring and refused to look at him. He eventually relaxed and let me hop down. Why does he do that? I never try to pick *him* up!

Day 113, Friday, February 15, 2019:
This morning, I got up before my human. After taking care of cat stuff, I played with my strings in the kitchen. When I was done, I didn't leave them piled up like last time. Instead, I stretched them both out alongside each other.

A bit later, I heard my human get up and go to the bathroom. I went to see him, but by the time I got there, he had returned to bed. I walked up the steps to the bed and stretched out on the blanket next to him. He gave me a back and belly rub, but it didn't last as long as the

---

[29]Tax season.

one yesterday. I spent a little more time on his lap in the basement before he went to work.

While he was gone, I watched things change outside. It got cold by the window, and very quickly a bunch of that white stuff fell out of the sky and covered everything. It was still falling when my human arrived home.

He gave me a plate of wet food, prepared a bowl of food for himself, and then took both of them to the upper room, where we ate together. After that, he started playing with the computer and papers, just like yesterday. Once again, I figured I should stay close to him, so I took a nap on my blanket chair.

Later in the evening, while he was watching TV, I walked on the table behind him and rubbed the back of his head with mine. He seemed a bit less stressed. He extended one of his paws out for me to sniff.

Day 114, Saturday, February 16, 2019:
This morning, my human slept in more than usual. I got up for a while before returning to take a nap next to him. After he awoke, he did his normal routine and went outside, but he didn't leave. Instead, I saw him push that white stuff around like he had done several weeks ago. From the front window, I watched him remove most of the white stuff from the driveway, sidewalk, and front steps. I saw some other humans doing the same thing. The human on the other side of the road pushed a machine around that tossed the white stuff back into the air. It fell back to the ground, though.

I got excited when my human came back inside the house instead of leaving for work. I ran around the house for a bit and jumped on my white string. While he was in the kitchen, I rolled a ball across the floor of the front room. I guess my human wanted to play, too, because he came into the room, picked up a ball, and rolled it toward me. It was the kind of ball that makes a lot of ringing sounds when it rolls. It left the carpet and rolled onto the hard floor near the front door. It wobbled back and forth for a rather long time before coming to a standstill. I took a few steps over to it and gave it a push. It rolled off the hard floor and down the stairs toward the basement.

That wasn't the end of our play session. My human picked up a plush chipmunk toy and placed it on the platform atop my scratching post. I couldn't let it stay there, so I reached up to grab it but ended up pushing it farther onto the platform. He moved it back to the edge. It took me a few more tries, but I finally knocked it from the platform. Later, I played with the white string in the front room and then in the upper room.

While in the upper room, I decided to check out the top of the table below the TV. It didn't go as I expected. When I jumped up there, I landed on a piece of paper I couldn't see from the floor. In the process of securing my landing, I slipped on the paper, and it ended up on the floor. I was okay but was intrigued by the paper. Having lost interest in the shelf, I jumped down to inspect the paper. I lay on it and started to play with the edge of it, but then my human came over. When I stood up, he took the paper and put it back on the table.

After taking the paper away from me, my human started to play with my white string. He sat down on the floor and pulled it across the carpet. I wasn't interested in playing with the string at the time, but I was certainly up for cuddling! I walked over to him and climbed onto his legs. I didn't stay there very long, but I enjoyed the attention he gave me. When I got up, he rolled one of my balls across the floor and into my paper bag. It was entertaining, but I didn't chase after it.

Later in the afternoon, I took the stairs up to the table and made my way over to the tall window. My human sat nearby and worked on the computer. He got up and pulled a string that was dangling above my head, and at the same time the bottom of the blinds moved up, which gave me a better view out the window. When he sat back down, I looked up and saw that, in addition to the string, there was a long, thin stick hanging down from the blinds. How long had that been there? The bottom of it was swaying left and right. There was a small shelf with some papers near the window. I stepped up onto the shelf to get a closer look at the stick. I reached up and gave it a slight tap. It moved some more! My human noticed what I was doing and tried to get my attention. I turned to look at him, and when I looked back, the stick wasn't moving anymore.

Day 115, Sunday, February 17, 2019:
Today, I spent a lot of time looking out the front window, the basement window, and the window in the upper room by the computer. At that last one, I decided not to play with the rod, like I did yesterday, because something more interesting outside the window caught my attention. There is a tree outside this window, and a bird was sitting on one of its thin branches! I sat and watched this bird for several minutes.

This afternoon, I jumped back onto the table that I just about fell off yesterday. It went better this time since I didn't land on any papers. I climbed all over the shelves that are on that table, including in front of and behind the TV.

I also climbed on top of the tall metal box of drawers. While I was up there, I noticed that the closet door was slid to the left, exposing the shelves on the side of closest to the metal box. I needed a closer look. I almost stepped on that tiny, unsecured shelf that had previously slid down the metal box (twice) but thought better of it. Instead, I stepped down to the top of a tall stack of narrow plastic boxes that sat below the small shelf. It was hard to do since the funny shelf was in the way, but my cat-fu lets me get into impossible places.

Only there was a problem: the tower of plastic boxes wasn't very secure. I steadied myself on it as I tried to make my way over to the closet, but it was so unstable that I couldn't make much progress. My human got out of his chair and started to come over to me.[30] I decided it was time to abort, so I jumped down to the floor.

I went back to the window. The bird was gone. I stood up and stretched with my front paws on the window. Then one of my claws got stuck on some strange mesh thing in front of the window. I tried to stretch again, and the same thing happened. Right after that, my human came over and got onto the table behind me. I didn't know that humans ever got on tables. Anyway, he played with the mesh thingy for a bit and eventually removed it. When he got down from the table, he took the mesh thing to the other side of the room and placed it behind the bookcase where one of my balls got stuck a while back.

I spent most of the rest of the day napping on the blanket chair while my human watched TV and worked at the table. Late in the evening, I asked to sit on his lap. We watched videos on the computer as I sat on his lap. He put one arm around me and gently stroked my back with his other paw.

Day 116, Monday, February 18, 2019:
I awoke to an amazing back rub this morning. It was so good, I purred loudly as my backside popped into the air and then fell over onto the blanket atop my human. Oh, it was good! It went on for quite a while but not long enough because my human had to get up and go to work.

---

[30]The plan was to secure her and the stack of parts bins or attempt to catch her if she fell.

Our morning routine was a bit strange. He did things opposite his normal order and first went to the basement to scoop my litter pan. By the time I got down there, he was back upstairs. While he took care of my food and water dishes upstairs, I hopped onto the platform between the curtain and the big glass door to survey my territory. I heard him come down to the basement briefly before he left, but he didn't come over to the bench.

I was happy to see him when he returned but a bit annoyed that it took him a while to get into the house. I waited at the door to greet him, but after he arrived, he stayed in the car room and made some noises before he came inside. Once he walked through the door, his priorities got corrected. The first thing he did was prepare my wet food. I took a few bites but then followed him upstairs because I was so excited to see him, plus I like to keep track of him. He eventually fixed his own food and sat down to eat in the upper room. He forgot my food in the kitchen, but that was okay because I ate most of it while he was making his own meal. A bit later, he went back to the kitchen and brought my leftovers to the upper room. I cleaned my plate since he went to the trouble to get it for me.

This evening, I got back onto the metal box of drawers. I sat on top of it for several minutes and observed my human. He got out of his chair and walked toward me, but he ignored me! He picked his camera up from the table, returned to his seat, and began taking photos of me.

Later, he went to the sink and moved the steps that I use to access my water bowl. He opened the two big doors under the sink and removed some boxes from the cabinet. Unlike the two smaller side doors that I had previously checked out, there wasn't a shelf behind these doors. That gave me plenty of headroom while I explored. It was easy to move around since he had removed those boxes. He went back to the table and left me to investigate this area unsupervised but returned several minutes later to close the doors. He didn't close them on me, though. We exchanged a few meows, and I stepped out of the cabinet of my own accord. He closed the doors and returned the small staircase to its rightful place. While he was there, he cleaned my water bowl and provided some fresh water. I walked up the steps and sat at the edge of the sink to supervise that operation.

While my human was in the bathroom cleaning up and getting ready for bed, I played with a ball in the hallway. I also found my white string and took it to the hallway to play with it for a while.

I visited my human in the bathroom. I'm still not sure how to open a door, but I know if I can see him through the crack, I can eventually work my way in there. I pushed a paw through the narrow opening as far as I could. That made enough room for me to push my head through, and the rest of my body followed. There must be an easier way.

On the metal box of drawers.

Oh, I almost forgot. Tonight, I got to explore a new place: one of the drawers in that big wooden box in the bedroom. Some of the drawers in that box are long and some are short. Tonight, my human opened one of the long ones. I stood on top of the pet steps and reached up toward the drawer. I could just barely see into it. It looked safe, so I took a leap and landed on . . . his shirts. That wasn't as exciting as I expected. At least it was a soft landing. I dug around a bit, but all I found were more shirts.

Day 117, Tuesday, February 19, 2019:
I received another great back rub this morning. What a great way to start the day!

Today, some more of that white stuff fell from the sky. I sat on my curved scratching pad in the front room and watched it through the big window.

In the evening, I spent quite a bit of time resting on my human's arm. He gave me a nice massage while we watched some cat videos on the computer.

My exercise tonight involved throwing my soft doughnut-like toy around the upper room. I picked it up with a claw and tossed it into the air. I chased it when it hit the ground and rolled.

Day 118, Wednesday, February 20, 2019:
I was a bit annoyed this afternoon because my human didn't come into the house right away when he arrived home. Instead, he played with that white stuff outside. Once he finally came inside, I let him know it was past my dinnertime. He listened to me and fed me right away.

While he was getting his own food ready, I played with some balls in the front room. I chased after a dark-purple one that I whacked into the kitchen. I left it there and went back to the front room. My human picked it up and rolled it toward me, so I chased it some more. Somewhere along the way, I switched to a pink ball. I hit it into the kitchen but didn't follow it. I chased it again after my human rolled it back to me. It was fun playing together.

When we got done playing, I followed my human to the upper room. I waited for him to finish eating and then sat on his lap. I rested my head on his upper arm and let one of my paws dangle over his arm.

Day 119, Thursday, February 21, 2019:
I was rather annoyed again today because, just like yesterday, my human not only spent too much time in the car room when he came home, but he was also late! I called to him in the car room when I heard him. He called back, but I could hear him walk away. After several minutes, he returned. He came through the door carrying his normal bag and some pink-and-gray thing I had never seen before. I ignored that and just let him know that I was annoyed by his slowness. He quickly provided my evening meal.

After I ate, I went to the upper room, where I discovered the blanket on the chair I frequently slept on was missing. It had been replaced with a soft pink-and-gray pet bed. I wasn't too sure about it because that blanket was *so* comfortable. I missed the old blanket but decided to give the new bed a try. I alternated between sitting on the bed and sitting on my human's lap several times that evening. The bed has soft sides that provide some nice support, but I wasn't sure yet if I liked it.

Day 120, Friday, February 22, 2019:
This morning, I did something a bit different. I normally face away from my human when I'm on his bed, but today I decided to turn around and look at him. He gave me a fantastic shoulder-to-tail back rub.

Today, I chased some balls and spent some time in my paper bag in the upper room. I also took a nap on my new pink bed. I rested my chin on the side and let a front paw hang off the edge.

In the evening, I followed my human to the kitchen. While he prepared a warm drink for himself, I played with my black string, which I had conveniently left in the middle of the kitchen floor.

Day 121, Saturday, February 23, 2019:
This morning, I looked out the basement window while I waited for my human. I heard him get up, but he didn't come to the basement. It was a bit too quiet upstairs, so I went to check on him. I discovered he was back on his bed. I walked up the steps and made my way to him. He reached out to pet me. After a lot of wiggling around to get comfortable, I settled down between him and his arm for a nap. We slept in for another hour and a half.

When I woke up later, I received another wonderful back rub and back scratch. I curled up and draped my head over his arm while he reached over with his other front paw and rubbed my belly. I really like days like this where we sleep in and cuddle.

Once we finally got up, I walked around the room while my human got dressed. That's when I found the blanket that used to be on my chair. It was in a corner of the room on a short wooden box next to the big wooden box of drawers. I hopped on top of the small box for a better look. I confirmed it was my blanket. Am I supposed to sleep here now?

This afternoon, I sat on the table and looked out the window in the upper room. The large tree outside that window kept me entertained for a while.

When it was time for a nap, I went to the bedroom, jumped on my blanket in the corner, and dozed off. A while later, my human came in and found me there. I got up and followed him into the other room. He moved my new pink-and-gray bed out of the way and put the original blanket back on the chair. I'm not sure why my human kept moving things around, but I was happy to have my blanket chair back.

My human provided my wet food a bit earlier than normal. Immediately after feeding me, he put his coat on and left. I played a bit while he was gone. I left my green-and-tan mouse at the door for him. He returned long after the sun had gone down. When I heard him come back, I went to the door to greet him. I spent some time on his lap while we listened to the radio. The lady on the radio said my name again and also sent purrs my way.

Soon after I received my radio purrs, my human got up and went to the kitchen. I followed him but stopped at the front room. I jumped up to the platform atop my scratching post and waited for him. When he walked by, he stopped to rub the top of my head. He held a cup of hot liquid with one of his paws and offered it to me. I liked the head rub, but after one sniff of that cup, I pulled back from the stench. He proceeded to the upper room. I followed him and got back on his lap while he drank that awful liquid.

Day 122, Sunday, February 24, 2019:
My human and I enjoyed some cuddling time this morning before he got out of bed and went to work at the shelter. I was excited when he returned a few hours later because I had a lot to tell him. I talked to him all the way to the bedroom and even while he changed clothing.

I spent a little time looking out the window next to the computer today. The birds didn't show up in the tree, so I went down to the front room to try another window. That one was a lot more interesting because things were moving around outside. I saw some leaves fly past and flop around in the dirt. I was so excited, I tried to grab them. I would have gotten them, too, if the window hadn't been in the way.

Later in the evening, I hopped onto one of the shelves in the closet in the upper room. The space available for me was quite narrow since the shelf was full of containers, but there was enough room for me to stand and perform an inspection of some of the stuff.

I also checked out the table with the TV and the metal box of drawers. Normally, there wasn't much exciting up there, but I like to keep tabs on it anyway. Today, though, I received a surprise. On top of the metal box was my human's dinner plate! It was mostly empty. He must have put it there after he was done eating. I nibbled on some of the crumbs.

After getting a taste of his food, I took a nap on my blanket chair. It's nice to have my blanket back where it's supposed to be.

Before we went to bed, I received some lap time on my human, along with a nice massage.

Day 123, Monday, February 25, 2019:
My human and I both woke up early today. It was too early to get out of bed, so I purred and kneaded the blanket while my human petted me. When I lay down again, still kneading, he put his arm around me. We went back to sleep for another hour and a half.

As usual, I waited in the basement for my human this morning. When he came down, we talked a bit before he left for the day.

I spent some time looking out the windows today. Most of the white stuff is gone. I didn't play with either of my strings but instead played with some toy mice. I got one of them stuck between the landing and the door to the car room. The car room's floor is one step below the landing, so when the door is closed, there is a narrow slot that toys can fall into.

I waited at the door when my human returned home. He came in and rescued the mouse that I had lost earlier. He tossed it up to me, so I hit it back to him. He picked it up again and lobbed it into the front room. I started to chase after it but passed it and kept running to the kitchen because it was time for dinner.

Later in the evening, my human performed the weekly routine where he collects the small plastic bags from throughout the house, puts them all in the larger bag in the kitchen, and takes it to the car room. I tried to sneak out there but couldn't get past him.

He got that long hose and stick from the closet and pushed it all over the basement floor. I didn't like that thing, so I waited upstairs in the front room. Once he put that monster away, we went to the upper room. He worked on the computer, and I took a nap on my blanket chair.

After my nap, I chased some toys around the upper room. My human joined in briefly when I batted a ball toward him and it hit one of his hind paws. He tossed it back to me. I also threw my white doughnut-like ring around a bit. It ended up in the bedroom. I left it there, even though I normally don't have toys in there. My human didn't say anything, so it must be okay.

Day 124, Tuesday, February 26, 2019:
I tried my best to talk my human into staying home this morning, but he went to work anyway. With the house to myself, I spent my day resting, observing the yard from the windows, and chasing some toys.

I had a bit of a scare this evening. While I sat atop the scratching post in the front room and kept an eye on my human in the kitchen, I suddenly heard a loud and repeating *thud-thud-thud* sound coming from the basement. I tried to figure out what it was. Just then, my human shot through the room and went downstairs.[31] The ominous, mysterious sound combined with my human's quick movement startled me so much I leaped from my post and took off to the upper room. During my leap, the post fell over with a *thud* of its own. I never saw one do that before. The loud repeating sound abated, and I soon heard my human return to the main level. He called me a couple of times, but I didn't answer. He came upstairs and found me hiding in the upper room. He explained what happened and said everything was okay, so I followed him back to the front room. I noticed the scratching post had returned to its normal, upright position.

With that excitement out of the way, I decided to get some exercise. I played with my toys—balls, mostly—in the upper room. I also retrieved my white doughnut from the bedroom and moved it to the hallway.

I sat in the upper room and watched my human as he did something strange tonight. He took cardboard tubes and cut them into narrow rings. I couldn't figure out if these were for me or for him. When he cut a ring from the tube, it would shoot down toward the table. He did this for a long time. I hopped onto the table for a closer look. I grabbed one of these rings with my teeth and took it to the floor. I played with it but lost interest rather quickly. I noticed later it had disappeared from the floor.

I took a nap on the blanket chair while my human played with his cardboard rings. When he was done, I asked for and received some well-deserved lap time.

We decided to go to bed a bit earlier than normal, so I returned to the blanket chair and waited while he prepared for bedtime.

Day 125, Wednesday, February 27, 2019:
This was a pretty boring day. I got up a bit before my human and waited for him in the basement. He came down but didn't stay long before leaving for work. I spent the day napping and looking out the basement window. This afternoon, a little bit of that white stuff fell from the sky.

---

[31]To stop the clothes washer's spin cycle and adjust an unbalanced load.

When my human arrived home, I was excited to see him. I took off running toward the kitchen when he came into the house, but then he returned to the car room. I went back to the door and found a couple of bags of groceries. He came back inside, so I took off again, but once again, he went back to the car room. I made my way back to the door and found even more bags. I called for him. He came back with even more bags, but this time he stayed inside. He set everything down and followed me to the kitchen. I waited patiently while he prepared my meal.

We spent our evening in the upper room. At one point, he pushed my yellow toy mouse in my direction. I reached for it and tried to pull it toward me but had some trouble because the table leg was in my way. He kicked the mouse toward me with one of his hind paws. It landed right at my chest, and the game was on! I chased that mouse all over the room and out to the hallway. It was some good exercise.

After that, I took a nap on the blanket chair, interrupted only by a brief stay on my human's lap.

Day 126, Thursday, February 28, 2019:
Wow! What a great way to wake up! Before we got out of bed this morning, my human gave me a long, fantastic, two-pawed, full-body massage. Every day should start that way.

As usual, I waited in the basement for my human, but he had already scooped my litter pan by the time I got there. I guess I was a little late making my rounds after that incredible massage. On his way out the door, he called to me, so I went to say goodbye before he went to work.

It was a cool day, so I spent a lot of the day napping, with some occasional window watching.

My human was home a bit late, but at least he fed me right away once he arrived. Later in the evening, I sat on the table behind him and sniffed the fur on his head. It smelled different than normal. There was also less of it than there was this morning.

While my human was working in the kitchen, I played with my black string near the kitchen table. I started under the chair, and as I tossed the string, I bumped my head on the chair. I was okay, though, and pulled the string out from under the chair and continued to play with it.

I spent some time looking out the basement window this evening before going back upstairs to nap on my blanket chair. As I dozed off, my human played with his cardboard tubes on the table, like he did a couple of days ago.

Before going to bed, I played with a ball and my white doughnut in the hallway.

Day 127, Friday, March 1, 2019:
I had a weird night. Normally, I can sleep next to my human with no problems, but last night, it was rather difficult. He kept waking up and making loud noises.[32] It would startle me so much that I'd run out of the room. I got to the point where I could tell when he was about to make one of those sounds before he made it and would preemptively leap from the bed and leave the room. I'd return after a while, only to have the same thing happen again. It was a bit aggravating. I'd never seen him do that before.

In the morning, just like yesterday, I said goodbye to him on the staircase before he left for work. After that, I enjoyed some time on the bench in the front room. I also chased some balls. It got so crazy that I ended up sliding on the rug by the front door, which caused it to wad up in the corner. My human put it back in its normal place when he got home.

This evening, my human made more of those strange sounds, so I didn't spend much time on his lap. Instead, I lay on the floor next to him while he worked on the computer.

Day 128, Saturday, March 2, 2019:
My human slept in much later than normal this morning. I went to check on him and tried to get him out of bed a few times, but each time he stayed there.

I played with some balls in the front room today. A few of them ended up on the staircase to the basement.

Tonight, I sat on one of my human's front paws, resting my head on his arm, when he suddenly let out a very loud noise.[33] It scared me so much, I extended my claws for maximum traction and leaped down as quickly as I could. As soon as I landed, he got up and ran to the bathroom. A few minutes later, he came back with something on his paw right where my paw had been. I think one of my claws got him when I jumped. I hoped he was okay. I didn't mean to hurt him. He ex-tended his injured paw so I could inspect it. After a brief sniff, I turned

---

[32]Sneezes due to seasonal allergies.
[33]Another sneeze.

my head and rubbed my neck against it. He then gave me a nice neck rub and back rub.

Day 129, Sunday, March 3, 2019:
Today, I noticed the ground was covered in that white stuff again. When my human returned from the shelter, he spent some time outside pushing that stuff off the driveway and sidewalk. That was entertaining. When he came inside, he went to the kitchen to prepare his meal, so I had to entertain myself. I batted balls around the front room.

I also played in both the front room and the upper room while my human watched TV and worked on the computer. In the process of chasing a ball, I slid on the rug near the front door, and it ended up in a pile in the corner again.

Day 130, Monday, March 4, 2019:
I got up early today to take care of some cat stuff and then returned to the bed to be near my human. When he woke up, he gave me the most fantastic belly rub *ever*! He started by scratching my neck. Then he moved on to a chest rub, and then down to my belly. I curled up in front of his paw and took it all in. I wished it would last forever. Unfortunately, he had to get up to go to work.

I was a bit annoyed when he arrived home because not only was he late, but he didn't feed me right away. He insisted on going upstairs to drop off his stuff and take his hat and coat off before he finally went to the kitchen to feed me. At least, once he did, he took my food to the upper room so I could eat along with him.

While my human did his weekly chore of moving the small plastic bags to the big one, I played with toys in the front room. I also whacked the toy chipmunk off the top of my scratching post since I noticed it was up there mocking me. I tried to get out to the car room when my human took the plastic bag out there, but I hesitated because it was really cold when he opened the door. As I contemplated my move, he closed the door.

Day 131, Tuesday, March 5, 2019:
This morning, I wanted to see if I could get another belly rub like the one I received yesterday. About the time my human was going to wake up, I joined him on the bed and lay down next to him. I made sure I leaned against his right side, just like last time. It worked! Just like yesterday, he started by scratching my neck before moving on to my belly. Oh, it was fantastic! I think he enjoyed it, too, because it

went on and on and on. He got up a bit later than normal, and I think it
made him late for work. I don't care, though. It was definitely worth it.

Once he got up, I tried to delay him a bit more in the basement.
There, we cuddled for a while before he left for work.

I got some exercise chasing some balls in the front room. In the
evening, I played with my little yellow mouse. I chased it out of the
paper bag in the upper room. My human rolled my white doughnut toy
to me as he entered the upper room, so I tossed it around a bit, too.

I spent some time on my human's lap early in the evening. Later,
I sat on the floor near him while he worked on the computer. He
reached down to me, but I slipped away from him. He claimed he
wanted to pet me, but I suspected he was trying to pick me up. After
that, I curled up on the blanket chair, where I kept an eye on him.

Day 132, Wednesday, March 6, 2019:
Another morning with another great massage before I even got out of
bed! My human is wonderful. That wasn't our only time together this
morning. When we went to the basement, I put my front paws and
chest on his lap and cuddled with him.

My exercise routine today consisted of playing with balls in the
front room.

When my human arrived home, I watched him bring several
items into the house. With his attention focused elsewhere, I managed
to sneak into the car room. On his way into the house, I heard him call
me. He must not have known I was in the car room because he turned
the light off and closed the door. A few minutes later, the door opened.
He called me again, but I didn't say anything, so he closed the door
again.

Left alone, I explored under the truck, like I did last time, but I
also got onto the chair on top of the thing he sometimes uses to push
the white stuff off the driveway.[34] From there, I got on top of a couple
of large plastic bins. I recognized those bins as the ones he pushes
down the driveway and out to the road about once a week.

It was pretty cold in the car room. I wondered why that room
wasn't as warm as the rest of the house. After several more minutes, I
was ready to go back to someplace warm. I heard my human come
down the stairs again. He opened the door and called me again. This
time, I was waiting by the door and eagerly went back into the main
part of the house.

---

[34]A garden tractor with a front-end loader.

After my adventure in the very cold car room, I needed to go somewhere warm. I found my human on his chair in the upper room and lay down on his lap to warm up. With the heat from his lap and paws, it didn't take long for me to get comfortable.

Before going to bed, I played with the white doughnut. Things got kind of crazy. I chased it all the way to the basement.

Day 133, Thursday, March 7, 2019:
My human got out of bed early today, so I didn't get a long early-morning back massage. As he changed his clothing, I trotted up onto the bed. To my surprise, he knelt down and gave me a brief massage before going off to work.

I played with my strings today. I found my white doughnut in the basement and tossed it around some more.

This evening, I checked up on my human while he was in the bathroom getting ready for bed. I could see him through the slit by the door, so I knew I should be able to get to him, but I still haven't quite figured out this door technology yet. I pushed my left front paw through the crack and reached in as far as I could when something un-expected happened. Something touched me! It was small, soft, and it lightly brushed the pad of my paw. I immediately retracted my paw. Then I heard my human giggling on the other side of the door. Did he see what touched me? Why was it funny? Right after that, I saw him reach down and use one of his paws to pull the door open just far enough that I could squeeze my whole body through. I joined him in the bathroom. Everything seemed normal, but that was freaky.

Day 134, Friday, March 8, 2019:
This morning, I rubbed against my human's legs several times as he scooped my litter pan. I wanted to let him know how much I appreci-ated him keeping that box clean for me. I didn't try to sit on his lap before he left for work.

Today, I explored the bathroom cabinet again. There wasn't as much stuff in there as there was in the past. Since there was more free space, it was easier to maneuver in there. I put my front paws up on one of the shelves in the cabinet to sniff the various items that were there.

I spent most of the evening alone since my human left the house again soon after he got home from work. He didn't return until well after sundown.

Day 135, Saturday, March 9, 2019:
My human and I stayed in bed much, much later than normal today. I received an amazing two-pawed back rub and belly rub. That is how every Saturday should start!

It was nice to have my human around all day, even though he was in a different room while I spent most of the day in the front room. I was fascinated, looking out the window. I couldn't see any of the white stuff anymore, but there were leaves bouncing down the sidewalk. Even without many leaves left on the tree, the branches moved around an awful lot.

On one of my human's many trips through the front room, he stopped and looked out the window with me.

Day 136, Sunday, March 10, 2019:
I received a belly rub earlier than normal today. My human also got out of bed earlier than normal.[35]

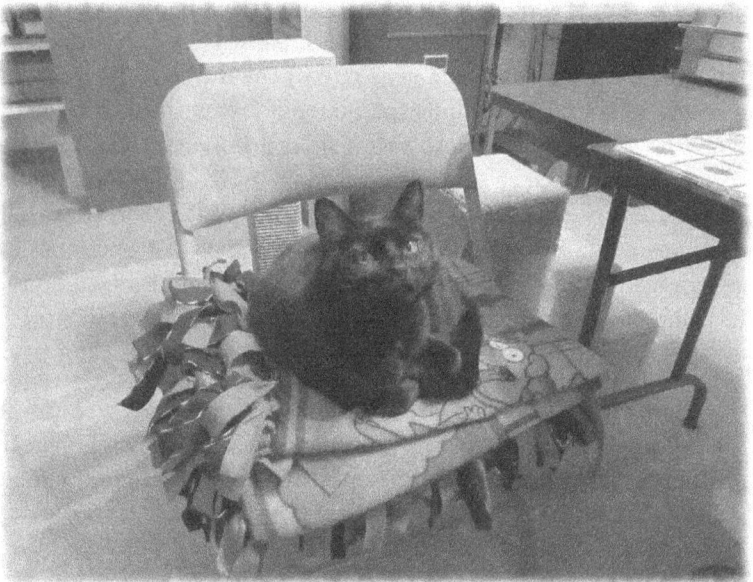

I was awoken from my nap due to the sound of the camera.

Like yesterday, I spent some time looking out the front window. My human opened the curtain a bit more, which provided a large sunbeam for me. I also spent some time looking out the window by the

---

[35]The start of Daylight Saving Time.

computer. From that vantage point, I saw something in the sky that got my attention. I don't know what it was, and it was gone quickly.

This afternoon, I played with some toys in the front room. I also chased my fluffy white mouse down the staircase.

I took a nap on the blanket chair while my human worked at the table. I awoke briefly to see him take a photo of me.

No evening would be complete without some lap time on my human. He gave me a nice neck rub as I sat on his lap and again later when I crawled up to lie down on his arm.

Day 137, Monday, March 11, 2019:
I played with a lot of things today, including my strings, a toy mouse, a ball with a feather-like thingy, and my white doughnut. I took my doughnut from the basement to the kitchen. I tossed it around the kitchen this evening while my human was preparing his meal.

I spent some time on my human's lap, but I got down and ran away from him when he tried to give me a manicure. Later, I took a nap on the blanket chair next to him while he worked at the table. Tonight, he played with a pile of little round metal discs.[36] I don't know what they are, but they seem to keep him entertained. I liked that it was a quiet activity so I was able to sleep well.

Day 138, Tuesday, March 12, 2019:
I didn't get much of a belly rub this morning. My human seemed to be in a hurry when he got up.

Today, I played with my fluffy white mouse. I also spent some time looking out both the basement window and the front window. The small bed that my human had temporarily moved to my chair in the upper room was now on one side of the bench at the front window. I still don't care for it very much.

When my human arrived home, he brought a large, empty cardboard box into the house and set it at the stop of the staircase. I jumped into it while he took his shoes off. I didn't stay there very long because I knew he would go right to the kitchen to make my dinner. He did.

My human cleaned the table in the upper room tonight. He had been doing that thing he does with those little round metal discs. I found a small stack of them on the table near my blanket chair. While sitting on my blanket chair, I pulled one of them off the pile and

---

[36] Cheap foreign coins, purchased by the pound.

pushed it along the table top. He seems to have a lot of fun with those things, but I just didn't get it. I'd rather play with something soft, like my doughnut or toy mice. I left the disc there and took another nap on the blanket chair.

Day 139, Wednesday, March 13, 2019:
I received a bit of a belly rub this morning. It wasn't as long as I would have liked, but it was better than nothing.

I played with my black string today. I moved it from the kitchen to the upper room. In the evening, I played with it on the floor near my human's chair while he played with those little metal discs on the table. He stacked them into piles. I was worn out from playing, so I got onto the blanket chair and dozed off to the gentle *clink . . . clink . . . clink . . .* sound of him playing.

Day 140, Thursday, March 14, 2019:
I totally missed my morning belly rub today. I was downstairs when my human got out of the bed. As he did his morning routine, I walked up the pet steps at the foot of the bed, went across the blanket, and begged for some attention. He gave me some loving in the form of a two-pawed massage of my back and sides. Like yesterday, it was over too soon.

I played with my black string in the upper room and kitchen today. Strings are so neat!

My human arrived home and provided my evening meal at a reasonable time today. He took both of our meals to the upper room so we could eat together. I really liked that.

After dinner, we talked for a while. He played with one of my toys—a highly reflective wad of metallic foil—and rolled it toward me, but I wasn't interested in it this evening. Rather, I climbed onto his lap and made my way up to his arm for some snuggle time.

After a brief amount of cuddling, I moved to the blanket chair for a nap while my human played with those metal discs on the table again.

Day 141, Friday, March 15, 2019:
I did a lot of playing today, spreading my toys everywhere throughout the house.

This evening, I made multiple trips onto my human's lap for some attention and massages. When I wasn't on his lap, I stayed nearby on the blanket chair and slept.

Day 142, Saturday, March 16, 2019:
My human stayed in bed longer than normal this morning. That was good for me because it meant I got plenty of back and belly rubs.

I spent a lot of time on the bench at the front window today. In the morning, I watched a bird walking around on the grass.

This afternoon, I sat on my human's lap for a while to receive a well-deserved massage. After that, I took a nap on my blanket chair. When I awoke from my nap, I decided I needed another massage. Fortunately, my human was still sitting on his chair and had a lap waiting for me.

After my second massage, I was still near my human and happened to look toward the window when I saw a bird fly by. I ran to the window for a better look, but the bird was gone.

Late in the evening, I cuddled with my human. I rested on one of his arms while the paw on his other arm alternated between operating the computer and stroking my back. As I lay there enjoying the attention, the lady on the radio said my name again.

Day 143, Sunday, March 17, 2019:
Today, I sat on the table next to the computer to look out the tall, narrow window in the upper room. Even though this window is far from the ground, something down there caught my attention. It was a squirrel! It was sitting on the grass, eating a walnut.

The squirrel wasn't the only thing on cat TV today. This afternoon, my human and I sat at the bench in the front room and looked out that window. We saw a neighbor go by on her daily walk. We also saw a bird up in the tree, perched on a small branch near the window. It was a small gray bird with a red head. It looked like it was cleaning itself.

That bird wasn't the only thing that needed to be cleaned today. This evening, I explored the cold floor room because my human had left the door to that room open when he took his dirty clothing in there. While I was in there, some cobwebs stuck to my long whiskers. When I went to the upper room to find my human, he tried to clean my face, but I got away from him before he could finish. He caught up with me when I lay down on my blanket chair. He managed to wipe the whiskers on the left side of my face. I jumped over to the pet steps so he couldn't clean the other side of my face. It wasn't until sometime later, while I looked out the tall window, that he caught me off guard and finished cleaning my face.

Day 144, Monday, March 18, 2019:
I think my human didn't feel well this morning. He got out of bed way too early. I heard him open a small cabinet in the bathroom and then heard some water running. He returned to bed, crawled under the blanket, and backed up next to me. Several hours later, he did it again, only this time he faced me. I stayed close to him instead of getting up to go on my morning prowl. I lay close to his chest, with my tail brushed up against his face.

When the sun rose, he must have felt better because he did all the things he normally does in the morning: prepared my food and water, cleaned my litter pan, cleaned himself, and then left for work.

While he was at work, I looked out the front window. I also took my white string from the upper room to the front room and played with it for a while.

When my human returned, I talked to him for quite some time. He prepared my food and set it on the kitchen floor. I didn't eat much of it until he took it to the upper room, along with his own meal.

After he ate, he put his mostly empty dish on the table. When I thought he wasn't looking, I took a sniff of his dish. He saw me, but he didn't seem to mind. He removed the fork from the bowl. That allowed me to get a better sample of his food. I took a few licks, but I didn't really like it. The meat and cheese flavors were nice, but there were too many spices.

There is a big red metal box on the table between the computer and the window. It has been there since I moved in. Tonight, I jumped on top of it since I had never been up there. Boy, it sure was dusty. It was cold on my paws, too.

Day 145, Tuesday, March 19, 2019:
This morning, I received a very pleasant back rub in bed. I wrapped my tail around my human's arm as he worked his paw up and down my back.

During the day, I played with my white string in the front room and the kitchen. In the evening, I played with several balls and mice in the front room. I also tried to play with one of my human's toys. It's a little metal and glass thing that he often looks through when he plays with his metal discs. I found it in front of the computer keyboard. I started to push it off the table, but my human suggested I play with some of my toys instead. He left the room, so I followed him. We went to the front room, where he picked up a few of my mice and took them back upstairs. I stayed in the front room. So why can he play with my toys, but I'm not supposed to play with his?

My eye has been doing that weird thing again today. It started yesterday, but today, it's really bad. My right pupil was dilated, while my left one was not. There was also some discharge from my left eye.

I spent part of the evening napping on the blanket chair. I also spent some time on my human's lap, where I received a nice neck massage.

Before bedtime, I followed my human to the bathroom. He sat on that white litter box contraption that looks kind of like a chair, but that didn't concern me. Rather, my interest was focused on a thin stream of water. It was coming from a spout in the big rectangular space where he often stands and gets wet. I hopped onto the edge of the rectangular box for a closer look at the water. I also sampled it. It was cool but was warming up. When he stood up, I jumped down and left the room, knowing the water was probably going to start falling from the ceiling soon.

Day 146, Wednesday, March 20, 2019:
My human was home late this evening. When he arrived, he smelled a bit like the shelter. I wondered why. This wasn't the normal time for him to smell like that. Regardless, I was happy because he immediately prepared my wet food.

My eye was still doing that weird thing today. It's kind of annoying.

I spent most of the evening napping on the blanket chair. I also sat on the table adjacent to the computer as my human typed on the keyboard. That was after I sat on his lap for a while. After all, no evening can go by without lap time.

Day 147, Thursday, March 21, 2019:
This morning, I spent some time looking out the window in the basement while I waited for my human. We socialized a bit after he finished scooping my litter pan. He noticed that my eye was getting back to normal.

Since my eye was doing better, I was a bit more active today. I entertained myself with my white string.

I greeted my human when he arrived home, then immediately ran to the front room to use my scratching post. Annoyingly, one of my claws got stuck. My human set his bag down and was coming over to help me, but I managed to free myself before he got to me. Maybe I should let him give me that manicure after all.

I played in the front room while my human prepared his meal. He picked up a white toy mouse I had left in the kitchen and tossed it to me. I chased it.

This evening, my human made a trip to the car room. I jumped at the opportunity to explore out there some more, so I bolted toward the open door before he even saw me. He tried to pick me up, but I ran under the truck, just like last time. He went into the house but quickly returned. This time, he didn't come toward me or even call me. Instead, he opened the back of the car. After removing something, he closed the car lid and went back into the house. I heard him walking around upstairs a lot since the car room is under the upper room and hallway. He didn't come back to the car room for about an hour. When he did, I was ready to come back in. As soon as he opened the door, I ran back into the house and went toward the basement. He went back upstairs, so I turned around and followed him.

I spent the rest of the evening with him in the upper room. I heard a long, strange growling noise outside, so I went over to the tall window to see if I could figure out what it was. In the distance, on the other side of the trees, I saw a human riding around in the grass on a small vehicle, similar to the one my human had used to push the white stuff off the driveway. It was pretty boring, not exciting like a bird or a squirrel, so I went to my human and sat on his lap.

Later in the evening, I played with a little gray toy mouse. It was one of the toys my human had brought up from the front room a few days ago. After that, I took a nap on the blanket chair, waking up occasionally to keep an eye on my human.

Day 148, Friday, March 22, 2019:
I got up to play with my black string in the hallway while my human slept. I noticed my human got up early but went back to bed. When he awoke a second time, he gave me a pleasant massage.

It was much warmer today than it had been recently. That wasn't the only thing different about today. When my human arrived home, he opened a window in the upper room. He also pulled the blind up. It wasn't the window I normally look out of, but it was one that looked just like it. Unlike the window I normally use, there wasn't a table next to this window. There was, however, a tiny ledge right in front of it, so I jumped up to the ledge. When my human returned to the room, he asked what I was doing. I didn't answer. I hopped down but got back up there again a moment later. That's when he moved my small cat tree—the one that is normally next to my paper bag—and placed it in front of the window. That gave me a more comfortable place to sit and observe this new view.

It didn't stay that way for very long. As the sun went down and it started to cool, my human closed the window and returned my cat tree to its regular location. Fortunately, by then I was no longer sitting on it.

Day 149, Saturday, March 23, 2019:
Today, my human and I played with my toy mousies. He put them on top of the scratching post in the upper room and also on my steps that lead up to the table. I batted them away because no mousie is going to look down on me!

I got my whiskers dirty while exploring today. My human picked me up and cleaned my face. I appreciated his effort, but I still found it rather annoying. I'm perfectly capable of cleaning myself when I want to.

I sat at the front window a lot today to keep tabs on what was happening outside. I saw a dog walking his human on the other side of the street. I also saw a bird fly by and land on a branch in the tree. It was another one of those little gray redheaded ones.

Later, I played with my big white mouse. I chased it into the kitchen.

This evening, I saw my human playing with his little metal discs again. While he entertained himself with those, I took a long nap on the blanket chair next to him.

Day 150, Sunday, March 24, 2019:
Today started off like any normal day. I saw my human off to the cat shelter, just like he did every week. But when he returned, things were different. He didn't go to the upper room to play with his toys, but instead, he took a nap on the sofa. I curled up on the blanket behind his legs for a while but then got up to do some cat stuff.

Later in the day, I found him still on the sofa, now with his legs stretched out. He was sound asleep. I thought he might not be feeling well. I walked up the steps onto the sofa and lay down on top of him. I normally face away from him, but today, I made sure I faced toward him so I could keep an eye on him. I reached out and held one of his front paws with one of my front paws. Even after he woke up, we both stayed there together, holding each other's paws. I did whatever I could to help him feel better.

Day 151, Monday, March 25, 2019:
Normally, the day after working at the shelter, my human goes to work. He didn't do that today. Instead, he stayed home and spent the whole day on the sofa. I checked up on him throughout the day. I also did a thorough examination of both of the cat trees in the living room because I hadn't done that in a while. In fact, until yesterday, it had been many days since we had spent much time in that room.

While he rested, I got some exercise. I played with some balls and mice in the front room and in the basement. Later in the day, a couple of plastic springy toys that I had lost under the refrigerator had somehow reappeared on the floor of the front room. I wondered how they got there.

I had a frightful experience this evening. While eating my canned food in the kitchen, my human was doing something with the refrigerator when things started falling on the floor, making loud noises and coming toward me.[37] I left my food and ran to the other side of the house. My human called me, but I still wasn't certain it was safe, so I kept my distance. I didn't return for a long time.

Day 152, Tuesday, March 26, 2019:
My human woke up several times last night. I stayed close to him most of the night. When he awoke near sunrise, he performed his normal routine and then went to work.

I watched things outside the front window today. I also played with some toys. I had some fun with my black string on the kitchen floor.

This evening, my human must have felt better because he went to the upper room instead of the sofa. I spent some time on his lap and received a neck massage. Then I took a nap on the blanket chair while my human worked on the computer.

My human went to the cold floor room in the basement a few times tonight. He left the door open, so I got to make a pass through the room. When I returned upstairs, he tried to grab me to clean my whiskers, but he wasn't very successful. He managed to clean a few of them before I got away. I left the room and cleaned them myself.

---

[37]Ice cubes fell from a tray.

Just before bedtime, I discovered that there were multiple blankets on the bed. I hid under a couple of them. When my human came into the bedroom, he asked what I was doing. Wasn't it obvious? Cat stuff!

Day 153, Wednesday, March 27, 2019:
I slept next to my human all night. Actually, I slept *on* my human most of the night. He extended his right front paw toward me and massaged my back, my side, and my belly. I really liked that. He normally does that as I knead the blanket right after I get onto the bed. I used to snuggle between his side and arm, but lately I've been lying on his arm and paw. Last night, I spent almost the whole night with my belly resting on his paw. It was nice.

I spent a lot of time looking out my windows today. It has been getting warmer, so it has been more pleasant to sit by the windows. I watched the sun set from the tall window by the computer while my human ate his meal.

This evening, my human and I played with one of my toy mice. He tossed it onto the table where I was sitting, and I batted it back to him. I'm good about sharing my toys with my human.

Day 154, Thursday, March 28, 2019:
I've been training my human to give me his arm at night. He has been getting pretty good at it. When I got on the bed last night, he put his paw next to me right away. I still kneaded the blanket, but then I lay down on top of his paw.

During the night, I got up to play for a while. I was quiet because I didn't want to wake my human. I was back by his side before he woke up.

I saw a bunch of water fall from the sky today. It disappeared right away when it reached the ground, unlike that white stuff that fell a few weeks ago.

Today, I played to get exercise. I chased a tiny gray toy mouse down the stairs until it got stuck between the landing and the door to the car room. My human retrieved it when he arrived home. He tossed it to me as I greeted him from the top of the steps.

After dinner, I sat on a table in the upper room and looked at a shelf. I've walked on that shelf before but didn't tonight. Instead, something on the shelf caught my attention. It was a narrow roll of brightly colored material.[38] I reached up and pushed it off the shelf. When it landed on the floor, I hopped down for a closer look. My human must have heard me because he came right over, picked it up, and put it back on the shelf. Then he knelt down, picked up one of my toys—a ball of shiny, crinkled paper—and tossed it toward me. Again, he can play with my toys, but he doesn't want me to play with his. I ignored the ball. Instead, I walked over to him and crawled up onto his lap. That was what I really wanted anyway. I turned around and faced away from him. Then I pushed my butt against his chest and rested my head on his knees. His front paws gave me a much-deserved neck massage.

After snuggling for several minutes, I got down from his lap. He returned to his chair while I sat next to him on my blanket chair. I watched him do that weird thing I saw him do a while back—cutting up cardboard tubes into rings. I chased after one of the rings when it fell onto the floor. He picked it up and put it in a plastic box that overflowed with cardboard rings. That box was conveniently placed on the table right next to my pet steps, so I climbed up the steps and swiped a different ring. I retreated to the floor and batted it around the room for several minutes. I got bored with it, though, and went back to my blanket chair for a nap.

Day 155, Friday, March 29, 2019:
Well, I guess I still have some work to do to train my human. I saw him off to bed last night but then left the room briefly. When I returned, I found him lying on his side with both of his arms hidden under the blanket. That left no arms for the cat. I went to the other side of the bed and eventually settled down with my butt aimed toward his face.

Today, more water fell from the sky. It was also colder than yesterday. While my human was at work, I explored the cold floor room. I think my human forgot to close the door to that room, so I couldn't pass on the opportunity to go in there.

This evening, I played with one of my toy mice. I chased it all over the upper room while my human worked at the table. That tuckered me out, so I took a nap on the blanket chair.

Day 156, Saturday, March 30, 2019:
The training has been going better. I received my human's paw last

---

[38]A roll of streamer material for a hobby project.

night as he drifted off to sleep and again this morning when he awoke. Before he got up, he gave me one of his patented belly rubs, followed by a neck massage. After that, we held paws for a while as I rested my head on the edge of the bed and looked at him. I'm glad I found a human like him.

I spent time looking out all of my favorite windows today: the basement door, the front room, and the tall window in the upper room by the computer. While looking out the windows, I noticed that there was both water and white stuff falling from the sky. While at the front window, my human came over and caressed me for a nice long time. We took turns rubbing the tops of our heads on each other. I lay down in the small pink-and-gray bed and leaned against his arm.

I took a nap on the blanket chair this morning while my human played with his metal discs at the table. When I awoke, something caught my attention at the doorway to the hall. I sat up and watched for a while. My human asked me what it was, but I didn't say anything. Eventually, I lost interest in it and went to look out the tall window. My attention turned to something in the tree. I hunched down to get a better look past the blinds but lost track of it when I heard my human leave the room.

This afternoon, I chased my tan toy mouse around the upper room. After a lot of exercise, I settled down for another nap on the blanket chair.

Day 157, Sunday, March 31, 2019:
I saw my human off to bed last night, as I always do. He gave me a belly rub as he went to sleep. While he slept, I got up to do some cat stuff and play with my white string. I made sure to get back on the bed before he woke up.

Today, my human worked at the shelter. I played with my white string some more while he was there. Then I returned to the bedroom for a nap. I stayed there until he came back. He greeted me but then went down to the cold floor room in the basement and closed the door. I waited in the soft floor room for him to come out. I didn't have to wait very long. When he opened the door, he held a large scratching post. It was similar to the posts I have but without a platform on top. He said it was for Elaine at the shelter and took it to the car room without letting me get a closer look at it. I noticed he left the door to the cold floor room open, so I went in there and explored.

I spent a lot of time looking out multiple windows today. The sun was shining brightly, and there was no water or white stuff falling from the sky. I wonder where all the birds went. I haven't seen them in a while.

Strangely, the door to the bedroom was closed part of the day. My human went in there briefly a few times throughout the day carrying blankets and sheets.[39]

Except for brief trips to carry things between the basement and bedroom, my human spent most of the day in the upper room playing with his metal discs. While he did that, I napped next to him on the blanket chair.

During the evening, I got down from the chair and asked my human if I could sit on his lap for a while. He made his lap available for me. After lap time, I returned to the blanket chair and took a bath.

Day 158, Monday, April 1, 2019:
Things were a little strange last night when I went to bed. The blanket on top of the bed smelled different. I cautiously inspected it as I stepped off the pet steps and onto the bed. It seemed less familiar than before. My human didn't seem bothered by it and got into bed like he normally did. Everything else seemed in order, so I kneaded the blanket for a while until my human gave me his right front paw to sleep on.

Overnight, I got up and played with my white string. Just like last time, I was back by my human's side before he awoke.

This evening, my human served my canned food as soon as he arrived home, but I was too excited to eat it. Instead, I followed him as he went to the basement to put away some supplies he had brought home with him.

A while later, I found him in the doorway leading to the car room. I tried to sneak past him, but I couldn't. He talked to me a bit as I walked around to see if I could find a way into the car room. I mistakenly let my guard down, and he snatched me! He scooped me into his arms and took me to the car room. I couldn't escape his firm grip, so I didn't even try. He walked around for a minute or so while I observed the room. He said, "See, there's nothing in here for a kitty," but he couldn't be more wrong. Couldn't he see all of the great stuff to climb on? I hardly ever got to explore this wonderland! He took me

---

[39]The door was closed to keep kitty claws off the waterbed while the bed sheets and blankets were being washed.

back inside and let me jump from his arms onto the steps. The door was closed before I could try to make a run for it.

After our brief visit to the car room, his dinner was ready (he had started it before we went out), so he took both his plate and mine to the upper room. After eating, he stayed in the upper room to play while I went downstairs to look out the window. I returned later and asked to sit on his lap. I don't think he has ever turned down a lap request, so he said "yes," and I walked across his lap. I turned around and pushed my right side up against his chest. It was nice to be close to him. After a few minutes, I left his lap and got onto the table to look out the window. After that, I got my evening exercise by chasing a few toys around the upper room, including my tan mouse. I really like that mouse. I chased it out of the room and halfway down the hallway.

The rest of the evening was spent napping on the blanket chair near my human while I observed him working at the computer and table.

Day 159, Tuesday, April 2, 2019:
I've never had any trouble getting onto the bed, but for some reason my human frequently has great difficulty doing so. Why doesn't he just use the steps at the foot of the bed, like me? It's so easy! Last night, once on top of the blanket, I walked to the side of the bed close to where he was standing. He stroked me nicely a few times and then walked around the foot of the bed and made his way to the other side. I took the more direct route and walked straight across the bed to be close to him. That's when he turned around and walked back to where he started, taking the long way again. Once more, I walked straight across the bed and looked up at him. Why didn't he just climb in? He motioned toward the foot of the bed and started to walk that direction. I followed, but he quickly turned around, pulled the blankets back, and hopped in while I tried to climb up the blankets to be close to him.

Whatever. Eventually, he figured it out. I walked across him a couple of times and then kneaded the blanket before settling down on his right front paw. He briefly gave me a belly rub before he drifted off to sleep. About half an hour later, he adjusted his position a bit. At that time, I hopped down and left the room to take care of some cat stuff.

In the morning, I didn't even notice him get up because I was busy in the basement, looking out the window. In fact, I didn't even greet him this morning until he came downstairs to scoop my litter pan. But before he left for work, I hopped onto his lap and demanded some attention.

I also didn't notice him this evening when he returned from work until he came into the basement. I was happy to see him and followed him upstairs. He provided my canned food dinner right away. I took a couple of bites and then ran into the front room. I waited until he had his meal prepared and took both of our plates to the upper room before I finished the rest of my meal.

After dinner, I followed my human downstairs again. He spent some time in the kitchen while I stayed in the front room. Soon, he came into the front room. We talked a bit while I sat on my curved cardboard scratching pad. He knelt down with his knees resting on my scratching pad. I walked onto his lap. I lay on his lap for a long time while he caressed me with both of his front paws. When I'd had my fill, I hopped down, and we both went back upstairs.

My exercise this evening consisted of a ball game. I batted a soft brown-and-tan ball around the upper room. The ball got stuck on one of my claws, and it took me a while to shake it loose. After that, I chased it behind the door.

Later in the evening, I asked for more lap time. My human provided it and gave me a gentle, mesmerizing neck massage at the same time. I curled my tail around his arm in pure contentment. Following my massage, I settled in for a nap on the blanket chair.

Day 160, Wednesday, April 3, 2019:
I tried something different last night. While my human got ready for bed, I sat on the top pet step and watched him. I waited for him to pull the blanket back and begin climbing onto the bed before I hopped onto the blanket. He got into bed much faster than he did last night. I stayed with him for a while and received my normal petting and belly rub, but as he drifted off to sleep, I left the room.

Once again, he woke up and was out of bed before I got to the bedroom. I went up to keep an eye on him as he got dressed. He did all of his normal morning business, including going into the basement to scoop my litter pan. I sat at the top of the steps as he put shoes on his hind paws at the door to the car room. He stood up and gave me a brief neck scratch before going off to work.

There wasn't a lot of sunshine today when I looked out the windows. I didn't exercise much today while my human was at work.

Tonight, I curled up on my human's lap. I purred as he gave me the best two-pawed neck massage I've ever had. He must have enjoyed it, too, because I think he also purred.

After my massage, I did some exploring. I jumped onto the table that holds the television in the upper room. My human had put a lot of plastic bags containing his metal disc toys on that table, so there wasn't much room for me. I saw something on the shelf under the television. I stood on my hind legs and reached up to the shelf for a better look. There were cardboard pieces that hadn't been there before. Whatever they were, they weren't very interesting. After that, I took a much-deserved nap on the blanket chair.

Day 161, Thursday, April 4, 2019:
Last night, I repeated what I had done the previous night. I waited on the top tread of the pet steps and watched my human get onto the bed. It seemed to be faster that way but still not fast enough. I walked on the blankets toward him, but it was difficult because he was still moving around.

Once he settled in, I kneaded the blankets. He put a paw out for me, but I wasn't done working the blankets. After I finished, I lay down on his paw for a bit. I got up during the night but returned to his side long before he got up this morning.

I played with some toys today. The last few days, I've kept my large stuffed white mouse in the kitchen, but it has gotten annoying close to my food and water dishes. I have to walk around it to get to my food. Someone should move it.

I spent most of the evening taking a nap on the blanket chair, but before that I asked my human if I could sit on his lap for a while. He agreed, and I climbed up on his arm and received a nice back rub. I hadn't sat on his arm for several days. It was nice to do that again. In fact, it was so good, I did it again before we went to bed.

Just before my human did his normal nighttime cleaning routine, he opened a drawer in the big box of drawers near the foot of the bed. I'd explored some of these drawers before, but it was a while ago. He left the drawer open, and I was able to support myself against it with my front paws while I stood on the pet steps. I could just barely see into it, so I jumped up for a better look. I think I'd been in that one before. It's where my human keeps his shirts when he's not wearing them. There were three stacks of them. I burrowed under a couple of the stacks until I got bored and hopped down.

Day 162, Friday, April 5, 2019:
Today, I found my big white toy mouse on top of a chair in the kitchen. How did it get up there? Well, it wasn't going to stay there if I had anything to say about it. I took a whack at it and knocked it to the floor.

This afternoon, I crawled up the post in the front room. It was hard to get to the platform on top of it that way. It was easier to just jump up there from my curved cardboard scratching block, but I was up for the challenge. I sat on top of it while my human prepared our evening meals. When he passed through the front room on his way to the upper room, I jumped down and followed him.

This evening, my human and I played with some toy mice in the upper room. I sat at the very top of the pet steps near the table and batted at the mice as my human tossed them up to me. Sometimes, the mice would get stuck on one of my claws, and I'd have to shake it off.

Day 163, Saturday, April 6, 2019:
My human stayed in bed much longer than normal today. I left the bedroom to go do my normal morning routine but later returned and lay down next to him. He awoke and gave me a really long belly and chin rub. We also held paws for a while.

It was much warmer today than it had been lately. My human pulled the curtain at the front window open farther than normal. That let more sunlight in. I sat on the bench by that window for a while to observe my territory.

Later in the morning, I heard some unusual sounds coming from the upper room. I went up there and discovered my human had opened one of the tall windows. It was the one that wasn't right next to the table. I tried to get a closer look, but I couldn't jump onto the ledge because he had left the blinds down. I saw him take the mesh thing he had removed several weeks ago and put it back at the other tall window—the one next to the table. Then he opened that window, too, and I was able to sit up there and take in the sounds from outside. I watched squirrels play on the grass. I also saw some birds fly by.

My human also opened the window in the small storage room upstairs. I jumped onto the wooden box that sat in front of that window for a better look. I was cautious at first because my human was messing with the window using a rag and a spray bottle.[40] I jumped down, but once he was done, I went back for a better look.

_____
[40]A long overdue cleaning.

That's when I noticed my human had squatted down on the floor. I decided lap time was more important than looking out the window, so I climbed onto his legs and lay down. Then he secured me and moved to sit on the wooden box, so I got to use his lap and look out the window at the same time. I enjoyed that.

Later in the afternoon, while I sat on the blanket chair, I happened to look toward the window near the computer and saw a bird fly by. I jumped off the blanket, hopped onto the table, and went over to the window for a better look. It was a small tan bird, and it was really close! I had to squat down for a better look because it was so close to the house. It was sitting on top of a square tube under the roof.[41]

This evening, I moved from the blanket chair and curled up on my human's lap while he worked on the computer. He held my left front paw and gently rubbed my right front paw. While I enjoyed that attention, the lady on the radio said my name again.

Day 164, Sunday, April 7, 2019:
This morning, I was exploring the cold floor room in the basement when my human got up. I didn't even know he was awake until he came down to scoop my litter pan. I was surprised but happy to see him.

I sat in a sunbeam at the front window today. When my human came home from the shelter, he opened the same windows he did yesterday. I moved to the tall window by the computer, where I sat and took in the sounds and smells from outside.

This afternoon, while I sat on one of the tables in the upper room, I reached onto a shelf and started to push one of my human's tools. From his chair, he told me "no," but then he got up, moved closer to me, sat down on the floor, and started to play with my toys. Success! I just wanted some attention from him. I hopped down and chased one of the toys he tossed but then walked onto his lap. I lay down and received a nice neck massage.

I saw a bird out the tall window, so I ran to the window for a better look. The small tan bird was back! He sat on the square tube outside the window. He wasn't the only bird. There were a lot of them out there today.

---

[41]A downspout that seems to gain a bird's nest every spring.

Later this afternoon, my human watched the television while he ate. I sat at the top of the pet steps and watched it for a while, too. It was the show with the four army guys who help people.[42]

I started the evening with a nap on the blanket chair but later switched to my human's lap. I lay down on his arm and let one of my front paws hang down. It was very relaxing.

Tonight, I sat on the table and looked at my human. He petted me and told me how pretty I was, but I already knew that.

Day 165, Monday, April 8, 2019:

Last night, my human got into the bed before me somehow. I ran up the pet steps just as he was getting settled under the blankets. I skipped my kneading routine and jumped straight to stretching out along his side to accept a belly rub. Once he was asleep, I got up to take care of cat things, but I made sure I was back by his side before he awoke. I arrived early, about an hour before he got up, and began kneading the blanket. That woke him up, so he gave me a belly rub and scratched my neck before falling back asleep.

I stayed in the basement as he performed his morning routine and then passed him as I ran up the steps as he was putting his shoes on. We talked, and he scratched my neck while I stood at the top of the steps before he went to work.

He opened the windows again so I was able to hear the birds and feel the fresh air. I watched out the tall window in the upper room for a while.

My human packed up all of the small plastic bags into one big bag and headed toward the car room. When I see him carrying the big plastic bag, it's normally a sign that I have an opportunity to sneak into that forbidden place, but this time, he quickly tossed the bag through the doorway before closing the door, so I wasn't able to sneak out there.

This evening, my human chased me around the house. It started in the kitchen, when I ran into the front room. Instead of going up or down the stairs, like I normally did, I turned and went into the room with the big cat tree. I ran all the way through it and back into the kitchen. I stopped to let him catch up and then took off again along the same route: kitchen to front room to cat tree room. I'm basically a miniature panther, so I'm really fast and there's no way he could catch me, but it's fun to watch him try. I was about to leave the cat tree room

---

[42]*The A-Team.*

as he entered it, but then he stopped, laughed, and scratched on the scratching post. I walked over to him and rubbed against the post. I won, as usual.

After our chase game, we went to the upper room. He played with his metal disc things, and I took a nap on the blanket chair.

Day 166, Tuesday, April 9, 2019:
I saw my human off to bed last night, like I always do, and received a nice belly rub as he dozed off.

This morning, I happened to be nearby when my human opened the door to the car room. I bolted through the doorway in a single leap before the opportunity vanished. He came out there and put some things into the big plastic bins, but then he went back inside the house and closed the door. I didn't see him again for several minutes, although I could hear him walking around. When he came back and opened the door, I apologized for running out there and sheepishly slunk back into the house.

My human left the house today, but wasn't gone as long as he normally was. When he returned, he brought some supplies into the house. I tried to sneak back into the car room, but he caught me this time and closed the door just as I started to make my move. He looked at me and made a sound that caused me to take a few steps back.

The windows were open again today. I watched and listened to some birds from the tall window by the computer.

I wanted to get on my human's lap this evening, but something was different. I hesitated because his legs didn't look normal. Usually, they are covered in heavy blue material, but tonight, his legs were mostly bare. I was concerned about landing on the parts of his legs that weren't covered. It turned out to be okay.

As usual, later in the evening, I took a nap on the blanket chair while he worked on the computer and played with his metal disc toys.

Day 167, Wednesday, April 10, 2019:
I cuddled with my human this morning (and received a nice belly rub!) before I got up to take care of some cat things. I met up with my human again as he scooped my litter pan. When he was finished with that, I followed him back upstairs and waited in the front room while he cleaned my water and food dishes. Before he left for work, he arranged several of my balls in a circle on the floor in the front room. After he went to work, I played with some of the balls.

I didn't feel very well today. My right eye felt a bit uncomfortable, and there was a little discharge from it. I might be coming down with a cold, or maybe it's just an allergy problem.

After my human and I had dinner, I sat on the table and complained about my eye discomfort. My human offered his lap, and I accepted. He gave me a nice neck rub and massage. After that, I took a nap on the blanket chair.

Day 168, Thursday, April 11, 2019:
I met up with my human this morning for another belly rub before he got out of bed. After that, I ran to the front room and waited for him to take care of his morning routine. Before he left for work, he knelt down next to the curved scratching pad that I was sitting on and looked at my eye. It's doing that thing again, and it's kind of annoying. I walked onto his lap for some cuddling. It was nice to receive some affection before he went to work.

Throughout the day, my eye got a bit better, but it still bothered me. I spent most of the day napping. After my human came home, I enjoyed his lap.

My human prepared my wet food tonight and set it on the floor. I waited until he finished preparing his own meal and took both of our plates to the upper room so we could eat together.

Day 169, Friday, April 12, 2019:
Good news! My eye is doing much better today. It's almost back to normal.

My human was being strange again. After he came home and provided my canned food, he returned to the car room. A while later, I saw him outside the front window, pushing a device all over the grass. The thing was growling at him almost the whole time. When it got quiet, he pushed the device onto its side and rubbed its belly with a large rag. It looked like it was wet. I'm glad he doesn't use a wet rag when he gives me belly rubs. He helped the device get back on its round paws and then wiped its back and sides with the same rag. After that, the device stayed quiet as he pushed it back to the car room.

I watched all of that from the bench at the window in the front room. From there, I could also see some flowers starting to bloom. They were below the window, right where the dirt lady had played.

When my human came inside, he prepared his own meal. He took it and what was left of mine (I had only eaten half) to the upper room. I finished my meal while he ate his. The rest of the evening, I alternated between napping on the blanket chair and getting back rubs on my human's lap.

Day 170, Saturday, April 13, 2019:
Today, I made multiple trips to the cold floor room. Every time I saw my human after doing that, he would try to clean my face because things kept getting stuck to my whiskers.[43]

I spent part of the morning looking out the front window while I received a massage from my human. I also spent some time looking out the tall window by the computer, searching for the birds. I only saw a few of them today.

I discovered a space under the head of my human's bed. I had to duck to get into it, but once I was there, I was able to walk around with plenty of headroom. My human came into the bedroom this afternoon and poked his head under there, apparently looking for me. I could hear a scratching noise, but I couldn't see anything.[44] After my human showed up, I came out and followed him to the other room, where I took a nap on the blanket chair.

As usual, I made multiple trips onto my human's lap today for neck rubs and massages.

Day 171, Sunday, April 14, 2019:
My human returned home from the shelter early today. That's a good thing because if the cleaning goes fast then it means there are fewer homeless kitties.

I spent some time in the front room today while my human worked in the kitchen. While his meal was cooking, I saw him make his way toward the car room. I quietly followed him. I tried really hard to slip by him, but he thwarted my attempt. He's getting good at that.

I followed him to the upper room when he took his midday meal up there. I spent some time on the blanket chair. Once he was done eating, I transitioned over to his lap. While I enjoyed a nice neck rub, I started to not feel well. I jumped down to the floor because I knew I was going to be sick. It wasn't much, but it's never fun. My human must have known what was going to happen because he put some paper towels in front of me before I got sick. I guess that made it easier for him to clean up. I appreciated that because I don't like things to be messy. Whatever it was, it passed quickly, and soon I felt better.

---

[43]Dusty cobwebs, usually.
[44]Mice in the wall, hence the previously mentioned mouse traps in the garage (where they enter and exit).

This evening, I followed my human to the bedroom when he went there to put his clean shirts away. When he was finished, I asked him to leave one of the drawers open for me. His shirts don't have enough cat fur on them when he puts them away. I fixed that for him.

Before we went to bed, my human and I had a nice cuddle session. I curled up on his lap and rested my head on his left front paw. His right front paw alternated between operating the computer and stroking both my head and my back.

Day 172, Monday, April 15, 2019:
Every seven or so days, my human takes plastic bags and the box of cardboard and empty cans to the car room. Today was one of those days, so when I saw him start to collect those things and place them near the door, I thought I'd have an opportunity to sneak into the car room. I knew I'd have to be quick. I followed him and tried to get close to the door. He told me to stay, but I complained that it wasn't fair for me to stay inside while he went out there. It kind of worked because he didn't go into the car room. Instead, he went down to the basement and scooped my litter pan. While he did that, I slipped behind the curtain and onto the bench to look out the window. He managed to sneak back upstairs and into the car room without me. I went up there and waited by the door for a second attempt, but he blocked my path when he came back into the house.

Later in the evening, we both heard a sound while we were in the upper room. It was someone at the front door. I followed my human down there. I couldn't see what was happening because he slipped out the door without me, but soon I heard tapping at the big window in the front room. I ran over to the window and jumped onto the bench to see what had made the sound. It was my human! He was standing there with the dirt lady. I sat on the bench for several minutes and watched as my human and the dirt lady talked. They looked at me and also down at the flowers below the window. I waited patiently for my human to come back inside.

Day 173, Tuesday, April 16, 2019:
This morning, I went to the bedroom when I heard my human move around on the bed. Since he was already awake, I got onto the bed and kneaded the blanket near him to get his attention. It worked! I lay down on his paw and received a long chin and belly rub. That was a great way to start the day.

I followed my human to the basement this morning. As usual, I checked out the window while he scooped my litter pan. I didn't see him leave, but when I heard the door to the car room open, I ran to the staircase just in time to see him disappear through the doorway. I went to the front room and sat on the bench to look for him. I saw him drag those two big plastic bins out to the end of the driveway. Then I saw him go away in the car. I think he saw me, too, because he waved to me as he passed in front of the house.

While my human was at work today, I got onto the kitchen counter. I had never been on the counter before, at least not any times my human ever knew about. There's a window right behind the sink. That window has a deep platform and a shelf. A plant lives in a pot on the shelf. Below the shelf, I found two pom-pom balls and one of my soft doughnut toys. How did they get up there?[45] I played with all three of them for a bit until they landed in the sink.

Late this afternoon, I saw my human outside while I sat on the bench in the basement. He was with the dirt lady again and was carrying a tool. What's she doing with my human?[46] They disappeared behind a tree near a small building. It was hard to see what was going on because of that tree in the way, but they emerged a few minutes later. They went different ways. The dirt lady disappeared behind her house, and my human came back to our house.

Day 174, Wednesday, April 17, 2019:
This morning, I received my usual belly rub from my human before he got out of the bed. After that, I got up and went to the front room. I sat on the bench and waited for my human.

I spent a lot of time looking out the window today. There wasn't much sunshine. Late in the day, some water started falling from the sky.

I sat on top of the scratching post in the front room while my human prepared our meals. When he was done, I followed him to the upper room and ate.

This evening, there were some strange noises coming from somewhere outside. They were a bunch of rumbling sounds. I found them a bit concerning.[47]

---

[45]They had been set aside, waiting to be washed.
[46]Going to help her figure out why her riding mower wouldn't start.
[47]Thunder.

I jumped onto the table below the television in the upper room tonight. There were some things in my way that my human had put there (bags of those metal discs he likes to play with), but I was able to maneuver around them. I also went across the metal box of drawers and onto the small plastic platform on the other side of it. I skipped that silly sliding shelf. The doors to the closet were slid to the middle of the opening, so I was able to walk from the plastic platform to a high shelf in the closet. I'd never been on that shelf. My human came over and moved a few things from the shelf, which made it easier for me to walk on it. I explored the shelf all the way to the other side of the closet before I leaped to the floor on the other side of the sliding doors.

Day 175, Thursday, April 18, 2019:
My human provided my evening meal right when he got home tonight, but then he left again for several hours. I don't know where he went, but when he returned, he had a present for me: a new toy mouse! He said it was a gift from a human he knows named Don. It's bright-green and fluffy. When my human pulled its tail, it twitched and bounced across the floor. It's quite entertaining. I played with it for a long time this evening. I tossed it all around the upper room and chased it into the hallway. I even grabbed it with a claw, carried it up to the table, and played with it there.

My new mousie!

I also played with a ball in the front room for a while, but returned to the upper room to play with my new mouse toy some more.

Before going to bed, I spent a lot of time on my human's lap. He rubbed my chin for me.

Day 176, Friday, April 19, 2019:
My human and I slept in this morning. Well, we didn't really sleep. Rather, my human didn't get out of bed when he woke up but instead, he lay there and gave me a long belly rub.

When we finally got out of bed, things seemed pretty normal. After he left, things got a little strange. He came back home much earlier than normal, or at least he tried to. I was sitting on the bench at the front window when I heard the big door in the car room start to open and saw the truck coming up the driveway. That's when things got weird. The truck stopped. I heard the door move again, and then the truck moved back to the road.[48] I played with my tan mouse for a bit before my human came home, still much earlier than normal.

This afternoon, I spent time in the upper room with my human. I watched the backyard through the tall window. After the sun went down, I took a nap on the blanket chair.

Day 177, Saturday, April 20, 2019:
My human was gone for part of the day today, so I played with my black string and some toy mice. When he returned, I spent a lot of time with him in the upper room, including cuddling on his lap and sleeping on the blanket chair. I also took a bath while I sat in a sunbeam that came through the tall window.

On one of my trips to the basement, I discovered the door to the cold floor room was open. I went in to investigate. I got into some dusty cobwebs. The next time I saw my human, he cleaned my face with a tissue. It was annoying, but I let him do it.

I saw something interesting today. Somehow, a small container of flowers had appeared on the desk in the upper room. I jumped up there for a closer look. They looked just like the flowers that had been outside the window of the front room. What were they doing in here?

Day 178, Sunday, April 21, 2019:
I had an embarrassing accident overnight. Somehow, I missed the litter pan while I took care of business. I tried really hard to cover it up. There are some absorbent white pads under the pan, so I pulled at the pad that I soiled and moved it up into the pan. When my human

---

[48]Almost forgot to wash the truck since it was out.

scooped the pan this morning, he replaced the dirty pad for me. He's good for things like that.

Today, I spent some time sitting on the perch in the small room, looking out the window over the driveway. I also made observations from the window in the upper room. The birds were active today.

I played with my white string a few times, including early this morning before my human got up. I also chased both my tan-and-green mouse and an oblong purple ball down the staircase.[49] Things got crazy with that ball. I didn't stop until I got to the cold floor room.

As usual, my evening was spent mostly on blanket chair naps and lap time with my human. Oh, and I helped my human look at the research book for his metal discs.

Helping my human with his research.

Day 179, Monday, April 22, 2019:

My human got out of bed so much earlier than normal today. He was so early, it caught me off guard. I was in the basement, looking out the window, and didn't even know he was up until he came down to take care of my litter pan. I followed him back upstairs to the bedroom. As he got dressed, I walked up the steps to the bed and reminded him that we hadn't enjoyed any cuddle time yet this morning. He agreed, and he lay down on the bed to give me a belly rub while I pushed my hind paws into his stomach.

When he returned from work, he provided my meal but then went back to the car room. I made my way to the basement and looked

---

[49]A plastic egg.

out the window. I saw him pushing that growling machine all over the grass again.

After that, my human entertained me some more. I saw him back outside that window, but now he was breaking sticks and placing them in a black metal orb with a grated door.[50] There was a small fire in the orb. He took large branches from the far side of my territory (near the stream) and brought them to the orb. He cut them up and added them to the fire. He did that for so long that I got bored and went to take a nap on the blanket chair.

Later in the evening, I sat on the bench in the front room and looked out the big window.

Day 180, Tuesday, April 23, 2019:
My human didn't seem eager to get out of bed this morning. He gave me a nice, long belly rub.

He stayed home today and spent most of the day playing with fire, like he did last night. I watched the fire for a while but got bored with it again and went to the upper room for a nap on the blanket chair. My eye was doing its strange thing again, but not as bad as last time, so it didn't annoy me quite as much.

An unknown human came into the house today.[51] I didn't get to see him very long. When I heard him arrive, I went to the hallway, where I was able to see him briefly before my human came upstairs. I wasn't sure what was going on, so I retreated back to the upper room and hid under the table. When I did that, my human closed the door to the upper room. The strange human left for a while but came back inside one more time before he left for good. Once he was gone, my human opened the door, and I once again had access to the whole house.

Day 181, Wednesday, April 24, 2019:
This morning, as my human left for work, I sat on the bench in the basement and looked out the window. The metal orb was still out in the yard, but there was no longer fire in it. Then I got a bit of a surprise: my human hadn't left for work yet but appeared in the backyard! He walked over to the orb and put a lid on top of it. He saw me and waved at me before he disappeared around the side of the house. I heard him leave soon after that.

---

[50]A chiminea.
[51]An air conditioner service person.

My human did another strange thing today. When he returned home (after he fed me, of course), he went back outside. From the basement window, I saw him pushing a device, but not the same one from a couple of days ago. This one was smaller, quieter, and flung small white pellets from the bottom.[52] I saw him drop those pellets over the entire yard as he walked back and forth with that thing.

When he came back inside, I asked for (and received) some well-deserved lap time. After that, I sat on top of the scratching post while he worked on the computer.

Today, my eye was still doing its weird thing. It hadn't gotten much better but also hadn't gotten any worse.

Day 182, Thursday, April 25, 2019:
I didn't get a very long belly rub today before my human got out of bed. I tracked him down in the basement before he left for work and asked for some lap time. He knelt down and provided his lap to me. I got onto his lap, but then he scooped me up and took me up the staircase to the landing by the car room door, where he sat down on one of the steps. I wasn't sure what was going on, so as soon as he sat down, I bolted from his lap and ran upstairs.

My eye was doing much better today, so I was a bit more active. I played with my white string in the kitchen and made observations from the various windows in between naps on the blanket chair.

This evening, I enjoyed some nice snuggle time with my human. He gave me a pleasant neck massage when I lay on his lap.

Day 183, Friday, April 26, 2019:
My human was home from work much later than normal today. I let him know that I was both concerned and annoyed by that. I think I got my point across because when he brought some supplies into the house, he immediately set them down and went to the kitchen to prepare my meal.

Tonight, I explored under the sink in the bathroom again. It had been a while since I last looked in there. There were fewer of those white rolls than before. In fact, I was able to go all the way to the back of the cabinet and lie down. I stayed there for a while. I watched my human go behind the plastic sheet into that small space where he got tortured by falling water.

---

[52]Grass fertilizer and weed killer.

Day 184, Saturday, April 27, 2019:
This morning, my human apparently wasn't feeling well. He got up very early for something to drink.[53] When he returned to bed, he buried his head under a towel. Rather than get up to do my normal routine of cat stuff, I stayed with him throughout the morning. I normally faced away from him, but since he wasn't feeling well, I turned around and kept an eye on him to make sure he was okay.

He stayed in bed much, much longer than normal. I think he felt better, though, because he gave me one of his paws to lie on. Once he awoke, I turned around so he could give me a belly rub. And what a belly rub it was! He caressed my neck, chest, and belly until almost lunch time. He even reached over with his other paw and gave me a back rub, too. Nothing beats a two-pawed, full-body massage! I couldn't remember the last time I had purred so much. We even held paws for a while before we got out of bed.

After lunch, he opened the window in the upper room just a crack. The birds were active today. I was entertained at that window for quite some time. Even when I went over to the blanket chair to rest, the birds at the window kept grabbing my attention. I ran back over there a few times to see what they were doing. There were a lot of little brown and white ones. Occasionally, one would land on the rectangular piece just below the roof, but most of them flew over to the tree or down to the grass. Later in the day, I took a nap in the sunbeam that appeared at this window.

My human spent too much time researching his metal discs this evening, so I helped him by taking a brief nap on one of his open books.

Day 185, Sunday, April 28, 2019:
I returned to the bed this morning after my human left for the shelter. It was rather cool today, and for some reason, whenever it got cold, the big bed was comfortably warm. I had a nice, long nap while I waited for him to return.

I got a lot of exercise today. I played with balls and toy mice in the front room and on the staircase while my human worked in the upper room. My human and I played together with my new bright-green mouse. I'm good at sharing my toys with him.

---

[53]Took a painkiller for a headache.

It was cooler today, so my human didn't open any windows, but that didn't stop me from watching the birds out there. They didn't seem as active today as they were yesterday.

I enjoyed my human's lap multiple times today. He was at the shelter this morning but was home with me for the rest of the day. I like days such as this, where I can have his lap any time I want.

Just like yesterday, I helped my human with his metal disc research today.

Day 186, Monday, April 29, 2019:
While my human was gone today, I played with one of my springy toys and also my tan mouse with the green tail.

After dinner this evening, my human and I went to the cold floor room. He worked at the workbench with some things he had brought home from the shelter. I jumped onto the workbench for a closer look. I recognized the things as shelves that fit in the kitty condos at the shelter. I had one of them for a while. It looked like he was fixing them. I got off the workbench to get out of his way. I asked to sit on his lap, but he kept standing and working on the shelves. Since he wasn't going to give me a lap, I focused my attention on exploring the room again. Fortunately, the work didn't take very long, and we were soon back upstairs, where I finally got to receive some lap time.

This was the day where my human collected all of the small plastic bags from around the house and took them and the box of cardboard, paper, and cans to the car room. Since I had been successful at sneaking out there when he had his paws full before, I thought I'd try again. It didn't work this time, so I didn't get to explore the car room tonight.

Day 187, Tuesday, April 30, 2019:
It was another cool morning, so after I saw my human off to work, I returned to spend some time on the warm bed. Later in the day, I got up to play with my tan-and-green mouse.

My human and I had dinner in the upper room, as usual. After eating, I got onto the table and sniffed his head a few times. Then I snuggled on his lap for a while. He gave me a back rub that was so intense, especially that spot on my lower back just in front of my tail, that it caused my legs to extend uncontrollably, pushing my butt way up in the air.

A bit later, I went to get a drink from the dish next to the sink in the upper room. The water was a bit stale, so I let my human know about it. He cleaned the dish and put some fresh water in it for me.

For some reason, my human types on the computer almost every night. His front paws spend too much time on the keyboard and not enough time stroking my back. So in order to redirect his attention to me tonight, I jumped onto his lap right after he started typing.

Day 188, Wednesday, May 1, 2019:
This morning, my human got out of bed earlier than normal. While he did his morning routine, my attention was directed upward at the big window in the front room. There was a bird standing on the roof! It was bigger than those tan ones I have been seeing. It had a bright-orange belly. I reached as high as I could on the glass to get a closer look. My human came over to see what I was looking at. We both stood there watching and talking about the orange-bellied bird for a while.

When my human returned from work, he had a big plastic bag that I hadn't seen before. It was full of yarn. I gave it a closer inspection after he set it down. Later, he put the bag in a box and said it was a present for Grandma so she could make hats.

This evening ended like every evening should—with a chin scratching while I lay on my human's lap.

Day 189, Thursday, May 2, 2019:
My human must have gone hunting today because he came home with several bags of food. He was late, but at least he fed me first before he put the food away.

This evening, I followed my human into the cold floor room. I ran in there as soon as he opened the door because it had been a couple of days since I'd been able to get in there.

After exploring the basement, I tried to get into the car room when my human brought more supplies in, but he prevented me from going in there.

Since my human was away a bit longer than normal, I made sure I got plenty of lap time this evening before we went to bed.

Day 190, Friday, May 3, 2019:
Today, I played with my green springy toy while my human worked in the kitchen. He even brought it upstairs for me when we went to the upper room.

Just as I always did, I spent some time on my human's lap today. This time, I positioned myself such that I rested mostly on one of his front paws. It was quite comfy!

Day 191, Saturday, May 4, 2019:
This morning, my human got that machine with the long hose out of the closet and took it to the basement. He moved my litter pan out of the way and pushed that thing all over the floor. Since it was loud, I retreated back upstairs.

I watched my human outside for a while. He had a long metal thing that he leaned against the house in front of the big window. It was close to where we saw that orange-bellied bird the other day. I saw him climb up the metal thing carrying a bucket. Was he hunting that bird? I didn't see any bird up there today. Even if there was a bird there, he was way too slow. How did this guy even survive this long? He came back down a couple of minutes later with the bucket full of gunk. I saw him empty the bucket and then move the metal thing. He climbed back up it and got more gunk. It was kind of entertaining.

Later in the day, my human opened several windows in the house. I sat at the tall one and watched lots of birds in the tree.

My human also picked up all of my toys in the front room and placed them in a straight line across the room. I had fun batting some of them away after he did that.

Day 192, Sunday, May 5, 2019:
I received a belly rub in bed this morning before my human got up. After we got out of bed, I went to look out the basement window as my human left for the shelter.

Upon returning from the shelter, I saw that my human had brought a piece of furniture home with him and set it on the table in the upper room. Since my nap on the blanket chair was interrupted, I got onto the table for a closer look. I recognized it as one of the pieces that was in my bigger room when I was at the shelter. It's a purple cube with big holes on the sides. It's a great place to take a nap when there's a soft bed placed in it. The top is solid, so it functioned as a nice perch, too. I wondered, why did he bring it home? I sat and watched him squeeze some thick liquid out of a couple of bottles onto a piece of plastic. He mixed the liquids together and put it into one of the sides. Then he secured the cube with some clamps.

After lunch, my human left the upper room. He called me a few times, but I was very comfortable on the blanket chair, so I stayed there.[54] A few hours later, he came back to the upper room. I left the room to take care of some things. When I returned, I found my human watching TV, so I stretched out on his lap and received a neck massage.

This evening, my human opened a couple of the windows. I sat at the tall window by the computer and took in the evening's sights and sounds before returning to the blanket chair.

Day 193, Monday, May 6, 2019:
My human left home later than normal today, which was great for me since it meant I received a longer belly rub. That was after I spent almost the whole night sleeping on or right next to one of his paws.

When my human left, I saw him take the box of yarn out to the car room. I tried to sneak out there, but as usual, I was stopped. Instead, I went down to the basement and sat on my bench to look out the window.

During the day, I played with some balls and toy mice before going to the upper room to take a nap on my blanket chair. That's where I was when my human came home, since he arrived much earlier than I expected. I normally meet him at the door, but since he was so early, I was caught off guard.

This evening, something really weird happened. My human and I were in the upper room. I was resting on my blanket chair and my human was quietly playing with his metal discs. The window was open, so there was a nice cool breeze going through the room. Suddenly, there was a horrendously loud sound that started with a huge *BOOM*.[55] My human and I were so startled by it that we both jumped out of our respective chairs. The sound turned to a rumble that faded away over time. I ended up on the floor and looked up at my human, who looked back at me. He seemed just as surprised as me. I don't know what it was, but it was scary. My human calmed down pretty quickly and reached out to me. After sniffing his paw and having him scratch my neck, I returned to the blanket chair. There were a few more rumbles later in the evening, but none were as intense as that first one.

Before we went to bed, I got up from the blanket chair and poked around on the table, where there were some plastic bags that contained my human's metal discs. There was a tiny bug trying to

---

[54]Called her to cuddle on the sofa, but she apparently wasn't interested.
[55]Thunder from a close lightning strike.

mess with them. My human heard me go after the bug and came over to investigate. He found the bug and took care of it. I stood guard over the bags of discs for a while longer to make sure everything was safe.

Day 194, Tuesday, May 7, 2019:
This was a pretty lazy day. After seeing my human off to work, I spent some time in the basement and looked out the window. I also played with my tan-and-green mouse.

This evening, I took a long nap on the blanket chair. It was easy to sleep because my human was very quiet as he worked nearby on the computer and played with his metal discs.

Day 195, Wednesday, May 8, 2019:
I spent most of last night wedged between my human's hip and one of his front paws. It was quite comfortable and has become my favorite place to sleep at night. As I almost always do, I got up early to take care of some cat things. After doing that this morning, I returned to his side. As he woke up, he pleasured me with a wonderful belly rub. It morphed into a neck massage. I love it when the day starts like that!

It was a rather cool day. I sat on the bench in the basement and watched some water fall from the sky.

When my human arrived home from work, I met him at the top of the staircase and told him all about my day. After he prepared our meals, we went to the upper room to eat. Later in the evening, I spent some time looking out the tall window while my human worked on the computer. I also snuggled on his lap for a while.

I gave myself a bath before I went to bed. I bathe myself fre-quently because not only does it keep my coat clean, but it also makes it very soft and shiny.

Day 196, Thursday, May 9, 2019:
This morning, I received another belly and neck massage. I wrapped my tail around my human's arm and pushed my back against his hip as he rubbed my belly. We also held paws for a while.

Before he left for work, we spent some time together in the basement. After he scooped my litter pan, I asked to climb onto his lap. When I did, he noticed that there was a small piece of litter stuck to my nose. He tried to remove it but just made it worse. No worry; I took care of it myself later in the day.

Today, I explored some cardboard boxes that are on top of a table in the storage room. Most of them are empty. My human came in when I was crawling around in them. I was so startled when I saw him that I jumped off the table.

My human talked on the telephone for a long time tonight. While he talked on the phone, I played with my yellow mouse. I stopped briefly when I heard him mention my name. I jumped onto the small desk below the television. I found a tool that my human left there and pushed it toward the edge of the table. I figured my human was spending too much time talking on the phone and not paying attention to me. It worked! He came over and talked to me a bit but also grabbed the tool before it fell to the floor. Having got my point across, I hopped down and played with my bright-green mouse. He later told me he was talking to Grandma.

Day 197, Friday, May 10, 2019:
This morning, my human and I held paws in bed before we got up. It made me feel good to hold my human's paw.

I explored the cabinet in the bathroom tonight. Nothing much had changed in it since the last time I was there. That wasn't the only cabinet I got into today. I also got to investigate the one below the kitchen sink. It wasn't really all that exciting, but it's my duty to keep tabs on all parts of my territory.

This evening, I sat at the front window and watched my human push that loud machine all over the yard. When he finished that, he came into the house and worked in the kitchen. While he was busy in there, I played with my black string.

Day 198, Saturday, May 11, 2019:
My human and I slept in today. The best part about that was the long massage he gave me. He started at my belly and worked up to my neck.

While my human watched videos on the computer this afternoon, I took a nap on his lap. Actually, I was half on his lap and half on one of his front paws. It was *so* comfy that I fell into a deep sleep.[56]

Later in the afternoon, I spent some time looking out the tall window. It was too cold, so the window wasn't open, but I still enjoyed sitting by it and watching the birds in the tree.

After bird-watching, I went to the front room for some exercise. I batted my soft blue and green pom-pom style balls around the room.

---

[56]And snored.

With my exercise routine done for the day, I returned to the upper room for a nap on my blanket chair.

This evening, my human decided I needed a manicure. He held me close to his chest and trimmed a couple of the claws on my left front paw. I let him know that was enough for one night and promptly hopped off his lap.

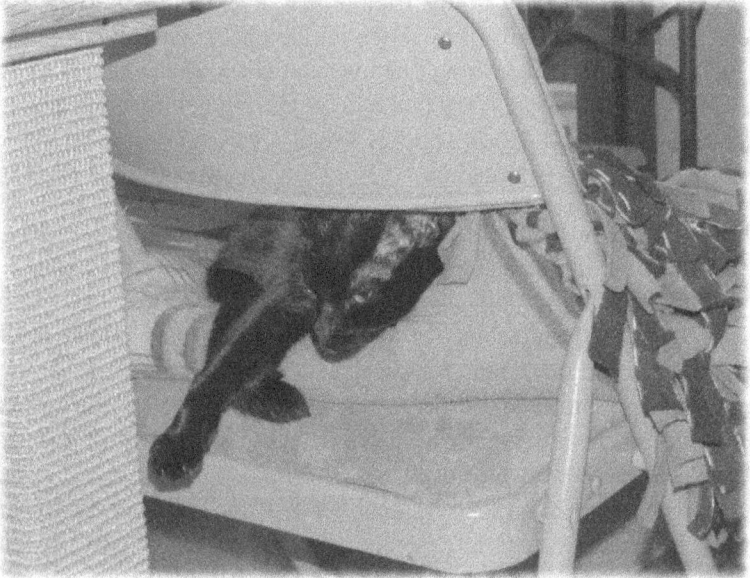

On the blanket chair near my scratching post.

Day 199, Sunday, May 12, 2019:
We didn't sleep in nearly as long today as we did yesterday because my human had to get up to go to the shelter. I also got out of bed early because I heard a bird outside the window. The blinds were closed, so I couldn't see it, but it was loud enough I definitely heard it. After seeing my human off to the shelter, I returned to the warm bed on this cool morning.

My human spent a long time at the shelter. By the time he returned, it was already lunchtime. While he ate, he put his hind paws up on the edge of my blanket chair. He left room for me on the blanket, but I wanted to be on his lap. I hopped onto his outstretched legs and settled in for a nice long nap. It ended up being several hours. What finally awoke me was his legs moving. He re-positioned his legs such that his hind paws were no longer on my blanket chair but instead were on the floor. He made a few strange sounds, too, as if he were in some kind of pain. I'm not sure why; I was comfortable the entire time.

Once I got up from his lap, I noticed a sunbeam coming through the tall window. I went over and sat in it while I gave myself a bath.

My human annoyed me this evening. He scooped me up when I wasn't expecting it and held me close to his chest. I refused to look at him and pushed back as best I could.

Day 200, Monday, May 13, 2019:
As has become our normal routine, this morning I awoke to a combined belly and neck rub from my human. We also held paws for a while before my human got up to go to work.

It was a bit warmer today, so I didn't spend as much time on the bed after my human left.

My human returned home at the normal time but strangely left again right after I received my wet food. I thought it was strange that he made my dinner and took it upstairs but didn't make one for himself. He didn't have his meal until he returned an hour later. I had nibbled at mine while he was gone but finished it when he ate his own meal. It's nice to have our meals together.

This evening, I got some lap time while my human was typing at the computer. I noticed that he types a lot less whenever I'm on his lap. When his paw wasn't typing, it was giving me a massage. After I'd had my fill of attention, I hopped down and went over to my blanket chair for a nap.

Day 201, Tuesday, May 14, 2019:
I received my morning belly rub today before my human went to work. While he was away, I got some exercise batting some balls around the front room.

This evening, I didn't get to spend too much time with my human because he was in the car room and wouldn't let me come out there. Instead, I took a nap on top of the big cat tree in the living room.

Day 202, Wednesday, May 15, 2019:
Today, my human had kind of a weird evening. When he came home, he left the car by the road. After we ate, he changed into a shirt I had never seen before and returned to the car room. Through the front window, I saw him move the truck out of the car room. Later, I heard some strange noises coming from that room. As the sun set, he moved the vehicles back into the car room and came back into the house to

clean up. I never did figure out what he was doing out there.[57] It kind of bugged me because I want to know what happens in my territory.

Day 203, Thursday, May 16, 2019:
It was quite warm last night. In fact, it was too warm to snuggle with my human. I wanted to be close to him, though, so instead of nestling right next to him, I lay down near him and just rested my head on his paw.

My human surprised me this morning when he got out of bed early. I had already gotten up and was on the bench in the basement, looking out the window. I spoke up when I heard him come down to take care of my litter pan. I asked to sit on his lap, and he readily complied. Since I knew he would soon leave for work, I wanted to get as much cuddling time in as I could.

While he was at work, I kept watch on my territory from the various windows. I also got some exercise by playing with my blue puffy ball.

This evening, I managed to get some more lap time with my human, despite him spending a good part of the evening in the car room and in the yard.

While in the yard, my human pushed that loud thing all over the grass again. I also saw the dirt lady. She came over to the front window and waved at me. I saw her pull up some plants from the dirt. She only removed some of them. Later, I saw my human pull the rest of them.[58]

Day 204, Friday, May 17, 2019:
Oh, what a wonderful belly rub I received this morning! I made sure I was on the bed when my human woke up, unlike yesterday. It paid off with a long massage of my belly. He also moved his paw up and scratched the top of my head right behind my ears. I didn't want it to end. It was so intense, I had to get up for a brief break. I walked around on the bed for a bit and talked with my human. Then he did something kind of rude. He grabbed me with his other paw and held me down close to his chest. We were almost nose to nose! I refused to look him in the eye. I mean, I like being close to him, but I'd rather cuddle with him under my own control.

---

[57]Welding parts to fix the lawn mower.
[58]Remnants of the tulips that had already blossomed.

Tonight, my human seemed annoyed. I found him in the upper room pushing a lot of papers around and typing on the computer.[59] He did that all evening, well past our normal bedtime. I decided I'd better leave the room, so I went to the top of the big cat tree in the living room and took a nap. I guess he was worried about me because he came to the living room looking for me. We talked for a bit while he gently caressed my head.

Later in the evening, I went to look for him. He was in the upper room, still working with those silly, annoying papers. I played with my yellow mouse while he continued whatever it was he was doing. I tried to sit on his lap at one point, but I wasn't sure about that because he wasn't wearing long pants. He must have understood my concern because he got up, left the room, and returned a few seconds later with a towel. He put the towel across his legs. After that, it seemed like his lap would be a safe place for me, so I cautiously walked onto it and lay down. He gave me the affection I sought. Cool air blew from the vents, but it was still quite warm, so I didn't stay on his lap very long. It was nice to have a brief cuddle session, though.

Relaxing under the table.

I spent the rest of the evening on the floor of the upper room. I waited for him to finish with his papers so we could go to bed.

Day 205, Saturday, May 18, 2019:
I found my human in the upper room this morning, He was still playing with those papers, so I let him be and went to the basement. I sat on the bench and watched water fall from the sky.

---

[59]Trying to figure out why the state had sent a letter claiming there was an error on a tax return from two years prior.

I got some exercise playing with balls in the living room and front room today. From the kitchen, my human rolled one of my green balls (with a bell!) toward me while I stretched out on the front room floor. It rolled right up to my paws. I grabbed it and looked at my human. He seemed pleased with himself. Humans are easily entertained. He had put all of the papers away by this point and seemed less stressed.

I continued chasing balls in the front room while my human worked in the kitchen. He was in there for so long that I got tired and decided I needed a nap. I climbed to the top of the big cat tree, which let me keep an eye on him while I dozed off and on. A couple of times, my human took a break from his kitchen work and came over to socialize with me.

After my human had lunch, we spent some time together on the sofa. I walked over him a few times and received some back rubs, and then I wedged myself between the back of the sofa and one of his arms.

I got up from our cuddling session when I heard a weird noise from in front of the sofa. My human had touched the handle on a door of the table with one of his hind paws. I hopped down from the sofa to check it out. He reached down and opened the door. I'd explored this dark space before, but that was a long time ago, so I went in for another look. Nothing much had changed since the last time I was in there. Still, it is good to keep up on those things.

Later that afternoon, we went to the upper room. Outside, the water was still falling from the sky. There were occasional loud noises from somewhere outside, but they seemed to be fading away. While my human quietly worked on the computer, I took a nap on the blanket chair.

This evening, my human prepared our meals and took them to the upper room. After we ate, I sat on his lap for a while. Once again, I was concerned because his pants were much shorter than normal. Like before, he got up, left the room briefly and then returned with a towel. This towel was a different color than the one before. It also had an image of a cat on it. I guess this is the appropriate towel a cat should use when sitting on a human's lap.

I was busy taking a bath on the blanket chair this evening when I was interrupted by a sound from outside. I hopped onto the table and quickly made my way over to the tall window. There was a human on the deck at the next house. I haven't seen this human before and didn't know who he was. I watched him for a while. I don't think he ever saw me. He went back inside his house, but I stayed by the window for a while longer and kept watch over my territory. Everything was good, so I asked my human to put the towel back on his lap for me. He did, and I settled down for some snuggling.

Day 206, Sunday, May 19, 2019:
I received my usual belly rub before my human left for the shelter this morning. The alarm on the clock sounded a couple of times before he got up. Each time it sounded, he turned it off and resumed rubbing my belly.

Several times today, I lay down on the blanket on my human's lap. We used the blanket instead of the towel for some reason. I also took a nap on the blanket chair while my human played with his metal discs. After my nap, I stayed on the blanket chair and took a bath. Before I finished, I got distracted by a bird. I ran over to the tall window to watch the bird for a while. When he left, I resumed my bath.

This afternoon, I explored the cold floor room in the basement some more. As I often did, I got some cobwebs stuck on my whiskers. When I returned to the upper room, my human cleaned them from my face.

I wanted to sit on my human's lap some more. Every time I sat on his lap today, he took the blanket from my chair and put it on his lap instead of using the cat towel. That seemed to work, but I don't know why he stopped using the cat towel.[60]

Day 207, Monday, May 20, 2019:
I watched my human clean my food and water dishes this morning. When he finished, I climbed onto his lap while he was still in the kitchen. Instead of staying on the floor, he scooped me up and sat on one of the chairs. I spent some time wiggling around on his lap before settling down for a massage. I'm glad we got to spend some time together before he left.

He surprised me, though, when he returned home a couple of hours later, much earlier than normal. I noticed he hadn't taken his bag with him like he normally does, either. I suspect he didn't actually go to work today. That's good news for me since it meant I got to spend more time with him.

---

[60]The material consisted of small loops, and her claws were starting to tear them out when she jumped down.

Later in the morning, I saw him go to the basement. I started to follow him, but I stopped as soon as I poked my head around the corner of the staircase. I was surprised at what I saw. He was in the basement but had leaned back to the staircase and was looking up at me. Did he know I was going to follow him? Am I really that predictable? He asked me "Prrrt?" and disappeared into the basement. Of course, I immediately chased after him and quickly caught up to him. We talked a bit while he gave me a back rub.

I received a special treat today. My human normally provided my canned food in the evening around the time he eats his own meal. I've noticed that when my human is home all day, he usually has two meals—one in the middle of the day, in addition to the one in the evening. Why did I only get one when he got two? During his first meal today, I asked him if I could also have something to eat. He said yes! He provided some of my canned food so that we could eat together.

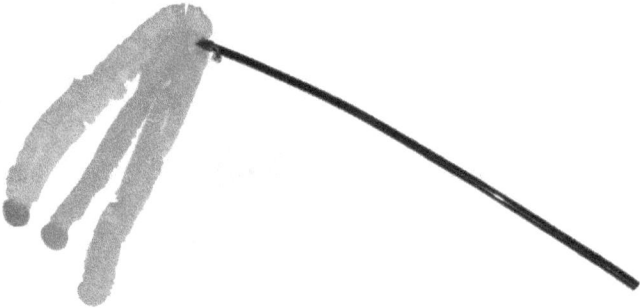

My new toy.

This afternoon, my human left for a while. When he returned just before dinnertime, he presented me with a new toy. He said it was another gift from Don. It has three long fuzzy strings with a soft pompom ball at one end of each string. The other ends of the strings are attached to a long stick and a bell. My human held the bare end of the stick and flicked the stringy end toward me. I swiped at the strings and balls as they bounced around. Later, when my human was busy in the kitchen, I dragged the new toy across the room, but it wasn't as much fun. It seemed to work better when my human and I played with it together.

Day 208, Tuesday, May 21, 2019:
On this cool morning, I got up early to take care of some cat stuff. After a while, I figured I should wake up my human. I climbed the

stairs to the bed and shouted "meow!" as I walked along the blanket toward him. He rolled over and gave me his paw. I lay on his paw, purred, and kneaded the blanket.

A bit later, I got up a second time and tried to wake him up again, but he must have been in a deep sleep because he didn't even move. It wasn't until I tried again several minutes later that he woke up and gave me my morning belly rub.

I was glad that my human stayed home again today. He took the new toy to the upper room, where we played with it for a bit. I watched the fuzzy strings crawl up my scratching post and onto my blanket chair. I ran to the top of the pet steps, where I reached for the strings. I grabbed them but then let them go. Then they fell down to the floor and moved around the bottom of my chair. I proceeded to go after them for a while before retiring to my blanket chair for a nap.

Like yesterday, I received part of my canned food in the middle of the day while my human also had his midday meal. That was another benefit of my human staying home all day.

After lunch, we spent some time at the big window in the front room. There wasn't much to see out there other than some water falling from the sky, but that didn't matter because what I really wanted was just to be close to my human. We talked a bit and took turns rubbing the tops of our heads against each other.

Later in the afternoon, we went back to the upper room. I took a nap on the blanket chair while my human played with his metal discs. Rested from my nap, I played with my new stick-and-string toy again. I took it to the other side of the room and batted it around. It was entertaining, but I still say it's more fun when my human and I play with it together.

Right after that, my human picked up one of my crinkly, sparkly balls and flicked it across the room. I chased it but it got away from me. I caught up to it, hit it again, and then chased it into the hallway.

Day 209, Wednesday, May 22, 2019:
I could tell by my human's morning activities that he planned to return to work today. I climbed onto his lap in the basement after he took care of my litter pan. I had to be sure I received some cuddle time with him before he left for the day.

More water fell from the sky today. I watched it through the windows. There sure has been a lot of that lately. The water is pooling up on the ground all over my territory.

I played with some toys in the front room and in the living room tonight while my human worked in the kitchen. I liked being near him.

This evening, I napped on my blanket chair while my human played with his metal discs. He sure likes to play with those. They aren't all that interesting, especially when you have a new stick--and-string toy to play with. Apparently, he agreed because as I started playing with my stick-and-string toy, he got up from his chair, came around the table, and sat down on the floor to play with it, too. He grabbed the bare end of the stick and made the balls and strings fly through the air. I watched it arc over my head and grabbed at the pompoms at the ends of the strings.

Day 210, Thursday, May 23, 2019:
Once again, my human had to go to work this morning. I followed him to the basement before he left. We talked for a while as he scooped my litter pan and added some new tiny rocks to it.

While he was away, I looked out the basement window from the bench. The sun didn't shine very much today. No water fell, either.

When my human arrived home, he prepared a meal for me, but not one for himself. He put my meal in the upper room. I ate most of it before returning to the basement. Outside the basement window, I saw my human push that loud thing with wheels all over the grass.

When he came back inside, I followed him to the bathroom. I asked him to open the cabinet under the sink, and he complied. This time, I didn't enter but just took a quick peek because something else had caught my attention. My human had turned a knob above the big white box. Some water was coming out of a small opening just above the box. I supported myself with my front paws on the edge of the box for a better look at the water. I'd seen this before and figured that the water would soon stop coming out of that small opening and start falling from the big thing near the ceiling. I didn't want to be around when that happened, so I got out of there.

While my human stood in that box and got wet, I played with one of my blue pom-pom balls in the front room and on the staircase. After he was done getting wet and dried himself off, I followed him to the kitchen. I played with my black string while he prepared his food. I hadn't played with that string in a while, so it was a nice change of pace. Once his food was ready, he took it to the upper room. I followed him. While he ate, I finished my own meal.

I rested on the blanket chair after dinner. Then I played with my big fluffy white mouse—the one with the black tail. That mouse is kind of neat because it has a bell that makes a fun sound, just like my stick and string toy.

Day 211, Friday, May 24, 2019:
While my human slept, I got up and played with my blue pom-pom ball. When my human finally awoke, we spent some time together at the front window. After that, I followed him to the basement. I figured he would leave for work soon and wanted to spend more time with him. I sat on his lap before he left.

I got a little scared today. There were bright flashes of light out-side and lots of loud rumbling. Water fell from the sky most of the day.

I was glad to see my human when he returned from work. After we ate, I decided we should both clean up a bit, so I stood on the table behind him and groomed the fur on top of his head. Once I was satis-fied that he was clean enough, I jumped down and went under the table. There I gave myself a bath while he worked on the computer.

Day 212, Saturday, May 25, 2019:
This morning, I received a full head-to-tail massage before I got off the bed. I love it when my day starts like that.

It was a quiet and relaxing day. There weren't any loud, dis-turbing sounds, like yesterday. My human spent most of the day in the upper room, where he played with his metal discs. I was in the upper room with him a lot and spent some time on his lap. He didn't have long pants on, so I was a bit uncomfortable about going onto his lap. He recognized my concern and grabbed a towel that he put on his lap for me. I really didn't spend that much time on his lap today because it was rather warm. When I wasn't on his lap, I was stretched out on the floor not far from him.

Something caught my attention in the evening. I was minding my own business on the floor in the upper room. I was near my scratching post when I saw movement in the corner of the closet. I quietly but quickly made my way over there to check it out. It was a spider! A little one. Where did it come from? How did it get in here? Alerted by my prowling, my human came over and got down on all four of his paws to see what I was seeing. When I turned to look at him, I lost track of the invader. My human grabbed a paper towel and returned to the floor. I never saw the spider again, so I think he got it. He praised me for doing a good job.

Day 213, Sunday, May 26, 2019:
It was another warm day. I spent some time looking out the window in the basement while my human was at the shelter. I'd noticed that room was a bit cooler than the others, so it's a nice place to go when it is warm. Plus, it's a lot of fun to look out the big window down here. A bit later, I took a nap on top of the big cat tree in the living room.

My human played with his metal discs again today. He sure has been doing that a lot lately. I helped him with his research again, but it was so boring, I fell asleep on one of his books.

I wanted to spend some time on his lap, but of course, he wasn't wearing long pants again. This time he moved my blanket from the chair to his lap. I like the blanket, and I like his lap, so when I can have them both, it's a great day.

There was a nice sunbeam coming through the tall window today. I spent part of the afternoon enjoying it while my human worked nearby.

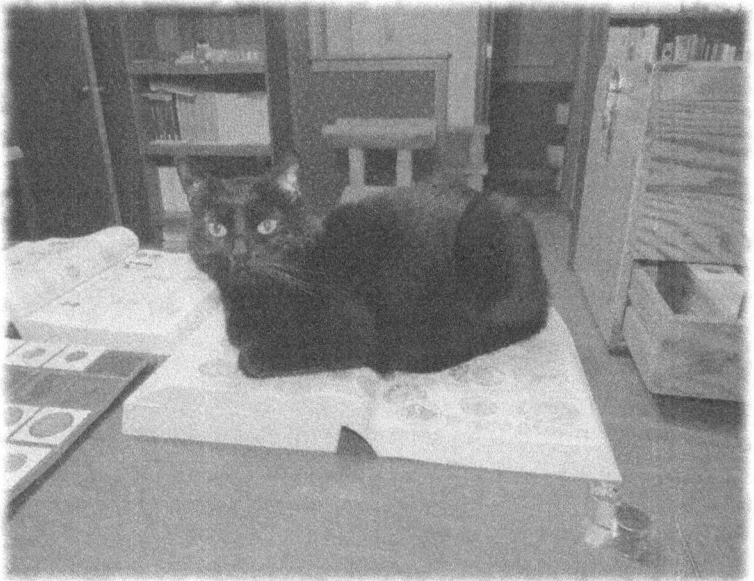

Getting bored with research.

This evening, things got a little strange. I followed my human to the living room, where he sat at a table and did some more work with metal discs. Why there and not in the upper room? I didn't know, and he never told me. Since he was seated, I decided his lap needed a cat, blanket or no blanket. I jumped onto his legs. He seemed happy to see me. I didn't stay there long. After I hopped down, we played with some of my toys, specifically the springy balls that Grandma and Grandpa gave me.

Day 214, Monday, May 27, 2019:
We slept in quite a bit today. My human gave me a belly rub, too, which I enjoyed. My human normally returns to work the day after going to the shelter, but today he stayed home for some reason.[61] That was okay with me because it meant a longer belly rub and plenty of lap time.

Something was wrong, though. My human didn't seem to feel well. Late in the morning, he left the upper room and went down the hallway. I stayed in the upper room since I thought he would return soon, but he didn't. Instead, I heard him call me from the other side of the house. I left the upper room and searched for him. I found him on the sofa under a blanket. He was lying on his side with his legs bent. I hopped up, walked across him, and made myself comfortable in the triangle between his legs and the back of the sofa.

I slept with him until it became too warm for me. While he was still asleep, I got down and made my way over to the big cat tree. I went all the way to the top and took a nap.

I woke up when I heard my human get up. My position at the top of the cat tree gives me a great vantage point to watch things that happen in my house. He didn't see me, but I saw him. He went all over the house. I didn't know what he was doing. He eventually came back to the living room. When he saw me, he walked over to the cat tree. At the top of the cat tree, I was at eye level with him, which was fun. He talked to me a bit and rubbed my head and back.

This afternoon, my human opened the shade that covers the sliding glass door in the kitchen. I looked out the windows for a bit. It's hard for me to see out those windows because they have wide frames that block the view, and unlike the door in the basement, there isn't a bench in front of them.

I went to the front room to look out that window instead since there is a bench next to it. My human came over, too. We sat on the bench together and looked out the window. Well, I didn't look outside

---

[61]Memorial Day.

very much because I was too busy crawling all over his lap and receiving his attention.

This evening, we spent some time in the upper room, like we
normally do. My human was busy with the computer and metal discs,
so I occupied myself on the floor. I played with some strange toys.
They've been here since I moved in. They looked like balls but have
wings. They have an interesting aroma. As I played with one near my
paper bag, somehow it came apart and made a small mess on the floor.
Catnip! Why was there catnip in that ball? It was kind of old and stale.

Observing a mouse and ball deep in my bag.

Right after that, something else caught my attention. In the back
of my paper bag, I saw my yellow toy mouse sitting in front of one of
my sparkly foil balls. What were they doing in there? I lay down and
stared at them in a trance. My human also came over to look at them.

I stayed put by my paper bag, even when my human left the
room to go get ready for bed. Not until he was in bed and called me
did I get up and go cuddle with him.

Day 215, Tuesday, May 28, 2019:
My human slept in again today, but I didn't. I went to the basement
and looked out the window while I waited for him. He finally showed
up to scoop my litter pan and add some fresh rocks to it. I followed
him upstairs all the way to the upper room, where I sat down on his
lap with the blanket. I had both of his front paws until he moved his

right front paw up to work on the computer. I moved around a bit to make myself comfortable with just his left paw and the blanket. I made it work, but I would have preferred using both of his front paws.

The blanket can be rather warm, and so can his lap. When I use both together (let's call it the *blanket lap*), it can easily get too warm. When that happened, I hopped down and sat below the table near him. It was a good time for a bath. After my bath, I noticed my human was still working at the computer, so I just stayed where I was and stretched out for a nap.

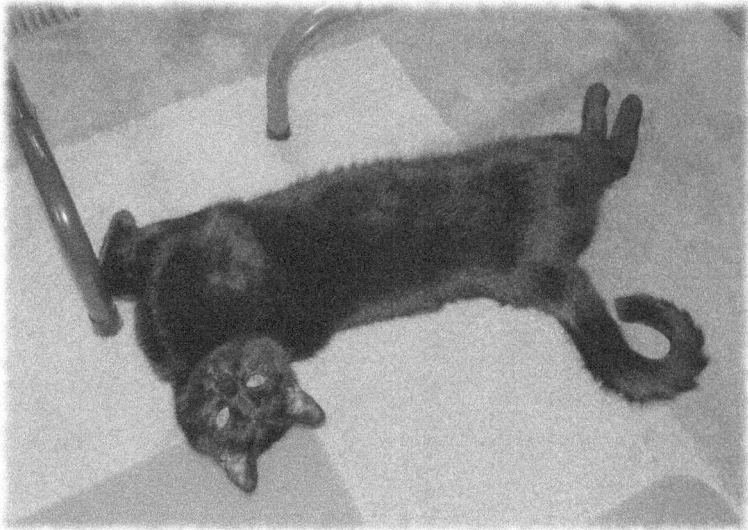

Relaxing in the upper room.

I made many trips to the blanket lap today. During one of those trips, I noticed my human's left front paw needed to be cleaned. I took care of that, along with a couple of my own paws.

After that, I got onto the table and cleaned myself a bit more. A kitty can never be too clean. I had let my guard down since I was bathing myself. Everything was fine until my human reached over and moved a book that was close to me. I wasn't expecting that and jumped when I heard it move. In the end, I took a nap on one of the books.

This evening, I got worried when my human locked me in the upper room. We were both in that room with the TV on when I noticed he left the room and closed the door behind him. He returned a minute later with my travel pod. Once again, he closed the door, this time trapping both of us in the upper room. I didn't know what was going on, but it worried me. My human seemed concerned, too. He put the travel pod on the floor with its door open and sat back down to watch the TV some more. There was a low rumbling sound coming from outside. It was noticeable because he had opened the tall window slightly. About half an hour later, the rumbling sound tapered off. After that, my human picked the travel pod back up and took it out of the room. I was happy that he never put me in it. I noticed he left the door open this time. He even left it open once he returned.[62]

Asleep on one of my human's books.

Day 216, Wednesday, May 29, 2019:
Just like the last several days, my human stayed home again. That meant I received lots of lap time. I really like it when he's here with me all day.

This morning, my human didn't just scoop out my litter pan. Instead, he completely changed it. The new one looked just like the old one, but I could tell it was different. I walked and sniffed around the perimeter of the new pan to inspect it. I determined it would work.

While my human kept busy in the upper room, I patrolled the house. Something caught my attention when I passed through the front

[62]All of this was due to an EF-4 tornado on the ground that passed about 10 miles from the house.

room. There was a human outside the big window! I quickly but cautiously walked over to the bench for a better look. The dirt lady was back! She was playing in the dirt again. I sat on the bench and watched her. I don't think she saw me.

While I watched the dirt lady, I also noticed my human went to the car room. A few minutes later, I saw him in front of the house with the dirt lady. Right after that, she looked up and saw me. My human sprayed some water on the grass while the dirt lady finished playing in the dirt. When she was done, my human sprayed water onto the dirt she had been playing in, on top of some flowers that weren't there yesterday.

My human took a couple photos of me this afternoon, including one where I sat on one of his books, trying to get his attention. Well, I guess it kind of worked.

Day 217, Thursday, May 30, 2019:
My human and I slept in this morning. As usual, I received a belly rub and a back massage.

Later in the morning, my human went outside and pushed that loud machine all over the grass. The temperature was kind of cool, so I went back upstairs and took a nap on the bed.

When my human came back inside, he spent a few minutes in that small water room. After that, he prepared lunch for us. We ate together in the upper room.

After lunch, my human became occupied with his metal discs again. He kept switching between typing on the computer and playing with the discs on the table. It was pretty boring, but I wanted to be near him. I took a nap on the floor close to him.

This evening, I followed my human to the upper room when he carried my food up there. He set it on the floor, where he normally does, but then went back to the kitchen. Since we normally ate together, I only took a couple of bites before returning to the front room to wait for him. I sat and waited patiently on my curved scratching pad while he finished preparing his own food. For some reason, it took a bit longer than normal. Once he was finally done, I again followed him upstairs, where we ate together.

After dinner, I took a nap, but rather than just lying on my human's lap, I got him to fold his arms in front of him, which created a cradle for me. I climbed up and dozed off. It was very relaxing.

Before we went to bed, we spent some time seated at the front window. There weren't many birds or other critters to watch tonight, but that was okay because I really just wanted to spend some time with my human.

Day 218, Friday, May 31, 2019:
This morning, I sat on my human's lap at the front window again. Just like last night, there wasn't much activity out there, but I enjoyed the lap time anyway.

Naturally, that wasn't the only time I spent on my human's lap today. This afternoon, I found my human working at the computer. I climbed onto his lap and rested my chin on his right arm. I thought that was nice of me because he could still operate the computer with his paw.

I stayed close to my human today. He has stayed home many days in a row now, which was unusual.[63] While he was busy in the upper room, I took a nap under the table near him. I was able to rest, but since I was close to him, I would be alerted if he got up.

This evening, I took a nap on my human's arms. It's the most comfortable spot in the house. After my nap, my human and I played with one of my small mouse toys. I sat on top of the scratching post while he tossed the mouse up to me. When it landed on the platform atop the post, I'd whack it back down to him. It was a lot of fun, at least when the mouse made it to the platform. My human can't toss a mouse very well, so sometimes it didn't land on the post. It was funny to watch him chase after the mouse, even when I didn't take a swing at it. Sometimes, I'd swipe at the mouse right away. Other times, I'd stare it down for several seconds before I sent it flying across the room.

While we played the mouse game, something grabbed my attention. I saw a bug crawling on one of the shelves in the closet. I stared at it intently to draw my human's attention to it. He's kind of slow, but eventually, he spotted the bug and dispatched it. I hopped down from

---

[63]Vacation days taken during the week of Memorial Day.

the post and watched the closet a bit longer to make sure there were no other intruders.

Day 219, Saturday, June 1, 2019:
I tried to wake my human up this morning. After I made my morning rounds, I trotted into the bedroom, jumped on the bed, and walked up to my human. I spoke to him several times as I made my way toward him, but he didn't move. Since he was still asleep, I gave up and curled up next to him. When he eventually awoke, he gave me my normal morning belly rub. We then held paws for a while.

My human eventually got up and made his way to the basement. Once he had finished scooping my pan, I asked if I could sit on his lap. He dropped to the floor and made a lap for me. He massaged my back and scratched the sides of my head as I purred and wrapped my tail around one of his arms. One problem with receiving back rubs is that they make my hind legs extend. When that happens, my butt and the base of my tail get pushed toward my human's face. On one paw, the whole thing is a bit awkward, but on the other paw, that back rub feels *so* good.

Later in the morning, I found my human working at the computer. I sat on his lap for a while until some birds on the other side of the window caught my attention. I went over and sat at the window for a better look. Birds are fun to watch.

There were a lot of birds today. A bit later, I was on the floor near my human when I heard some birds close to the window. Eager to get back up to the window, I skipped the pet steps and leaped directly onto the table in front of my human. Unfortunately, I landed on the computer's keyboard. It slid out from under me and caused me to briefly lose my balance. My feline gracefulness allowed me to quickly recover from the situation, and in no time, I was at the window, watching the nature show.

Before we had lunch, my human approached me as I sat on the table behind him. I thought he might grab me, so I got up and made my way down the steps. He followed me. On his way out of the room, he grabbed my strings-and-stick toy. He rang the bell on the toy and chased after me. I shot off down the hallway, through the front room, and into the kitchen. He might be a lot bigger than me, but I'm a lot faster than him. I left the kitchen and proceeded into the living room. I lost him! That's when I heard the bell and saw the three strings dancing at the other entrance to the living room. They exited the room, and the sound of the bell faded, so I cautiously crept toward that doorway. When I got there, I saw the strings disappear around the corner in the front room. Again, I carefully followed them. Next, they disappeared into the kitchen. I picked up the pace because it seemed like they were moving faster. When I entered the kitchen, I was a bit startled to see my human right around the corner instead of my strings. It surprised me so much, my tail got all puffy. My human laughed and then knelt down to pet me. I ran away and retreated to the safety of my curved scratching pad. He came over and stroked my back and my tail. *You won this time, human!* After our chase game, we sat at the bench by the front window and watched some birds. My tail gradually returned to its normal size.

My human prepared our lunches soon after our chase game. He took mine to the upper room. I started to eat but stopped when I saw him leave. He assured me he would be right back with his own food. He didn't lie. After he returned and sat down with his own food, I resumed eating my meal.

After lunch and the excitement of the earlier chase, I thought it was a good time for a bath. While my human was preoccupied with the computer, I sat on the floor near his hind paws and gave myself a complete head-to-tail cleaning. I followed that with a brief nap.

Day 220, Sunday, June 2, 2019:
I spent the morning looking out the basement window since my human was away at the shelter. After a somewhat longer than normal time at the shelter, he arrived home and prepared our meals. While he got the food ready, I exercised by first running a complete circuit through all the rooms on the main level of the house. Next, I grabbed my big fluffy white mouse and chased it out of the kitchen, through the front room, and halfway down the staircase toward the basement. I left the mouse near the door to the car room. After all that exercise and a good meal, I took a nap on top of the big cat tree.

Later in the day, I followed my human to the basement. I entertained myself with a puffy red-and-blue ball while he worked with some boxes. I started to run upstairs but stopped when I heard the door to the cold floor room open. I quickly turned around, ran back down the steps, through the soft floor room, and toward the cold floor room. I received a bit of a surprise when I nearly smacked my nose into the closed door. I hit the brakes hard and looked up at my human to figure out what was going on. I thought he had opened the door, but for some reason, it was closed. He laughed and then opened the door. I don't know why he thought that was funny.

I spent most of the afternoon and evening near my human in the upper room. I made several visits to his lap and to the tall window to look out over the backyard. As the night wore on, I took a few naps on the floor.

Day 221, Monday, June 3, 2019:
Sadly, my human returned to work today. I heard him leave as I sat on the bench in the basement.

Something kind of strange happened today while my human was gone. I heard a loud noise outside. It was a sound I had heard before, but it was much louder this time. I made my way to a window, and the dirt lady was driving a small machine all over the grass in my territory.[64] I had seen her on that device in the past, but she always stayed in her own territory.

I was excited to see my human when he returned home. I met him on the staircase and talked to him. He prepared a dinner for me but not one for himself. Instead, after serving me, he returned to the car room for a while.

Later that evening, he made some more trips to the car room. On his final trip out there, I quietly stood by the door and attempted to sneak out there since I hadn't been there in a long time. Alas, it didn't work. He must have known I was on the other side of the door because he blocked my path right away. I'll have to be even stealthier next time.

While my human was in the bathroom this evening, I asked to see the cabinet under the sink. He opened the door, but to my surprise, I couldn't get in! The last time I explored this small compartment, I could easily enter and maneuver in the tight space, but this time, it was almost completely full of those rolls of white paper. I poked my head in for a better look but decided against trying to jump into the extremely limited space.

Day 222, Tuesday, June 4, 2019:
So, I was in the basement this morning when I heard my human come downstairs. I remembered that yesterday he went to work after spending many days at home with me. I figured that might happen

---

[64]She mowed my lawn while I was at work. I had planned to mow that evening, but there was a chance of storms. Fortunately, it didn't storm, but it was nice to come home and have one fewer chore to do.

again, so as soon as I saw him, I ran to him and hovered as close to him as I could. He stepped to the side a couple of times, but since I was a lot faster than him, I kept in lockstep with him. There was *no way* he was going to leave for work today without spending some quality time with me first. He quickly understood that I was serious. He dropped to the floor and provided a lap for me. I crawled on his lap for a long time and received many back rubs from him. I got off his lap briefly to adjust my position before I lay down on his lap to receive a massage. After a while, I figured I'd made my point. I hopped off his lap and went over to the bench to look out the window. He was free to go to work.

It was a pretty quiet day without my human. I looked after the house and watched the backyard from the basement window. I didn't see any water fall from the sky today.

When my human arrived home, I inspected several bags of supplies he brought. It appeared he had gone on another one of his hunting trips for human food. Quite successfully, I might add.

I spent some time in the cold floor room because my human had gone in there with a basket of clothing. I shot into the room as soon as the door opened. At least I didn't nearly hit my nose on the door, like last time. I found a couple of tiny bugs in the corner. I wondered if I should tell my human about them, but I didn't.

I took a nap this evening after a long, hard day of watching over the house. My human seemed preoccupied with the computer, so I stretched out on the other side of the room.

Just before my human left the room to go clean up for bed, I moved to the blanket chair for another nap. He came in and found me there before he went to bed. Normally, he would just call me to come to bed, but this time, he did something evil. He knelt down and showered me with affection. Immediately after that, he pinned me down and grabbed one of my front paws in a pitiful attempt to trim my nails. I let him clip one of them, but that was it. It was annoying. I wasn't mad, though. I followed him as he went off to bed. At least he gave me some nice affection as he drifted off to sleep.

Day 223, Wednesday, June 5, 2019:
Like yesterday, I was already up and in the basement when my human got out of bed. He was up earlier than normal. I approached him when I heard him enter the room, but he turned and went toward the door into the cold floor room. I followed him but got worried when I saw

him roll a big red-and-black container on wheels.[65] He unraveled a long string from it and stuck it into the wall. Then he picked up a big floppy tail that was attached to the container. He reached down and touched the container. Suddenly, it screamed at him! I got out of there as quickly as I could. That thing continued to scream, so I didn't stop in the soft floor room. I ran all the way to the long hallway upstairs. The screaming lasted for several minutes and then stopped as quickly as it started.

A few minutes later, I heard my human come up the steps, so I went to the end of the hallway and peeked around the corner. I was relieved to see that he was unharmed. He spoke with me briefly, then sat on one of the steps and motioned for me. I trotted down the steps and climbed onto his lap. I knew he would leave for work soon, but I was so happy that the angry, screaming container didn't hurt him. I just wanted to rub myself all over him.

While my human was at work, I played with my black string. I also performed my usual window watching, and I took a few naps.

I waited patiently at the door this afternoon when I heard him arrive, but he didn't come into the house right away. I don't know what he did out there, but I was glad that it wasn't very long before he was inside and socializing with me. He quickly prepared our meals, and soon we were eating in the upper room.

After dinner, I lay down meatloaf style (with all four of my paws tucked under me) under the table and stared into one of the corners of the room. I did that because, well, it's a cat thing.

Once my staring session was done, I played with my black string some more. I had left it on the floor near my human's chair, but since he was now sitting there, I moved it to the floor across the room, where I had more space.

Day 224, Thursday, June 6, 2019:
The temperature was a bit cooler than it had been recently, so I spent most of the night snuggled next to my human. As the sun came up, I left my human on the bed and went to take care of some cat things. As frequently happened, I was on the bench in the basement when my human came downstairs sometime later. I got onto his lap as soon as I could. We shared a moment together before he left for work.

---

[65] A wet/dry vacuum.

We spent more time together this evening. We played with one of my toy mice in the upper room. I sat atop the scratching post and batted the mouse when he tossed it up to me.

After we played with the mouse, I relaxed by the tall window and watched the yard while my human worked on the computer.

This evening, my human opened the door to that tiny room off the hallway. There was a stack of nested boxes on the floor in there. I jumped into the top box to see what was in it and to get a closer look at the shelves above it. Sadly, it wasn't very interesting. I quickly hopped out and tracked down my human.

It turned out my human wasn't doing anything interesting, either. He was on his way to that other tiny room where he stands under the water, so I left and went to find something to do in the front room. I found my big fluffy white mouse and played with it while my human tortured himself with water.

After chasing my toy mouse, I went to the basement to look out the window. That's where my human found me before he went to bed. I'm not sure why he came down there. I would have found him on the bed eventually. I humored him and followed him all the way upstairs, where I joined him on the bed.

Day 225, Friday, June 7, 2019:
This was a pretty relaxing day. I mostly rested and watched out the windows, starting with the big one in the basement. I also played with my white string in the kitchen and in the upper room.

On days where my human doesn't wear long pants, I've trained him to move my blanket to his lap whenever I want to sit there. Today was one of those days. In fact, I got him to put the blanket on his lap many times this evening.

Day 226, Saturday, June 8, 2019:
This morning, I played with my white string while my human went through his morning routine. I had left it in the upper room but took it to the front room to play with it.

My eye started to act up again today. It was kind of annoying, but I couldn't complain much because it hadn't happened for quite a while.

This afternoon, my human took a nap on the sofa. I was elsewhere in the house when he went to the living room, and by the time I found him, he was fast asleep. It was too warm to snuggle next to him, so instead, I climbed to the top of the big cat tree and took a nap up there. That way I was able to remain comfortable but still be close enough to hear him when he awoke.

My human went back upstairs after his nap. I followed a bit later, but since I wasn't done napping, I walked up the steps to the table and made my way over to my blanket chair. I curled up on the blanket to continue my nap.

While my human got ready to go into the water room this evening, I asked him to open the door to the cabinet under the sink. He did. It was still full of lots of rolls of white paper, so I couldn't walk into it. This time, though, my human removed a big jug that had always sat just behind the door and put it on the floor. That made some room for me to get deeper into the cabinet, even with all of the paper rolls. I couldn't quite get all the way in, but I could get far enough to see that the stacks of paper appeared to go all the way to the back. Satisfied, I exited the cabinet and left the room. I wanted to make sure I was far enough away from danger before the water started to fall. I found my black string and played with it for a while.

Once my human dried himself off, he got ready to go to bed. The only problem was, the bed wasn't ready for him. Or me. I had never seen this before. The blanket and sheets were missing! My human found them and put them in a big pile on the bed. I sat on the top pet step and watched as he stretched the sheets over the corners of the bed and then pulled them tight along the edges. He then unfolded the blanket and spread it out on top of the sheets. With that done, everything seemed in order, so I hopped onto the blanket as my human squirmed his way between the sheets. He put his arm out for me. I wedged myself between his thigh and paw.

Day 227, Sunday, June 9, 2019:
This morning, I went to the basement to see my human off to the shelter. After he left, I went back upstairs and returned to the bedroom for a nap. I curled up on the blanket near the pet steps. When I'm on the bed with my human, I like to be near his front paws, but when I'm by myself, I like to be on the part of the bed normally occupied by his hind paws. It's just one of those things.

I got a bit of a surprise when my human returned from the shelter. He carried a white box with a black tail. The box was about the size of me, but its tail was long and thin.[66] I recognized it from the shelter as a box that sometimes roars loudly. I watched as he pulled

---

[66]A handheld vacuum cleaner from the shelter that had stopped working.

tools from the tool chest and split the white box into two pieces. He spent a few minutes fiddling with some parts inside the box before he put the two halves back together. He grabbed the end of the tail, shoved it into a strip of plastic on the table, and then warned me that there might be a loud noise. I saw him reach over to the white box and touch it briefly. Sure enough, the box let out a brief but loud roar. He extracted the tail from the plastic strip and wrapped it around the box. I watched him take the box down the hallway and heard him go all the way to the car room. When he returned sometime later, the white box was no longer with him.

Later in the afternoon, I sat on the table in the upper room and observed my human. He had received some packages with a bunch of those metal discs again and had dumped them out on the table. He looked at them and stacked them into piles. He put some of them in plastic containers. I was on a part of the table without any discs, minding my own business, when some movement caught my attention. I bolted a few feet over to one of the plastic containers that my human had been dropping discs into. A bug! My actions alerted my human to the intruder. He grabbed the container and put it on the floor. I jumped down to help but lost track of the bug. My human had found it, though, and knocked it free from the container. He disposed of it and praised me for a job well done.

I kept an eye on things for a while longer to see if there were any other intruders, but I didn't spot any. Satisfied, I curled up on my human's lap for some well-deserved relaxation.

That was just one of several lap sessions I had with my human today. The best one was later in the afternoon when he put his hind paws up on the chair where my blanket normally resided. He put the blanket to his lap, so I made my way onto the blanket. I ended up sleeping on top of one of his front paws for at least half an hour. I couldn't even begin to describe how great it feels to sleep on a human's paw.

This evening, I spent some time in the basement, looking out the window, while my human worked in the upper room. When I went up there to check on him, I was a bit surprised to see the square table from the kitchen had somehow moved to the upper room. It was between the closet and my scratching post. I jumped on top of it and found that my human had placed some small bags containing discs on part of it. The other part was still empty, but the empty space grew smaller as he put more and more bags on the table. The door to the closet was open, and from the empty spot on the table, I was able to get a closer look at some of the higher shelves in the closet. Unfortunately, there wasn't much exciting to see up there.

My eye was still doing its weird thing today. By the end of the day, it seemed like it was getting better—my right pupil was beginning to return to normal.

Day 228, Monday, June 10, 2019:
My human got up earlier than normal this morning. I went upstairs and found him playing with his metal discs. He didn't do that very long before he started his normal morning routine. I was going to follow him to the kitchen when he went there to prepare my water and dry food dishes, but I got distracted in the front room by my white string. I tossed it around for a while. After my human left for work, I switched and played with my black string.

It was a great day for me since my eye was feeling much better. I think it'll be completely normal by tomorrow morning.

After dinner, I spent some time on my human's lap. I soon spotted an inviting sunbeam coming through the tall window near the tool chest. It looked like the perfect place to take a bath, so I moved from my human's lap over to the corner of the table and proceeded to clean myself.

Later in the evening, I was in the basement, looking out the window, when I heard my human walk through the room. He carried a basket of his clothing into the cold floor room. While he messed with his basket, I slipped into the cold floor room. I didn't stay very long, though, and bolted out of the room as soon as he turned around and started to walk toward the door.

Back upstairs, my human asked me if I wanted to be brushed. I didn't need the grooming, but the attention was nice. The only problem was, he couldn't find the brush. I had given up on him and went to the storage room to look out the window over the driveway when he finally found the brush and came looking for me. I talked to him a bit and walked around on the platform by the window as he brushed me. I kept moving to make it easier for him to get to all sides of me.

I played with my black string a bit while my human worked at the computer. Later, I sat on top of my scratching post and was entertained by my human. He tried to toss a mouse toy up to me multiple times. I think he tried to get it to land next to me on the platform, but he kept missing. Once it was on the platform, I decided I didn't feel like playing that game, so I hopped down and rubbed the sides of my head against his knees and paws. He stroked me a few times. After that, he got up and returned to the computer. I hopped onto the blanket chair and curled up for a nap.

Day 229, Tuesday, June 11, 2019:
I followed my human around the house this morning as he took care of some tasks before he left for work. I asked him for some lap time. We sat on the floor of the front room for a while. It was much easier to sit on his lap today because he wore long pants. While we sat there, he rolled one of my balls across the floor. I watched it but didn't chase it because I preferred to spend time on his lap. After I transferred some of my fur to his shirt and pants, I let him go. I sat on the bench by the big window and watched him drive away. I watched outside for a while longer and then went to take a nap.

When my human returned home, I greeted him at the door and then ran to the front room. As he made his way upstairs, I excitedly followed him. I knew he would soon prepare our meals. Strangely, when he went back downstairs, he didn't go to the kitchen but instead went back to the car room. I heard the big door go up. I got worried that he forgot to feed me and was planning to leave again, but I soon heard the door move a second time, and he returned inside. This time, he went straight to the kitchen and started to fix our food. He served mine right there in the kitchen. I was so hungry, I ate half of it before he even finished preparing his own food. Once his was finally done, he took both of our plates to the upper room. I finished my meal and then looked out the tall window while I patiently waited for him to finish eating.

When my human was done eating, I asked for some lap time. He put his hind paws up on my chair and moved the blanket to his lap, just like he did a couple of days ago. I stepped onto the blanket but only briefly as I used it to make my way over to his chest. I lay down on his left arm with my hind paws supported by his paw. That has become my favorite napping position.

Later in the evening, I played with my black string under one of the tables while my human played with his metal discs on top of the table. When I got bored with the string, I went to see what my human was doing. He was moving metal discs from piles on the long table to bags on the kitchen table that was still in the wrong room.[67] I made my

---

[67] Organizing coins by country.

way to the kitchen table via the platform of my scratching post to get closer to him. Doesn't he know that it's hard to walk on the table when it's covered in lumpy bags?

After I made sure I had his attention, I hopped down, stretched out under the kitchen table, and took a nap.

Day 230, Wednesday, June 12, 2019:
As usual, I demanded lap time from my human this morning before he left for work. I let him take care of my litter pan first because that's important, but once it was scooped, it's lap time!

I rested and observed my territory through my various windows today while I waited for my human to return. I was on the bench at the front window when I saw a car approach and back up into the driveway. It was him! I ran down the staircase and greeted him as he came through the door.

After we had our meals, I wanted some time on my human's arm, just like I did yesterday. He provided his arm to me. It was *so* relaxing.

Later in the evening, I walked on the table to inspect my human's activities. He was playing with those bags that held his metal disc toys. I'm not sure what he does with them, but he seems to be entertained by them.[68]

Tonight, I lay on the floor next to my pet steps and grabbed my big fluffy black-and-white mouse. When I did that, my human got out of his chair and came over to me. He got down on the floor and played with it, too.

Soon after that, he went to the hallway. He returned with my bright-green mouse—the one that buzzes and wiggles when he pulls its tail. He put it on the base of my scratching post and pulled the tail a couple of times. It was mesmerizing! Once I gathered my wits, I slunk up to it and grabbed it by surprise. I chased it all over the room, around the big table, under the computer table, past my human, and eventually through the hallway and into the storage room. It was the most exercise I'd had all day.

After that excitement, I returned to the upper room and played with a ball. It was soft and had a few flaps that made it easy to grab with my teeth or my claws, and it had a bell. I found it in the short tube of the cat tree. I didn't know how it got there. I tossed it around

---

[68]Rearranging the bags (countries) into alphabetical order.

the room much the same as I did the green mouse, but with a bit less vigor. All in all, it was a great evening.

Day 231, Thursday, June 13, 2019:
My human left the windows open overnight. It was noticeably cooler than the previous evenings, so I spent some extra time cuddling with him.

Like yesterday, I waited in the basement while my human took care of all of his important morning chores, like preparing my water and dry food and also cleaning up my litter pan. When he came to the basement, I asked for his lap. I didn't spend as much time there this morning.

When my human returned home, he didn't come into the house right away. I went to the front window to see if I could spot him. I found him on the other side of the window, giving the flowers a drink of water. He saw me and put one of his paws up on the window to acknowledge me. After he gave the flowers some water, I saw him walk back in the direction of the car room. I heard the big door move, so I figured he'd be inside soon. I ran down the half flight of stairs and met him as he came through the door.

After dinner, I sat on his lap for a bit. He put the blanket on his lap before I jumped up there. That was nice of him. I didn't lie on his left arm this time, but instead, I turned around and rested my chin on his right arm. I thought it'd be good to change things up.

Later in the evening, I got up on the table and talked with him for a while. He made a quick motion toward me with both of his front paws, as if he was going to grab me, so I quickly moved down the table. He didn't actually try to get me. I think he was just faking me out. I got up on the kitchen table, and he did the same thing. It's empty now. Why is it still in the wrong room? I hopped down and ran over to the half wall next to the sink, where my water dish was located. He came over and again reached toward me, but slower this time. We cuddled a bit. As he massaged my sides, he leaned over and kissed the top of my head a few times. I'm getting used to him doing that now, although it still kind of surprised me.

The telephone rang tonight. He sat and talked on the phone for a long time, so I figured that would be the perfect time to jump onto his lap and rub myself all over him. I made sure to shove my butt toward his face a couple of times, too.

The windows were open again tonight. During one of my trips onto my human's lap, something at the tall window caught my attention. I went over to get a closer look. There was a bug flying between the open window and the mesh. My human came over and saw the bug, too. He flicked the mesh a few times, and soon the bug left.

Day 232, Friday, June 14, 2019:
I met my human at the door when he arrived home, but once again, he didn't come into the house right away. Instead, he set his bag down and then closed the door. Then I heard some activity at the front of the house, so I ran over to the bench in the front room. Like yesterday, he was out there giving the flowers a drink of water.

When he came inside, he served me dinner but didn't make one for himself. After eating and multiple cuddle sessions on his lap, he got up and said he needed to leave. It was a rather unusual time for him to go since he normally stayed home after a day at work. While he was gone, I spent time looking out the windows and napping.

My human finally returned home well after the sun went down. Right after he came inside, he started talking to someone on the phone. I lay down on the floor in the upper room while he sat on his chair and talked. Part of the conversation was about me because I heard him say my name. When I heard that, I got up, walked over to him, and jumped on his lap.

We finally went to bed much later than normal.

Day 233, Saturday, June 15, 2019:
My human left the house for a while this morning but returned before lunchtime. He returned with several bags of supplies and food items after what was apparently a very successful hunting trip.

He prepared meals for us, after which we spent most of the afternoon in the upper room. I was on his lap a lot, usually at my request. Once, though, he picked me up and held me close to his face. I liked being close to him, but I was annoyed that he did that.

We played together, too. He tossed one of my balls onto the short cat tree from across the room. I hopped up there and batted it down. After that, we played with one of my toy mice on the pet steps.

This evening, after the sun went down, I spent some time at the bench in the front room. I watched some bugs flying around slowly on the other side of the window. They were usually dark, but they would light up occasionally. It was neat.

Day 234, Sunday, June 16, 2019:

My human spent the morning at the shelter, like he does every week. I met him at the end of the hallway when he came home. We had lunch a bit early and then spent some time in the upper room. Soon, though, he went to the living room and lay down on the sofa under a blanket. I joined him and nestled myself on top of the blanket in the triangular cavity formed by his legs and the back of the sofa. After a couple of hours of snuggling on my human's legs, I went over to the short cat tree by the window. I jumped up to the platform and looked out the window briefly before I gave myself a bath in the sunbeam.

My human got up briefly but was soon back on the sofa. I wanted to stay close to him, but it was a bit too warm to cuddle again, so I went across the room and climbed to the top of the big cat tree. There, I watched over him between catnaps.

Early in the evening, I followed my human to the upper room. I sat on his lap for a while. He put the blanket on his legs to make a space for me. I curled up on the blanket and rested my head on one of his front paws.

I spent part of the evening looking out the front window again for those bugs that lit up. I also went into the bathroom while my human was in there and asked to look under the sink. It had been a few days since I last inspected it. He opened the door and removed the same jug as before, so I was able to walk into the cabinet. Nothing much had changed in there.

Day 235, Monday, June 17, 2019:

I sensed that my human wasn't feeling very well, so I spent most of the night close to him, even though it was rather warm. When he got up in the middle of the night, I waited patiently on the bed for him to return. After he came back, I kneaded the blanket by his side for a few minutes and then curled up next to him. I finally got up early in the morning to perform my morning patrol. I didn't see him again until he got up and went to the bathroom. He greeted me from the hallway as I sat in the front room. He seemed to be doing better.

I went downstairs to look out the basement window. I jumped off the bench when I heard my human come into the room. I waited patiently as he scooped my litter pan. He lay down on the floor and socialized with me for a brief time.

When he returned in the evening, I noticed that he came inside right away. I guess the flowers didn't need a drink tonight.

We had dinner and then spent the rest of the evening in the upper room. He worked on the computer while I catnapped on the floor. Between naps, I spent time on his lap, even lying on his chest and arm once while he had his hind paws up on my chair.

Day 236, Tuesday, June 18, 2019:
I spent most of the night with my human again, although he seemed to be doing much better. It was nice to cuddle with him. I got up early to take care of some things and left him to sleep a bit longer. I was surprised when I heard him get up but not come down to the basement. Instead, I found him in the upper room, typing on the computer. It looked like a good time to sit on his lap. He put the blanket on his legs for me. I curled up on the blanket and purred as he stroked my back. Eventually, I hopped down so he could leave for work.

I was in the basement when he got home from work. I got so excited when I ran up the stairs past him that I misjudged the last step before the middle landing and whacked one of my paws against the tread. It hurt a bit, but I didn't let on. I just kept running up to the front room. Besides, I'm too graceful. I just acted like I *meant* to do that.

We had dinner together. Well, at first my human put my food on the kitchen floor while he prepared his own meal. I think he'd know by now that I won't eat there unless I really have to. I'd much rather wait for him to take both of our plates to the upper room so we can eat together. He got the message, and once his food was ready, we went to the upper room to eat.

I didn't exercise much tonight but instead switched between resting on the floor, cleaning myself, and spending time on my human's lap (on the blanket).

During one of my trips to his lap, I faced the window when something caught my attention. I leaped off his lap and onto the table near the tall window. I jumped onto the tool box (fortunately, it was closed) and put my front paws up on the wall to the right of the window. It was a bug! It shot up the wall and out of my reach. My human must have seen it, too, because he also jumped onto the table. Since he's a lot longer than me, he was able to reach it with one of his front paws. After he got down from the table, he praised me for a job well done. It felt nice to be appreciated.

Day 237, Wednesday, June 19, 2019:
Well, that was embarrassing. I missed my litter pan this morning. I tried to cover it up by pulling the absorbent pad under my pan up into

the pan, but it didn't really help. My human took care of it when he came downstairs. He removed the soiled pad and replaced it with a fresh one. It's nice to have him around to do things like that for me.

As usual, before my human went to work, I sat on his lap. I found him at the car room door, putting his shoes on his hind paws. When he was done, I made my way onto his legs. I snuggled with him and received a back massage. Everything was good until he moved a bit unexpectedly. He reached behind himself for something. Not really sure what was going on, I decided to hop down. I went down a couple of steps and then turned around to look at him. He had one of my toy mice in his right front paw. He tossed it down to the basement, and I chased after it. After spending the morning playing with my mouse and looking out the basement window, I went upstairs to catch up on my sleep.

When I heard my human return home, I went to meet him at the door, but like earlier in the week, he didn't come in right away. I went up to the bench in the front room and found him giving water to the flowers again. Once the flowers were done drinking, he came inside and prepared our meals. We ate in the upper room, as usual. After dinner, I spent some time on his lap.

Before going to bed, I took a bath on the blanket chair. I like my fur to be soft and shiny, so frequent baths are required.

Day 238, Thursday, June 20, 2019:
After taking care of my litter pan this morning, my human lay down on the floor. I walked over to him and put my front paws on him. He rolled over onto his back, so I climbed onto his chest. I lay there facing him while I received a pleasant back rub. I enjoyed spending time with him before he left for work.

I played with my bright-green mouse today. My human and I also played with another mouse and a ball. I chased after them when he tossed them onto the short cat tree in the upper room. I'd throw them back to him, and he would toss them up to me again. While we played with the ball, I accidentally caught a couple of my claws on one of his paws. I felt bad. I didn't really feel like playing anymore after that. I just lay there while my human gently stroked me with his front paws. I rested my head on one of his paws for a while. A human's paw makes the best pillow.

Later in the evening, I sat on top of my scratching post and watched my human as he rearranged a bunch of his books. At one point, he removed the blanket from my chair and moved the chair over to the bookcase for his own use. Thankfully, he put both the chair and the blanket back when he was done.

Day 239, Friday, June 21, 2019:
Like yesterday, I received a back massage while I lay on my human's chest in the basement. I always try to spend at least some time with him before he leaves.

The sun was late today. When I looked out the window this morning, it was much darker than normal. For a while, a lot of water fell from the sky.

I heard my human arrive home, but he didn't come into the house. I also didn't see him outside when I went to look for him, at least not right away. After a few minutes, I saw him in the distance. He walked over to the flowers but didn't give them any water. He waved at me on his way to the car room before he came into the house.

As usual, I enjoyed some lap time after dinner. Tonight, I took a nap under the table while my human worked on the computer. We didn't play much tonight.

Day 240, Saturday, June 22, 2019:
This morning, my human didn't lie down in the basement but rather sat down like he used to do. I helped myself to his lap. We spent a long time cuddling before I got up and returned to the window.

I was still in the basement when I heard a loud sound coming from the staircase. I sat in the corner of the room farthest from the steps and waited as the sound grew louder. I soon saw my human backing down the steps, pushing and pulling that growling thing with the really long tail. At the bottom of the steps, he turned and began pushing it back and forth across the floor in this room. I managed to sneak by him and ran upstairs to get away from that hideous thing.

I ran all the way to the upper room and sought refuge, but it didn't last. He started pushing and pulling that thing in the hallway and soon came into the upper room. I saw my opportunity to escape again when he stopped briefly. I quietly slipped out of the room, down the hallway, and made my way to the living room. There, I climbed the big cat tree. I'd only ever seen that monster on the floor; I didn't think it could climb up something like my cat tree. Once that thing finally stopped growling, my human put it back in the small room near the front door. He then came over to the cat tree and comforted me.

This evening, my human left the house briefly. When he returned, he had an ice cream cake with a photo of me on it! How did he do that? He said he planned to take it to the shelter tomorrow to share with the morning volunteers. He said it was to celebrate the 10th anniversary of his work with the shelter. I didn't get any of the ice cream.

Day 241, Sunday, June 23, 2019:
I got an early start on my exercise this morning. I played with my puffy blue ball while my human slept. I kept my activity in the basement so I wouldn't wake him up.

Before my human went to the shelter, I had him sit on the basement floor so I could climb onto his lap. I knew he'd be gone a while, so I rubbed as much fur onto his shirt as I could.

Curled up near some of my toy mousies.

This afternoon, I spent more time on my human's lap, but this time, we were on the living room floor. He was playing with his metal discs on the table but took a break to give me a back rub. When I was done with my back rub, I hopped into the tube on the short cat tree near the window, and he returned to his toys. I lay there and kept an eye on him while he worked.

I also spent some time with my human in the upper room. There, I curled up on the floor while he played with his metal discs on the table.

My human took a nap on the sofa later in the afternoon. It was too warm to snuggle, so I went up to the top of the big cat tree for my own nap.

Day 242, Monday, June 24, 2019:
It cooled down a bit last night, so I spent most of the night with my human. I stretched out next to him so he could put his paw on my belly and shoulder. When he rolled over in the middle of the night, I changed sides so I would still be in front of him.

This morning, I could tell my human was going to leave for work. I didn't get to sit on his lap in the basement but he stopped at the door to the car room and sat down for me. I happily jumped onto his lap and accepted a long neck and back massage from him. It lasted so long, I think it may have made him late for work, but that didn't concern me.

I played with some of my toys in the front room today. My human had arranged them in multiple lines on the floor. He had moved all of them a few days ago when he fought with that growling beast with the long tail.

This evening, I sat and observed the backyard from the tall window in the upper room. I saw the dirt lady drive her machine all over her yard and then my yard. About that time, my human left the room and went outside. I went to the basement for a better look. I saw my human walking around with a long stick. He walked along the edges of the grass, holding the stick, and sometimes the stick made a loud sound.[69]

Later, things got weirder when I saw my human with something that looked like a really big brush. He pushed it all over the patio outside my window. He moved all sorts of small twigs and leaves to the grass so the patio was empty.

When my human came back inside, he did his periodic routine where he takes the small plastic bags from various rooms in the house and places them into a big bag before he takes the big bag to the car room. I thought about trying to slip through the doorway and go out there with him but decided against it, mostly because he was right there at the door, so I never had a good opportunity.

Day 243, Tuesday, June 25, 2019:
This morning, I tried to wake up my human. I thought I'd heard him

---

[69]An electric trimmer/edger.

move around, so I went into the bedroom. It looked like he was still asleep, but that didn't stop me from hopping onto the bed and kneading the blanket for several minutes. I also purred loudly. He didn't respond to either of those activities, so I gave up and went back to the basement.

My human eventually came to the basement. As usual, I could tell he was going to leave for the day, so I asked to sit on his lap after he scooped my litter pan. When he sat down, I wiggled on his lap for quite some time before I settled down. Then I received the best back scratching *ever*. He used both paws to rub my lower back right in front of my tail. It was incredible! It was so intense, I almost couldn't stand it. He followed that up with a full head-to-tail massage.

This evening after dinner, I needed more lap time. I waited until my human was typing at the computer before I told him to put the blanket on his lap for me. He obeyed. I have trained him well.

I also asked to look inside the bathroom cabinet again. He opened one of the doors and took the jug out for me, but after glancing into the opening and seeing it hadn't changed since my last excursion in there, I decided not to walk into it.

Day 244, Wednesday, June 26, 2019:
I made my human late for work again today, although it wasn't as bad as it was a couple of days ago.

While I lay on my human's blanket lap this evening, I got really excited. I saw a bug crawling up the wall in about the same spot as before. I jumped off the blanket and onto the table. I made my way over to the corner, where the bug was climbing. It was lower than before, so I was able to reach it without jumping onto the toolbox. I grabbed it but then lost track of it. My human came over and tried to find it, but he didn't seem to have any luck, either. I hopped onto the toolbox and sat for a while with my attention focused on the wall, but the bug never came back.

I also spent some time this evening relaxing on my human's arms. He had his hind paws up on my chair and was watching TV, so it seemed like a good time to curl up on his chest and arms.

Day 245, Thursday, June 27, 2019:
Today, I had a bit of a scare. As I walked up the dark stairs from the basement, something entered the top of the staircase. My tail got puffy as my fur stood on end. I arched my back to make myself appear bigger. The light came on, and that's when I got a better look. Whew!

It was just my human. He stroked my back and tail as he passed me on his way to the basement. I turned around and followed him. My tail slowly returned to its normal thickness.

This afternoon, I watched my human through the front room window as he gave the flowers some water. Then he came inside and made our meals. After I ate, I got onto the table behind my human and groomed the fur on his head.

Before we went to bed, I spent a long time on my human's lap.

Day 246, Friday, June 28, 2019:
My human annoyed me this morning. After he took care of my litter pan, he didn't sit down for me. Instead, he picked me up! What aggravated me even more was that he then kissed me! I refused to look at him during any of that. I think he got the message because he didn't hold me very long.

He went back upstairs for a few minutes but then sat down at the car room door. I decided I wasn't mad at him, so I hopped onto his lap. We snuggled for a while before he left for work.

While he was away, I played with my tan mouse in the basement. I also played with my white string. Between my play sessions, I took some naps.

This afternoon, I saw my human give the flowers more water. Then I saw him do something strange. He gave a bunch of water to one of the trees. It wasn't the big tree right outside the window but the smaller one on the other side of the driveway. I wondered why the big tree didn't get any water.

Later in the evening, my human picked me up again. What's his obsession with that? At least he didn't hold me as long this time. He also didn't try to kiss me. Instead, he set me back on the floor, at which point I walked to the other side of the room. He got down onto the floor and picked up one of my small toy mice. He put it on the table near the pet steps. I shot up the steps and onto the table to get it, but once I got on top of the table, I lost interest. Since he picked me up twice today, I decided not to give him the satisfaction of seeing me get excited about a mouse.

Day 247, Saturday, June 29, 2019:
I got to enjoy the whole day with my human. I sat on his lap for a while using the towel he puts on his bare legs. We also played with some toy mice while I sat on my scratching post.

This afternoon, I took a bath while sitting in a sunbeam. It came through the tall window. That was nice because I could clean myself yet still be close to my human while he worked on the computer.

This evening, I received a belly rub in the upper room. That was a bit strange because my belly rubs usually happen on the bed, but I still enjoyed it.

I spent most of the day in the upper room because that's where my human was working. While lying on the floor near him, I happened to look over at the closet. The doors to it were open. I hadn't been in there since that time I found the spider. I was overdue to explore it again, so I went over and put my front paws on the second shelf up from the floor. The open space on the shelf was pretty narrow, but since it wasn't very high, I was easily able to calculate the jump required to stick the landing. I walked along the shelf and inspected the items there. I didn't notice anything different from the last time I was there, but it was good to check.

Around bedtime, I popped into the bathroom while my human was sitting in there. He opened the cabinet below the sink for me and also removed the large bottle that was behind the door. Last time, I think I only took a quick peek inside, but this time, I walked all the way in. There were still a bunch of those white paper rolls in there, but maybe not as many as before.

I stepped down from the cabinet and left the bathroom altogether. I figured he would soon get into the small room where the water falls on him, and I didn't want to see that.

Day 248, Sunday, June 30, 2019:
My human was at the shelter longer than normal today. When he returned, he didn't stay home very long. I saw him pick up a box, and then he said he had to return to the shelter. His second trip didn't last nearly as long as his first trip.

When he arrived home the second time, he prepared our meals. After we ate, I spent a very relaxing day in the upper room, never far from my human. It was kind of warm, so I didn't spend a lot of time snuggling with him, but I made several short trips onto his lap throughout the afternoon and evening.

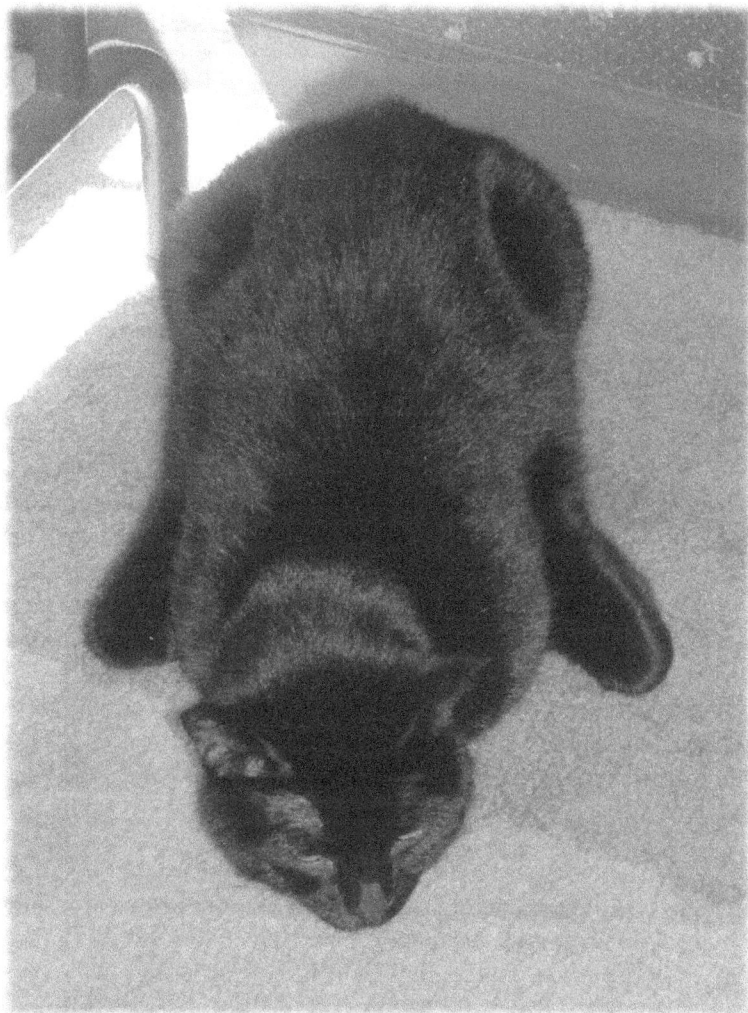

Resting in the upper room near my human's hind paws.

Day 249, Monday, July 1, 2019:
I followed my human from the basement to the front room this morning. When he sat on the steps near the front door, I hopped onto his lap. I demanded my morning cuddle session since I thought he would leave soon. It turned out he didn't.

Even though he stayed home, my lap time was limited because he spent a lot of time outside. In the morning, I saw him on the other side of the basement window. He had a loud machine with a large stick that shot a stream of water very forcefully. He spent a lot of time pointing the stick at the patio, and as the water hit it, the patio appeared cleaner. It was a bit terrifying how strong the water looked. I watched it in horror from the bench until I couldn't stand it anymore and backed away. I went upstairs because I figured I was safer up there.

During the afternoon, he came inside, thankfully without the water stick. I enjoyed some lap time with him while he worked on the computer.

Later in the evening, I heard the water stick machine running again, but this time in front of the house. I didn't go to inspect it.

When the water stick machine finally quieted down for the evening, my human came back inside. He performed his weekly routine of gathering the small plastic bags and the boxes with paper and cans. In addition to consolidating the plastic bags, he emptied the small box of paper into the larger box and then set the small box at the top of the steps. I tried to sneak out to the car room when he went out there but didn't have any luck. Failing that, I went to the front room and looked out the window. I saw my human pushing the two large plastic bins out to the end of the driveway. When I heard him come back inside, I went up the steps, where I found the smaller box he had emptied. It was rectangular and had two elongated holes that he sticks his paws through to carry it. The box was just my size, so I jumped into it. I hadn't been in that box before, and it is always fun to try out a new box.

Day 250, Tuesday, July 2, 2019:
This morning, my human didn't come down to the basement when I expected him, so I went looking for him. I found him still on the bed but with the blanket pulled away, as if he was about to get up. As I walked along the edge of the bed toward him to get closer to him, he pulled the blanket back over himself. That created a soft spot for me right next to him. I plopped down and pushed a thigh against his body. He reached over and gave me an extended belly rub. It was nice to spend time together. We even held paws for a bit.

While I was lying there enjoying the attention, I heard some loud sounds outside in the direction of the window.[70] Those sounds startled me, so I jumped off the bed and left the room.

My human must have gotten up about the same time because he soon came down to the basement. He sat down and presented his lap,

---

[70]Construction equipment for a project across the street.

which I happily accepted. After several minutes of wiggling around and rubbing as much of my body against his as I could, I settled down on his legs. I rested my chin on his right arm while both of his front paws massaged my back and sides. We spent a long time together. He picked up my soft purple pom-pom ball and handed it to me. I grabbed it with the claws of both front paws and held it against his leg. He also picked up one of my tiny mice—the sparkly blue-and-purple one—and put it on one of his hind paws. I didn't have much interest in it because I was too busy enjoying my massage.

Rather than go to work today, I wanted him to stay home with me. And guess what. He did! Maybe if I sit on his lap for a really long time every morning, he will stop going to work. It was nice to have him home all day, but like yesterday, I didn't get to spend as much time with him as I wanted because he went outside with that loud water stick again. While he did that, I played with the purple pom-pom ball in the basement until I got it stuck under a board.

Day 251, Wednesday, July 3, 2019:
My human brushed me this morning. I enjoyed the attention. He used a metal brush, so it felt like an intense back scratching but with a really wide paw and lots of tiny claws.

Later in the morning, I spent some time on the V-shaped top of the small cat tree in the upper room. While there, my human gave me another back scratching (with his paws this time) and a back rub.

My human left the upper room briefly. When he returned, he had some of my soft pom-pom balls. He tossed them at me one at a time. They were all different colors. After he threw the last one, I chased the green one around the room. By then, my human had returned to his chair. A couple of times, the ball ended up near his hind paws. When that happened, he pushed it back to me.

During the afternoon, I took a nap on the open pages of a large book. It was a book my human looked at frequently when he played with his metal discs. I don't think he minded, but I noticed he didn't play with the discs as much while I was there.

This evening, I wanted to take a nap on my human's lap, but his legs were bare. He noticed my predicament and covered his legs with my blanket. I jumped onto his lap as soon as the blanket was in place. I curled up on the blanket and snuggled between his paws.

Day 252, Thursday, July 4, 2019:
This morning, I slept with my human until I was startled by his sudden

movement and a loud sound.[71] I leaped from the bed and bolted from the room.

Later in the morning, I lay down on my human's lap while he sat at the front window. It was nice to get a back massage while I snuggled on his lap.

I followed my human to the basement when he went to scoop out my litter pan. When he was done, he got down on all four paws and looked under the board where I lost my purple pom-pom the other day. I couldn't reach it, but he could. He pulled it out for me.

That weird thing where one of my pupils gets really tiny and the other gets really big to compensate started to happen again. I hoped it didn't last very long.

This afternoon, I took a nap on my human's lap while he worked on the computer. He positioned one of his arms just perfectly, so I was able to rest my chin on it.

After my nap, I checked out the small cat tree again. I found my tan-and-brown ball up there. I knocked it to the floor and chased it around the pet steps near the sink.

This evening, I found my human in the upper room with the TV on and his hind paws up on my blanket chair. I climbed onto him and nestled into his folded arms. It was nice to take a nap on his chest. I was so comfy, I stayed there for a couple of hours. My human started to wiggle a bit toward the end, though I wasn't sure why. He eventually held me tighter and got up briefly, only to sit back down again. That annoyed me, so I jumped down.

This evening, there were some strange sounds that seemed to come from somewhere outside. There weren't a lot of them, but occasionally, I'd hear some kind of muffled boom. I have no idea what they were.[72]

Day 253, Friday, July 5, 2019:
Ugh, that eye thing is *so* annoying. It was not as bad as it has been in the past, but I still wished it would just go back to normal.

I spent a lot of the evening in the basement, sitting on the bench and looking out the window. I also went to the upper room and inspected some shelves in the closet.

Day 254, Saturday, July 6, 2019:
This morning, I found my human working in the upper room. I talked

---

[71]A sneeze.
[72]Fireworks.

to him and convinced him to follow me down the hallway, down the steps, and to the front room. I got him to sit on the bench while I scratched on my curved scratching pad. When I was done, I jumped onto the bench and made my way to his lap. We sat there for a while and looked out the big window. We even got to see a bird in the yard.

It was a good day for a bath. I cleaned myself under one of the tables in the upper room while my human worked nearby.

This evening, I got some more exercise chasing the green pom-pom ball that my human brought up to the room a few days ago.

My eye was still acting up, but it seemed like it started to get better later in the day.

Day 255, Sunday, July 7, 2019:
I played with my green ball again today. I chased it all over the upper room, over by the steps near my water dish, into the bathroom that my human never uses, and back into the main part of the upper room.

My human lay down on the floor near me today for a while. He gave me scratches and a back rub. It was nice to spend some time with him.

Later in the afternoon, I took a long nap on the small cat tree. I woke up when my human started taking photos of me, but once he was done, I got comfortable again and went back to sleep.

My eye was much better today. In fact, it was almost back to normal.

Before going to bed, I followed my human into the basement. He took care of my litter pan and then lay down on the floor for some reason. He was on his side and looked at me. I went over to him and rested my front paws, head, and chest on his body with my hind paws still on the floor. It was a little awkward, but it felt nice to be close to him. He moved one of his front paws such that I could stand on it so I didn't have to extend my legs as far.

Day 256, Monday, July 8, 2019:
Oooooooooooohhhhh! Catnip!

Day 257, Tuesday, July 9, 2019:
Wow, things got crazy last night. That catnip was intense. As it wore off, I followed my human around the house. He went into the basement and took care of my litter pan. I brushed against him, but he didn't sit down like he normally does. Instead, he went back up the stairs and went to the car room. I tried to follow him, and even though

I was quick, he somehow managed to block me. When he came back inside, I grabbed my black string and ran all over the house with it. At one point, I think I even had it up on top of the small cat tree in the upper room. Before the night was over, the string ended up on the floor in the upper room, where I finally settled down. That was fun. I hadn't played with my black string in a long time.

I slept it off this morning. I eventually moved my black string back to the front room. That's where I waited in the afternoon for my human to return. I watched him from the front window as he gave the tree and the flowers some water before he came inside.

After dinner, I asked my human if I could spend some time on his lap. He moved the blanket to his legs, and I made my way onto the blanket. I curled up and lay on top of one of my human's front paws. I received a back massage from his other front paw.

Before I went to bed, something kind of embarrassing happened. I got onto the table and walked between my human and the computer, making sure I carefully stepped over his front paws. I made my way to the end of the table, where there was a towel. I walked onto the towel. Then I looked over at my chair and saw that my human had put my blanket back on it. I tried to jump to it. Unfortunately, the towel I was standing on slid out from under me. I didn't have enough forward movement to make it all the way to the blanket. I grabbed the blanket with my front claws and ended up pulling it off the chair as I hit the floor. I landed on my paws and acted like it was no big deal. My human noticed what happened, but he didn't say anything. He just folded the blanket up and put it back on my chair. He's pretty cool like that.

Day 258, Wednesday, July 10, 2019:
A buff tabby cat visited me today. He didn't come into the house but stayed outside on the patio. I saw him while I sat on the bench and looked out the basement window. He lay down on the patio and took a nap. Was that why my human spent so much time cleaning the patio last week? To make it ready for this visitor?

I kept an eye on him. I didn't even leave the bench to greet my human at the door when he arrived home. I only got off the bench after my human came into the basement. He looked out the window and saw the buff tabby, too.

Day 259, Thursday, July 11, 2019:
The buff cat was back this morning. I saw him lying on the steps that

lead up to the deck. I wondered if he was there all night or if he came back to visit me. I stayed by the window and watched him, even as my human left for work.

My eye thing started again, but this time it's the other eye. I wished it would clear up so my eyes would be normal again. It bothered me a bit, so I didn't do much today.

This evening, I spent some time on the blanket after my human put it on his lap.

Day 260, Friday, July 12, 2019:
The buff cat wasn't outside my window this morning. Since I didn't have to worry about him, I demanded lap time from my human as soon as he appeared in the basement.

I took it easy today since it was rather warm and my eye thing was still going on. It was getting better, though. I took a nap on top of the big cat tree in the living room.

When my human arrived, he fed me, but then he left without eating anything himself. He returned a while later but then left again. He finally returned about the time the sun disappeared. I could tell he had been at the shelter. I wondered why he was at the shelter in the evening because he normally only went there in the morning.

My human ate much later in the evening. That was strange because I normally ate with him, but I had already eaten. It was so upsetting to me that when I told him about it, he went to the kitchen and prepared a second small meal for me. I enjoyed having dinner with him, even if it was late in the evening.

After my second dinner, I jumped onto my human's blanket lap. With him gone so much today, I had a lot of cuddle time to make up.

Day 261, Saturday, July 13, 2019:
Good news! My eye was much better today. It's almost back to normal. Now I just hoped it would stay that way for a while.

I got plenty of lap time in the basement this morning. Since my human stayed home today, I got to enjoy lots of lap time.

Today, my human and I played with my yellow mouse. I sat atop the cat tree in the upper room and batted at it when he tossed it up to me. I enjoyed playing with my very own human.

After lunch, I received a special treat. My human brought a small plate of catnip to me in the upper room. I enjoyed smelling it and licking it up. I also rolled around on the plate and the floor where I had spilled some. Oh, it was good!

With the catnip in full effect, I lay down on the floor near what remained of my treat. I became startled when my human walked over and lay down on the floor near me. I popped up as quickly as I could and leaped to the top of the cat tree. I turned to look at him as I lay back down. He sat up and started to rub my head. Okay, all was good. It was quite relaxing. In fact, I ended up taking a long nap on the cat tree.

Early in the evening, I got some exercise with my plush green ball. I was on the floor near my human when the ball rolled and struck one of his hind paws. He pushed it back to me. I played with it a bit longer before switching to the larger plush white ball with red dots. I chased that one around the room, past the steps near my water dish, and into a small adjacent room—the room that has one of those human litter devices.

Day 262, Sunday, July 14, 2019:
This morning, I went to the basement and discovered the buff cat was back. He was lying on the patio. When my human came down, he also saw him. We sat at the bench and watched him together. I chattered at him as he stared at us. Then he started to clean himself! The nerve of that guy, lying down on my patio so relaxed that he just decided to take a bath! I complained about it to my human. I sat there and watched the buff cat get up and walk off the patio. Soon, I lost sight of him. I ran upstairs to look for him through another window, but he was gone.

When my human returned from the shelter, he went into the cold floor room. I followed him, but he turned to the left while I went to the right. There were some cobwebs over there that I wanted to eat. I stayed in the basement after my human went upstairs. I returned to the other room to use my litter pan. Unfortunately, I didn't stand quite right and ended up missing the box. There was a pad under my pan that caught my mess. I tried to clean it by folding the pad up, but there's only so much I could do without thumbs.

This afternoon, I took a nap on the cat tree in the upper room. I also took a bath while I was up there.

Later in the evening, I found my green pom-pom ball in the upper room. I batted it around the room for some entertainment.

Before I went to bed, I followed my human to the basement. He went there to scoop my litter pan. That was when he discovered the mess outside the pan. Like the last time that happened, he didn't say anything about it. He just cleaned it up and replaced the pad with a fresh one. I rubbed him with the top of my head to show my appreciation. I think I have a good human.

Day 263, Monday, July 15, 2019:
I tracked down my human in the bedroom this morning. He was out of bed already, but he sat down and provided a lap for me. We spent several minutes together before I got up and returned to the basement.

After my human took care of my food and water, he came down to the basement. I figured he had forgotten about our earlier cuddle session, so I asked him to sit down again. It was nice to get some extra lap time before he went to work.

Today, I sent a letter to the Purrfect Pets shelter. That was the shelter I lived at for quite some time before I moved to my current house. Below is a copy of the letter.

Dear Purrfect Pets,

It has been almost nine months since I left the shelter and moved into a house. There is plenty of room and lots of vertical space for me. I get to look out several windows and watch the birds, squirrels, and rabbits. Many of the windows have benches or ledges that I sit or lie on to take in the view and sometimes even a sunbeam. This house also has plenty of toys—mice, balls, strings, and springy things.

I share this house with a human. It is wonderful to have my very own human. He will produce a lap any time I ask for one. His paws are good for giving me fantastic head-to-tail back rubs and the most incredible belly rubs. Sometimes, he and I play with the toy mousies, or we bat a ball back and forth. I like to sit on top of one of the cat trees or scratching posts and bat the mousies back to him when he tosses them up to me.

It's very quiet here, and I like that. Sometimes, I'll just lie on the cat tree or on the floor near my human while he works. He has been good to me. The other day, I accidentally missed the litter pan while doing my business. I did my best to take care of it, but to no avail. When my human found it, he cleaned it up without saying a word. I rubbed the top of my head against him to show my appreciation.

I have included some photos that my human took. He takes lots of photos of me. In one of them, I am helping him with his research. I like to help whenever I can. The other one shows me on my curved scratching pad. If you've never had one of these, I highly recommend it. It is comfy to sit or lie on, and it's great for scratching.

Thanks for all you did for me while I was at the shelter and for helping me through my surgery.[73]

-Blackie

One of the photos I sent to Purrfect Pets.

Before I went to bed, I chased my red-and-white ball around the upper room. My human tossed the fluffy, multicolored pom-pom ball to me, so I chased that, too.

Day 264, Tuesday, July 16, 2019:
I had an extra-long lap time with my human this morning. For some reason, he left for work a bit later than normal.[74] While he was gone, I nibbled on my dry food, carefully picking out the nice treats that were

---

[73]Surgery to remove a bladder obstruction.
[74]Due to a morning dental appointment.

mixed into it and eating those first.[75] After that, I played with my white string.

This afternoon, I was in the basement, looking out the window and waiting for my human to arrive home, when something crazy happened. I saw a cat and another human. The weird thing was that the human picked up the cat, brought him over to my window, and set him down near me. The human didn't bother me, but the cat freaked me out! He was a big black-and-white tomcat. He sat there and looked at me. I let him know, in no uncertain terms, that he was in *my* territory, and he needed to leave. He sat there for a bit but eventually walked away. He turned around and looked at me from under the steps before hiding behind a bush. Soon, I saw my human show up and walk over to the other human. They stood there for a while until the black-and-white cat walked away. My human later told me the cat's name was Sir Bennington Ozark but that people call him Benny.

Benny outside my basement window.

Once my human came inside, he prepared our meals. I was so excited about what had happened earlier that I ate half of mine in the kitchen while my human was still fixing his own food. I followed him

---

[75]Dental treats.

upstairs once his dinner was ready and finished my meal up there. Right after I was done, I went back to the basement and looked out the window for any more intruders. Fortunately, I didn't see any.

I went back upstairs and talked to my human for a while before I went to look out the tall window near the computer. From there, I was able to look down on most of the backyard and observe a larger area than I could see from the basement window. I didn't see any other cats from there, either. I went back to the basement to keep an eye on things at ground level.

I put him in his place.

Later in the evening, my human and I played together. I sat on top of the cat tree in the upper room while my human tossed a toy mouse up to me. It got a little scary at one point when I was flopping around, trying to get the mouse. I fell off the end of the perch! I caught the ledge with my front paws and pulled myself back up. Soon after that, I decided I was done playing and hopped down. A few minutes later, I saw that the mouse was back on top of the tree, so I ran back over and jumped up there. After knocking the mouse to the floor, I noticed the tan ball with the bell somehow had made its way to the top of the tube just under my perch, so I reached down and whacked it to the floor. I chased the ball into the hallway but left it there and went back to the basement.

Before bedtime, I went back upstairs and spent some time on my human's lap.

Day 265, Wednesday, July 17, 2019:
No cats visited me today, but I spent a lot of time looking for them.

When my human came home, I went to the front window and watched him water the flowers and the tree. There weren't any cats with him, either.

He got the message.

I played with my human on the living room floor this evening. We started by tossing some balls around. My human also picked up a purple jack and spun it on the base of my scratching post. I was mesmerized, watching it spin, and sometimes I'd hit it and knock it onto the floor. Then we went over to the three-layer ball thingy that Grandma and Grandpa gave me. We whacked at the balls in it and watched them slide around in their tracks. We also tossed some toy mice.

Day 266, Thursday, July 18, 2019:
This morning, I sat on my human's lap in the basement until one of my pom-pom balls flew by. I jumped from his lap and chased it toward a bookcase. As soon as I was off his lap, my human stood up and used that opportunity to leave for work.

During the day, I played with some toys, including my purple pom-pom ball.

This evening, my human tried to entertain me by playing with mice in the upper room. I wasn't very interested in them, except for the big black-and-white one that sat on top of the scratching post. I took a swipe at it and knocked it to the floor.

Day 267, Friday, July 19, 2019:
I left my human in bed this morning and went to the basement but, after a while, I went back upstairs. I found my human in the bedroom. He was up, so I walked up the pet steps and asked him for some lap time. He sat on the edge of the bed and presented his lap to me. I spent several minutes snuggled on his lap. Satisfied, I hopped down and returned to the basement.

My human resumed his normal morning activities, which included going to the basement to scoop my litter pan. While he was down there, I asked for some more lap time, hoping he had forgotten that I had just received several minutes of his attention. Apparently, he had because he sat down for me. I climbed back onto his lap for more affection.

While I sat on his lap, he gave my back a pleasant scratching. He also cleaned my whiskers. I had gotten into some cobwebs earlier in the morning and ended up with dirty whiskers.

I also had many lap visits this evening in the upper room. Each time, my human prepared his lap with my blanket.

Day 268, Saturday, July 20, 2019:
I spent most of the night sleeping near my human. I also got up during the night and played with my black string for a while.

When my human got out of bed, I tried the same thing I did yesterday. I got him to sit down on the edge of the bed so I could sit on his lap. He cleaned my whiskers again since I had gotten into some more cobwebs. I found the cobwebs in the cold floor room overnight. The door to that room was normally closed, but it had been open the last few days.

My lap plan didn't work entirely, though. I went to the basement to wait for my human while he took care of other things, and when he arrived, I tried to get on his lap again. Only this time, he picked me up! He sat down, rolled onto his back, and placed me on his chest. I hopped down to show my annoyance and then turned around and climbed back on top of him under my own power.

Once I got off his chest and he was able to get up again, I noticed he went over to the cold floor room and closed the door. I guessed I wouldn't get to eat any cobwebs for a while.

Day 269, Sunday, July 21, 2019:
I spent some time looking out the front window today while my human prepared our meals. After lunch, I jumped to the top of the short cat tree in the upper room and cleaned myself before settling down for a nap.

My human was in the upper room most of the day, so that's where I was, too. I alternated between lying on the floor and snuggling on his lap with the blanket. I curled up next to him several times and frequently rested my chin on one of his arms while I pushed my hind paws against one of his front paws.

Early this evening, there was a bright flash followed immediately by a loud sound. My human left the room right after it happened. I followed him. He went to the living room and looked out the window near my short cat tree. I jumped to the top of the tree and brushed my sides against him while he stroked my back and sides with his front paws. He looked out the window for a long time. Outside, it was rather dark, and there was a lot of water falling from the sky.

I wanted to stay on the cat tree and continue to receive his attention, but he went back upstairs. I tried to convince him to stay but was unsuccessful. On his way to the upper room, he stopped briefly at the top of the steps. He poked his head around the corner and called me. I decided to follow him. When I got to the upper room, he sat on the floor. I climbed onto his lap and stayed there for several minutes, ensuring I maintained his attention.

Later in the evening, my human left the upper room. I heard him enter the car room, so I went to that door to see if I could also go in there. When he opened the door, he blocked my path. He also wasn't alone. A moth flew into the house! My human tried to catch the moth, but he couldn't. I was greatly entertained watching him try. He went upstairs, but I stayed on the staircase and watched the moth. My human returned a moment later with a small, flat piece of plastic at the end of a metal stick. He used that stick to get the moth.

Day 270, Monday, July 22, 2019:
I had a nice nap this afternoon when I got on my human's lap (with the blanket) and rested my chin on his arm.

This evening, I heard my human go to the car room. I followed him from a distance and watched him go out there and come back inside, but I didn't try to go out there myself.

Later in the evening, my human lay down on the floor in the upper room. I talked to him a bit and lay down near him. We each had a brief nap.

Day 271, Tuesday, July 23, 2019:
I have my human trained really well. He knows to sit in the basement every morning so I can spend time on his lap. He also gives me full-body massages during my lap time. I like that because it helps me transfer some of my loose fur to his clothing. That way, even when he is away, he has a reminder of me and knows to hurry home.

When I heard him arrive home today, I went to the front room and hopped onto the bench by the big window. I watched him give water to the tree and the flowers before he came inside to fix my dinner.

After dinner, I got him to put the blanket on his lap. I curled up on it and rested for a bit. When I got down, I stayed close to him while he worked on the computer.

Day 272, Wednesday, July 24, 2019:
This morning, I heard my human moving around, but he didn't come down to the basement, even after preparing my water and dry food. I went to see what was going on. I found him in the bedroom, getting ready for work. I climbed onto the bed and asked nicely several times to sit on his lap. He finally sat on the edge of the bed for me. We spent a lot of time together, which was really nice. He gave me a wonderful two-pawed chin scratching. I lapped up as much of it as I could. When I was satisfied, I hopped down and followed him to the basement. Our cuddle session was so great that I didn't try to trick him into a second one, like I'd done before. We looked out the window together to see if there were any visiting cats, but there weren't any this morning.

This afternoon, I was going to clean myself on the small cat tree in the upper room when one of my mouse toys flew at me. I batted it down and chased it. After tossing it around the room for a while, I returned to the top of the cat tree and resumed my bath.

This evening, I was looking out the front window when I heard my human coming down the hallway. I hopped from the bench to my curved scratching pad. I gave it a good scratching as he came through the room on his way to the kitchen. While he was in the kitchen, I jumped to the platform atop my scratching post. That turned out to be a good idea because on his way back through he stopped and gave my back a scratch. Even better, he picked that really sensitive spot right in front of my tail. Oh, he's good.

I followed him to the upper room and got onto the table. After we talked for a bit, I went to the top of the scratching post in this room, but for some reason, I didn't get my back scratched again.

Day 273, Thursday, July 25, 2019:
Something kind of weird happened today. I heard my human arrive home, but I was too busy keeping an eye on things from the basement window to go greet him. The buff cat was back and was lying on one of the steps that go up to the deck. After several minutes, my human still hadn't come into the house. I stayed in the basement and watched the buff cat in my territory. Soon, I saw my human outside. He walked toward my window but stopped when there was a sudden commotion. The buff cat leaped from the step and took off toward the dirt lady's house! I think they were both surprised. My human came over to the window, but I ignored him because I was too busy looking for the buff cat. He was long gone, though.

With that excitement over, my human came inside. I paced between the kitchen and the front room, waiting as patiently as I could. Every time I entered the kitchen, I told him how late he was and how slow he was at preparing dinner. He finally listened to me and put my plate on the floor. Most of my food had been eaten by the time his food was ready, but he was nice enough to take my nearly empty plate to the upper room so I could finish while he ate.

After dinner, I spent some time on his lap before I followed him to the basement. He went into the cold floor room, but I stopped at the window to see if the buff cat was back. He wasn't, so I continued on to see what my human was doing. He was busy at the table. With him occupied, I explored the room since it had been a few days since I was last there. When I finished exploring, I decided my human needed to sit with me on his lap. He agreed and sat on the stool. After wiggling around a bit, I curled up and rested my chin and a paw on his arm while he caressed my head and back. It was nice. I wondered why we didn't sit in that room more often.

After our snuggle session, I hopped down and looked around the room a bit longer. I got startled and froze in place when I heard a loud roaring sound start up.[76] Fortunately, it didn't last very long. I'm glad I didn't have to listen to it much because it was pretty scary.

Day 274, Friday, July 26, 2019:
Today, things were pretty chill. I looked for the buff cat at the basement window, but he hasn't been back since he ran away yesterday. I spent some time looking out the front window, too, but there wasn't much happening out there, either.

Day 275, Saturday, July 27, 2019:
I waited for my human in the basement this morning. When he arrived, I gave him time to scoop my litter pan and then demanded some lap time. He sat down, just like he always does. We spent quite a bit of time together.

When I finished my lap time, I saw my human go into the cold floor room. The door closed behind him. I waited for him until I heard loud sounds start coming from that room. It had been quite a while since he spent time in that room with the loud sounds, except for that brief period a couple of days ago. I wonder what goes on in there.

After a few hours of intermittent loud sounds, my human emerged from the basement and prepared our meals. We went to the upper room to eat. After lunch, I spent some time curled up on my human's arms while he sat with his hind paws up on my blanket chair. When I got down from his arms, he returned to the cold floor room.

Later in the afternoon, everything repeated. He came upstairs, made our evening meals, and then returned to the basement. After my meal, I played with the red-and-white ball in the upper room. I knocked it around the room, out the door, and down the hallway to the bedroom. I left it by the bed, close to my pet steps.

Day 276, Sunday, July 28, 2019:
This morning, I cuddled with my human before he got out of bed. After he got up, I went to the basement and discovered the buff cat had returned! He lay on his favorite step and looked at me. I told my human about him as soon as he came down to scoop my litter pan.

My human went to the shelter today. I stayed by the basement window and watched the buff cat. He was gone by the time my human returned, so I went to find my human, who hadn't come into the house yet. I looked for him from the front window. There I saw him giving

---

[76]A wet/dry vacuum. I thought she had left the room and didn't see her until I turned the machine off.

the flowers some water. When he was done with the flowers, he came inside and fixed our lunches. After that, I went upstairs to nap because my human went to the cold floor room and started making noises.

In the middle of the afternoon, my human came upstairs and turned the TV on. He sat on his chair, so I figured that was a good time to rest on his arms.

After spending some time with my human, I got down from his arms and went to the short cat tree on the other side of the room. Once at the top, I sat down and had a bath and a nap. Later in the afternoon, I enjoyed a sunbeam coming through the tall window behind my human.

Strangely, my human and I didn't eat dinner together today. He prepared my meal, but not one for himself. Instead, he returned to the basement and made more annoying sounds. It wasn't until much later in the evening that he finally ate. I wanted to eat with him but he didn't give me another meal. Instead, he presented me with some of my tasty dental treats.

Day 277, Monday, July 29, 2019:
As I always do, I demanded some lap time with my human while we were in the basement this morning. He normally caresses me with both of his front paws, but today he started with both and then switched to just one. I turned my head and saw that his other paw was still there but was motionless. Apparently, he needed a reminder, so I cocked my head to the side and smacked the top of my head against his idle paw. He should know by now that both paws should be used when giving me a massage. He got the message and resumed stroking me with both paws.

I was so excited to see my human when he returned from work that I ran all over the house. I followed him from room to room as he settled in for the evening. After all that running, I needed to rest, so I lay down on a mat at the front door. That mat was perfectly sized for me. My human soon walked by on his way to the kitchen. I think I surprised him because he stopped and seemed concerned. He knelt down to check on me, but I thought he was going to grab me, so I hopped up and jumped onto the first step down to the basement. I turned to look at him and saw that he had stopped, turned around, and gone to the kitchen. Whew!

Later in the evening, my human performed his weekly task where he picks up the small plastic bags and places them in the larger plastic bag from the kitchen. I knew that meant he would soon take the big bag to the car room. I quietly followed him. I tried my best to sneak out there behind him but was unsuccessful.

With my exploratory trip to the car room canceled, I followed my human back to the upper room. He put the blanket on his lap, so I curled up on the blanket. He slowly scratched my chin back and forth while he worked on the computer.

Before I went to bed, I played with one of my sparkly crinkly toys.

Day 278, Tuesday, July 30, 2019:
This morning, my basement lap session included a two-pawed belly rub followed by a two-pawed chin scratching. It felt amazing! There was no place else I wanted to be. It was so relaxing that I almost fell off his lap, but I managed to catch myself. I think he learned his lesson that two paws are required when he massages me in the morning.

The buff cat didn't visit me today. I spent the day at the basement window looking for him. And resting. Lots of resting.

In the evening, I sat on my human's lap and received more chin scratches. Just before bedtime, I played with my black string while my human stood under the falling water.

Day 279, Wednesday, July 31, 2019:
As usual, this morning I sat on my human's lap in the basement before he left for work. That was, until I thought I saw a bug. I hopped out of his lap to pounce on it, but there was nothing there.

While my human was gone, I spent some time looking out the basement window to see if the buff cat would stop by. I also played with my purple pom-pom ball.

This evening, I sat on the blanket on my human's lap while he gently caressed my back. I also went to the storage room and looked out the window over the driveway while my human stood in the small room across the hall in the falling water.

Day 280, Thursday, August 1, 2019:
My human could have just gone outside this morning if he wanted to stand in water. I sat on the bench in the basement and watched it fall from the sky.

While my human was at work, I played with my tan-and-white mouse. After that, I took a nap.

I followed my human into the cold floor room tonight. I explored the room while he stood near the workbench and played with pieces of wood. I ended up with some cobwebs in my whiskers. My human cleaned them up for me. With my exploring done and my whiskers cleaned, I left the cold floor room just in case those loud noises started.

Later in the evening, I spent some time on my human's lap in the upper room. I didn't stay there very long because I got started when he suddenly shook and made a loud sound.[77]

Day 281, Friday, August 2, 2019:
This morning, I once again climbed onto my human's lap in the basement, only this time he put his arms around me, and then he stood up! He walked halfway up the stairs and sat down where he would sit to put his shoes on. I didn't know what was going on, so as soon as he relaxed his grip, I jumped from his lap and left the area.

Today, I watched for the buff cat at the basement window, but he didn't show up. I wondered where he went. As the day wore on, my left eye started to do that weird thing again.

This evening, I tried to follow my human to the car room, but he wouldn't let me go in there. I went to the bench in the front room and looked out the window to see if I could spot him. At first I couldn't, but then he walked by the window. He held a bowl in with one of his paws. He walked past a moment later in the other direction, still carrying the bowl.[78]

After some time, my human came back inside. I followed him upstairs because I wanted to lie on his lap. He put an arm around me as I pushed my back against his chest. I rested on him in my current favorite position: with my chin on his arm and my front paws tucked under myself. That let me push my hind paws against his left front paw, and it left his right front paw available to stroke my head and back. I did this several times tonight.

I explored the office and storage room some more. I jumped onto the desk and found a large plastic tray.[79] I walked across it to the other side of the desk. There wasn't anything interesting up there, so I hopped down and followed my human to the bedroom.

_____

[77] A sneeze.

[78] A container of water for a project in the garage.

[79] A scale.

Day 282, Saturday, August 3, 2019:
This morning, my human stayed in bed much longer than normal. After my morning routine of looking out the basement window, I returned to the bedroom to check on him. I found him awake, so I stretched out next to him for a belly rub. That belly rub lasted for over half an hour, and it was great! He also reached up and scratched my chin for a bit and massaged my back. When he finally got up, I returned to the basement.

I stayed in the basement and waited for him to show up. I knew he would because humans are creatures of habit. When he showed up, I asked for lap time. Just because we had just spent all that time together a few minutes before didn't mean we wouldn't also do our normal lap cuddling routine. This time was a bit different. Instead of sitting on the floor, my human moved the curtain back from the window and sat on the edge of the bench. I jumped onto his lap and received a long back rub. We looked out the window, too, but there wasn't much to see. The buff cat wasn't there.

Despite multiple affectionate periods with my human, I didn't really feel that well today. My eye was acting up some more and getting worse. I spent most of the afternoon trying to sleep it off. I took a nap at the top of the tall cat tree in the living room while my human worked in the upper room. I slept some more after dinner, but I wanted to be closer to my human, so I took a nap on the short cat tree in the upper room.

Day 283, Sunday, August 4, 2019:
Ugh. That eye thing is so annoying. Not only was the pupil thing happening, but there was some liquid discharge that accumulated in the corner of my eye. Because of my eye problems, I spent most of the day napping on the floor of the upper room or on top of the short cat tree.

Today, my human made several brief trips to the basement, but I didn't feel like following him. I just rested and hoped my eye would get better. Between naps, I spent some time on his lap using the blanket. I lay on him using my new favorite position I wrote about a few days ago. It was comfortable, plus I received a back massage.

Day 284, Monday, August 5, 2019:
I went to the basement this morning to look for the buff cat. He wasn't there. Instead, there was something strange outside my window. In the

rocks near the steps, there was a large round purple thing about the size of my human's head.[80] It just sat there and didn't move.

I sat and watched the purple thing until my human came into the room. After he scooped my litter pan, he sat down for me. I spent some time on his lap. He gave me an intense back rub, but it wasn't enough. As he stroked my back, I pushed with my hind legs so his claws would rub deeper into my fur. I pushed my butt up as high as possible so I could enjoy the deep massage. My human got the hint and started to scratch my back with more vigor.

My left eye got better today, but just like last time, the problem shifted over to my other eye. So far, it's not very bad, but I hope it gets better soon.

After I finished dinner this evening, I spent some time looking out the tall window. I also walked along the table to get behind my human. I groomed the thin fur on top of his head while he ate.

When my human finished eating and turned his attention to the computer, I went over and squatted next to the keyboard. I thought about sitting on his lap. He got the blanket and motioned for me, but I decided not to use it. I wanted him to see my eye. He spent the next several minutes slowly and softly stroking the top of my head.

Later in the evening, I was ready for lap time. I got back on the table and approached him. He put his hind paws up on my blanket chair and motioned for me to climb aboard his lap. I crawled onto his chest and plopped down on his left arm. He folded both of his arms under me and reached for my left front paw with his right front paw. I enjoyed being close to him and holding paws with him.

Day 285, Tuesday, August 6, 2019:
This was a great morning! My human got up early, so I spent more time on his lap before he left for work. It would have been even better if my eye was back to normal but it wasn't. It was much better, though.

Just like yesterday, I rested on my human's chest while he caressed my head and back.

My human tried to scare me this evening. He walked out of the upper room. I stayed there and minded my own business. He returned a few minutes later and immediately made a short but sudden move toward me. I jumped back because I thought he might pick me up. I quickly realized he was just messing with me, so I stood up and

---

[80] A balloon that had floated in from somewhere.

pushed my head toward him. He reached down and stroked my head and my back.

My human was up later than he should have been. I got on his lap and tried to convince him it was time for bed. I didn't have much luck, so instead, I got down and played with my green pom-pom ball.

Day 286, Wednesday, August 7, 2019:
Meow-ow! What a great day! Not only did I enjoy some lap time in the basement this morning, but my eye is back to normal! The only thing that would have made this day better was if my buff friend stopped by. I looked out the window for him but didn't see him.

I got on my human's chest a couple of times this evening, just as I have done every day recently. I like the way he cradles me with one of his arms and pets me with the paw of his other arm.

This evening, I spent some time on the floor of the front room near the steps. As my human walked by, he reached down toward me. I got a little scared, just like last night, but again he didn't pick me up. He also didn't pet me for some reason. Instead, he proceeded to the living room. I followed him. He messed with some books on the shelf and then went to the kitchen. I saw him get a plate and a container. He opened the container and poured some of its contents onto the plate. It wasn't one of my plates, so I wasn't all that interested. He took the plate upstairs and then called for me a couple of times. My curiosity got the better of me (it's a common cat problem), so I went upstairs to see what he was up to. He put the plate on the floor. CATNIP! I licked it up and rubbed my head all over the plate. Oh, it was wonderful! After that, I got really relaxed and stretched out on the floor.

Day 287, Thursday, August 8, 2019:
My human and I looked out the basement window this evening. He sat on the bench, and I sat on his lap. Then he started to give me a back rub. It got pretty intense. He rubbed that sensitive spot right in front of my tail and then moved his paws around to my thighs, squeezed, and kept rubbing. The sensation caused my hind legs to extend as far as possible, and then next thing I knew, my hind paws weren't even touching his lap anymore! He set me back down pretty quickly. It was crazy, but it felt good.

Later in the evening, I followed him into the storage room. He opened the closet door. I quickly hopped into that small space. It had been a long time since I had explored that tiny room, so I jumped at the opportunity. My human soon left the storage room, but I stayed and inspected the closet a bit longer. When I was done with the closet, I went back to the upper room, where my human was, and took a nap on the floor.

My human brought out the white sheet again today and set two identical wooden objects on it.[81] I inspected the objects as he took photos of them.

Inspecting more wooden objects.

Day 288, Friday, August 9, 2019:
I watched my human outside when he returned from work. He soon came inside and prepared our meals. I'd normally run ahead of him to the upper room and wait for him to deliver my food, but today I stopped at the top of the steps for the basement. I turned around and waited for my human. When he drew close, I ran to the basement. He put our food down and followed me. We looked out the window but didn't see anything interesting. He then suggested that we go upstairs to eat, and I agreed.

This evening, I spent some time on my human's chest and arm. He gently caressed my back and the top of my head. I also followed him to the bathroom. He opened the sink cabinet for me and removed that big bottle that's always in my way. I poked my head into the space

[81]Clocks I had made for my niece and nephew.

but didn't walk into it today. It didn't look much different than it did the last time I went in there.

Later in the evening, I went back to the basement to look out the window in case the buff cat came back. He didn't.

Day 289, Saturday, August 10, 2019:
After my normal morning lap session, my human said he needed to leave for a while. He left and returned a few hours later. Then I saw him push that loud machine all over the yard. I also saw him give water to the tree and the flowers.

When he came back inside, I followed him to the cold floor room. While there, I found some more tasty cobwebs. We soon left that room and went back to the soft floor room. There, I sat on my human's lap. He said he needed to clean my whiskers. He ran one of his front paws along the sides of my face. I didn't understand how that could be cleaning them when he didn't lick his paw first.

Later in the afternoon, my human prepared another plate of catnip for me. He set it on the floor near my cat tree in the upper room. That's some really good stuff! I licked some of it and then brushed the sides of my head on the rest of it. I spilled a lot of it on the floor, so I rolled around on it and continued to rub my head all over it.

The catnip might have had an effect on my human, too, although I didn't see him get too close to it. He lay down on the floor near me and looked up at the television. I crawled over to him and lay with the front half of my body on his chest and my hind paws on the floor next to him. He reached over and put one of his front paws next to me. We had never lain like that before, but it was nice.

This evening, my human emptied my upper room water dish and took it to the kitchen. I followed him but stopped in the front room. As he returned, I got ahead of him and went upstairs since I knew he would go back up there. Then he surprised me when he took off after me! He chased me up the stairs and into the room. I stayed ahead of him. When I got to the upper room, I turned around, arched my back, and puffed my tail. That was enough to stop him. He came to a halt as soon as he got to the doorway. He didn't seem scared, though. Instead, he just laughed at me. He slowly approached me and stroked my back. He then returned the water dish to the sink. With my tail almost back to its normal size, I jumped to the top of the cat tree and onto the short wall, where I watched him fill my dish with fresh water.

Later in the evening, I got another whiff of the catnip and then chased my yellow toy mouse around the upper room.

The catnip kicked in.

Day 290, Sunday, August 11, 2019:
I was enjoying my routine morning lap time in the basement today when my human made a sudden loud sound.[82] I jumped off his lap and turned to look at him. I guess he thought I was done with lap time because he stood up and went upstairs. I followed him a few minutes later and found him in the bedroom, changing his clothing. I walked up the pet steps and stepped onto the edge of the bed. I asked him if I could have some more lap time. Once he finished getting dressed, he sat on the bed for me. I climbed onto his lap to finish my morning lap session.

My human spent more time at the shelter today than he normally does. While he was there, I lay on the bench in the basement and looked out the window. When he returned, he came down to the basement and opened the door to the cold floor room. I followed him in there because I wanted to find some more cobwebs. He went upstairs and left me in the cold floor room. A few minutes later, I went upstairs

---

[82] A sneeze.

and found him. He complained about my dirty whiskers again and insisted on cleaning them himself.

Today, my human and I played together in the upper room. I
went to the top of the cat tree while he sat nearby and tossed my
yellow mouse up to me. He also tossed the little black-and-white one.
I enjoyed that because it made a rattle noise whenever it moved. I
batted the mice back down to him and watched him chase after them.
When I got bored with that, he reached up and gently rubbed my neck.
When he started to caress the top of my head, I put my chin down on
the yellow mouse that was still between my paws. It's fun to play with
my human, but it's even more fun when he showers me with affection.
Later in the evening, I played with the yellow mouse by myself while
my human worked on the computer.

Before I went to bed, I found my human in the bathroom. He
had that stick with the tiny brush that he likes to push into his mouth
for some reason, but that's not what interested me. Above my human's
litter device was a shallow wooden box. The door to it was open, and I
wanted a closer look. I jumped onto the lid of my human's litter device. Then I put my front paws on the white box behind the seat to
support myself. I stretched my neck as far as I could for a closer look
at that wooden box. There was a shelf inside it. There were some bottles and tubes in it, too. It was fascinating, but I couldn't figure out
what it was.

Day 291, Monday, August 12, 2019:
I got annoyed this evening when my human picked me up. I was on
the table talking with him when he just grabbed me. He held me on his
lap, close to his chest. As I normally do when he subjects me to that, I
refused to look at him. As soon as he loosened his grip, I jumped from
his lap and onto the floor. I paused briefly at my scratching post and
then made my way up the pet steps and back to the table. I waited for
him to provide a lap and then casually walked onto it. When will he
learn that *this* is the proper way to get a cat on his lap?

Later in the evening, I was relaxing on the floor in the upper
room when my human got up to leave the room. On his way out, he
knelt down and rubbed my belly. It was a bit strange because my belly
rubs normally happen on the bed. It felt nice, though.

After my belly rub, I got some exercise playing with my little
yellow mouse.

Day 292, Tuesday, August 13, 2019:

My human spent much longer preparing his food today than normal. Thankfully, he was kind enough to make my meal first. I ate half of it in the kitchen before he was even done fixing his own food. When he was finally ready, he took both of our meals to the upper room.

After dinner, my human spent a lot of time in the cold floor room. I couldn't see what was going on because the door was closed. I spent part of the evening in the soft floor room waiting for him and part of the evening on the landing at the top of the staircase. From there, I followed him as he made multiple trips between the basement, the upper room, and the car room. I tried to get into the car room once, but he blocked my path.

We went to bed after he finished working in the cold floor room and got cleaned up. I stretched out alongside him for a brief belly rub. I would normally get up and go do some cat things as my human falls asleep, but tonight I did something a bit different. I got up and jumped onto the big box of drawers near the foot of the bed. I put my front paws up on a large plastic basket that was on top of it. It held some of my human's clothing. After checking it out, I hopped down to the floor and left the room to do some cat things.

Day 293, Wednesday, August 14, 2019:

This morning, I was in the basement, looking out the window, when I decided I wanted more cuddle time with my human. I went back upstairs and found him still in bed. I snuggled up next to him and put my hind legs around his right arm. He rubbed my belly and chest.

I played with my yellow mouse today. Unfortunately, it broke, but I still played with the piece that had the tail.

This afternoon, I watched my human water the tree and the flowers. He seemed to have trouble watering the tree because some of the water blew back onto him.

Later in the evening, my human and I played with the small black-and-white mouse and the larger bright-green mouse—the one that buzzes and moves when my human pulls its tail. My human tossed the black-and-white mouse up to me as I sat on the table. I batted it back down to the floor. I chased the mouse when he tossed it on top of the cat tree. From there, I threw it back to him. He also tossed a pink plastic ball up to me that I batted away.

My human brought my tan-and-green mouse up from the basement, so I played with it for a bit. I noticed the two parts of my little yellow mouse were no longer on the floor where I left them.

Day 294, Thursday, August 15, 2019:
After our morning snuggle session in the basement, my human went over to the door to the cold floor room. He opened the door, briefly reached in, and then quickly closed the door. He had something in his paw. It was my yellow mouse toy! It was back in one piece! I guess he fixed it. I was happy to see it but decided not to play with it right away. My human took it back to the upper room, where I normally played with it.

When my human returned home from work, he came into the house to feed me but then left again. He returned again after the sun went down. I was happy to see him. I sat on his lap without the blanket because he wore long pants. I climbed onto his chest and stretched out on his arm.

Day 295, Friday, August 16, 2019:
I was entertained today watching my human water the flowers and the tree. Things with the flowers were normal, but when he sprayed water on the tree, it looked like some of the water fell back on him. He kept moving around, trying to avoid it. I didn't understand why he wanted to avoid the water when he willingly stood under water every day in that small room. I'm not sure if I'll ever understand humans.

When he came inside, he went to the basement and scooped my litter pan. I tried to keep him from leaving the room but was unsuccessful. That was okay, though, because next he cleaned his front paws and prepared our meals. I waited on top of the scratching post in the front room for him to get the food ready. He was pretty quick about it today, and soon I followed him to the upper room to eat.

While my human was leaning back on his chair, I got onto the table behind him and groomed the fur on top of his head. Once he was cleaned to my satisfaction, I went over to the tall window and enjoyed a sunbeam.

Later in the evening, I climbed onto my human's arm and chest. I stretched out and received a back massage. After that, my human pointed out my repaired yellow mouse. I played with it for a while. I ended the evening stretched out on the floor, taking a nap with my chin resting on my paws.

Day 296, Saturday, August 17, 2019:
When I walked into the upper room today, I found the bright-green mouse sitting on top of the scratching post. I took a swipe at it and knocked it to the floor. It hit the base of the post with a loud *clunk*.

It was nice having my human home all day today. Since he worked in the upper room, I spent a lot of my day there, too. I mostly stretched out and relaxed on the floor.

This afternoon, I took a bath on the short cat tree. After my bath, I went across the room and climbed the stairs up to the table and made my way over to the tall window. There I found a sunbeam coming through the window. I sat and enjoyed it for a while.

I followed my human to the cold floor room this evening. He was only in there briefly, but I stuck around a bit longer. There were some cobwebs near one of the walls I had to check out.

Day 297, Sunday, August 18, 2019:
This morning, I got trapped! My human came down to the basement, but I didn't go meet him because I was busy in the cold floor room. The door had been left open for some reason. Just as he arrived, I heard the door close. Then I heard him cleaning my litter pan. Did he not know I was in there? I scratched at the door and said "Meooow?" That was enough to get his attention, and soon the door opened. Whew! That was close. I'd hate to be trapped away from my litter pan all day.

My human spent some time at the shelter this morning. I got excited when he returned because I knew we would soon eat, plus I figured I'd have him for the rest of the day.

I spent most of the afternoon alternating between naps and sitting on my human's lap or arm while he stroked my back and the top of my head. I also spent a little time sleeping on the cat tree in the upper room.

This evening, my human and I played with some toy mice. Mice can be a single-player game, but it's more fun with two players. I sat on the top step near my scratching post and waited for him to toss a mouse up to me, or set one on the step, or set one on top of my scratching post. Then, I'd hit it back down to him. Sometimes he had to chase them. He also put the bright-green mouse on top of the post and pulled its tail so it would buzz and wiggle around. I tried to hit it down to him, but it got stuck on my claws. I worked hard to get it freed up and thrown to him. At one point, he put the small tan-and-green mouse on top of the post. He flicked it across the room, and I ran off the steps after it.

My human left the upper room but returned a few minutes later with a treat for me—a plate of the most excellent catnip! I licked it up in small doses and then rubbed the sides of my head all over the plate. My human lay on the floor near me and watched me, but he didn't eat any of the catnip.

Later in the evening, I was relaxing on my human's lap when I thought I saw a bug on the wall near my window. I jumped onto the table and ran over there, but when I got there, I couldn't find it. My human looked for it, too, but he didn't find it, either.

As the night wound down, my human opened the door to that tiny room with the shelves in the hallway. Before he closed the door, I jumped into the stack of empty boxes that live in there.

Day 298, Monday, August 19, 2019:
A couple of strange things happened today. The first one happened before the sun came up. I was on the bed sleeping near my human when we were both awakened by an unusual noise. It was a short, high-pitched sound that happened three times.[83] I looked at my human. His head was up, and he was looking around the room. A strange light appeared on the wall above that box of drawers I had climbed on the other day. My human got up and grabbed something off the top of the box. I followed him when he went to the upper room across the hall. He stuffed a string into that thing and then left it on the table. After that, we both went back to the bedroom and got back in bed.

When my human got up, he failed to do his normal morning routine. He came down to the basement, where I was waiting for him, but after scooping my pan, he didn't sit on the floor to give me his lap. Instead, he went back upstairs.[84] Fortunately, he came back down a few minutes later. I was still sitting there on the floor near my pan, trying to figure out what had happened, when he came in and sat down. I climbed onto his lap and brushed my head against one of his paws.

My human came home with boxes full of food. He brought the food in using the tote boxes that were normally in that small room near the hallway. After the boxes were emptied, he stacked them and

---

[83] A low battery alarm from a cell phone.
[84] I had forgotten to clean and fill her water and dry food dishes.

set them in the hallway. I had to jump into them because it was not normal to see those boxes in the hallway.

While I was in the boxes, I noticed my human going around the house collecting the small plastic bags that he keeps in some of the rooms. I knew what that meant! He'd go to the car room! I slunk down the staircase and hid in the basement. When I heard the door to the car room open, I quickly shot up the steps. I *almost* made it, but my human stopped me. It was the closest I had gotten in quite some time.

I waited until my human came back inside. I didn't really try to sneak out there a second time. But right after that, something strange happened. I followed my human to the front room. He opened a small door high up on one of the walls. I thought about jumping up there, but he closed the door before I had a chance. Before he closed it, he grabbed something from the shelf behind the door. There was a red thing in the shape of a loop and a long, wide, black string with another loop at the end. I chased the black string as he dragged it along the floor. He pushed the red string toward me, but I stepped back. I got a bit closer and inspected it. He held me down and put the red loop around my neck. *What was happening?* I thought. The ends of the red strap were on my back. He pulled them down toward my chest and clipped them together. It didn't hurt, but it felt weird. After a moment, he picked me up and took me to the front door. He opened the door and we went outside! He sat down on the front steps and set me on his lap. I wasn't sure what to make of that. It was quite warm out there. It was also very loud.[85]

I continued to sit on my human's lap as he stroked my head and rubbed my neck. I watched a couple of other humans walk by on the other side of the street. I don't know who they were. I don't think they saw me. After they passed, I cautiously stepped off my human's lap and onto the step closest to the door. It was all very weird. My human picked me up, and we went back into the house. As soon as he set me down on the floor, I took off toward the living room. The thick black string followed right behind me. My human came over and detached the black string from my back. Then he reached around and unhooked the ends of the red strap. I popped my head free from it. The whole experience was something hard to describe.

My human went to the upper room, but I stayed in the living room for a while to process the recent events. Once I regained my

---

[85]Cicadas.

composure, I went upstairs and played with my big black-and-white mouse. Then I got onto the table and stretched out to relax.

A bit later in the evening, I watched my human walk out of the upper room, followed by the sound of a door opening. I chased after him and found him in the small storage room across the hall. The door to the closet was open! I shot into it before my human could close it. My human left the room but kept the closet door open for me.

Day 299, Tuesday, August 20, 2019:
I enjoyed my normal lap time this morning. Then I played with some pom-pom balls in the basement.

This evening, I was minding my own business, stretched out on the floor of the upper room, when my human walked in grasping something with one of his front paws. He set it on the floor near me. It was one of my purple pom-pom balls, but something was different about it. It had an enchanting aroma. It smelled of catnip! I brushed the sides of my head against it, then grabbed it in my mouth, secured it with my front paws, and kicked at it with my hind paws. I rolled from side to side while I kicked at it. I chased it when it got away from me. I ran around the upper room kicking and chasing it for a long time. It was great!

Day 300, Wednesday, August 21, 2019:
I hadn't played with my white string much lately, so today I picked up where I had left it (on the floor of the front room) and took it to the basement to play with it. It was a good time.

When my human arrived home, he carried a bag with a scent that greatly interested me. I followed him to the upper room, where he set the bag on a table. He pulled something out of the bag and worked with it for a bit. It was a piece of cardboard with some soft skinny things. He worked the things free from the cardboard and presented them to me. They were toy fishies! Were they for me? I wasn't sure at first, but he set them down and left them with me. I played with them as he left the room. I tossed one of them around and chased it into the hallway. I took the other one down to the front room and sat close to it while I kept an eye on my human. He was in the kitchen, preparing our meals.

After dinner, my human went back to the bag and pulled some-thing else out of it. I was relaxing on the floor and not paying much attention until he came down to the floor and set three new toy mice in front of me. They had a great scent. Their tails were thick and fairly firm, which made them easy to grab. I spent a good part of the evening chasing my new mouse toys all over the upper room. I even took one up to the table and played with it behind my human. It got stuck in some of his toys, though. He turned around and freed it up for me. I figured it might be better to play on the floor, so I batted it off the table and chased it to the floor.

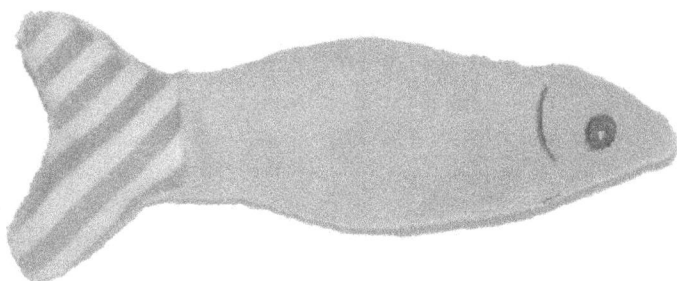

My new fishies.

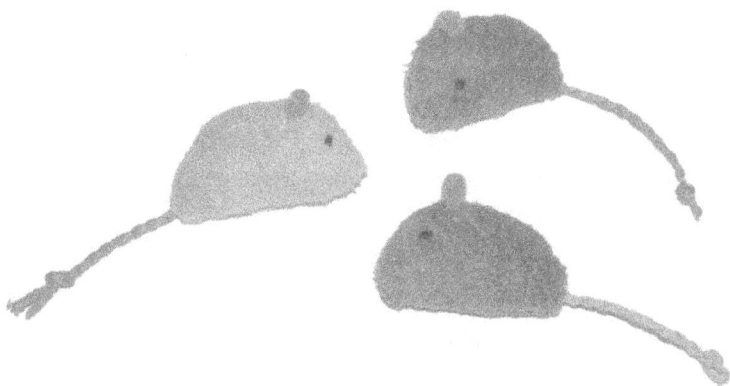

My new mousies.

Later in the evening, my human brought one of my fishes back into the upper room and set it near me. I had been relaxing but was ready for some more fun, so I tossed it around the room for a bit.

I was so grateful for my new toys that when I sat on my human's lap this evening I let him give me a manicure, at least for one and a half of my paws. This was a really good day.

Day 301, Thursday, August 22, 2019:
I played with my white string again today. When I was done, I put it back where I like to keep it: on the floor in the doorway between the front room and the kitchen.

I also played with my new fish toys today. I took the purple one all the way to the basement and played with it some more down there.

When my human arrived home, I sat on the scratching post and waited for him to fix our meals. Then I followed him to the upper room to eat. Well, I followed him at first, but since I'm faster, I passed him on the staircase.

After dinner, I played with one of my new mouse toys. I chased it around the upper room and even carried it up the pet steps to the table. From there, I dropped it to the floor and jumped down after it.

Later in the evening, my human and I played with one of my new mouse toys together. I sat on the short wall between my water dish and the cat tree and watched as he tossed it up to the top of the cat tree. I stepped down to the wedged platform of the tree and flung it back to him. He threw it back up for me to bat down again. We did this several times. A few times, it landed on top of the paper bag on the other side of the tree and he had to chase after it. I thought it was a good idea to make sure my human got plenty of exercise.

Oh, I almost forgot. After dinner, I snuggled on my human's lap with his arm wrapped around me. I started with just one of my paws on his arm, but he lifted me up and put both of my front paws on his arm. Then I rested my head on his arm and accepted a back rub for several minutes.

Day 302, Friday, August 23, 2019:
I watched my human water the tree and flowers again today. This time, he managed to keep himself dry.

When my human came inside, he took something new to the upper room. I wasn't sure what it was. He put it on the table so I climbed up and checked it out. It's a little bit smaller than me. It had a round metal base with a long tail, a long but very skinny neck, and its head was an empty cone with a small round thing inside. My head could fit inside the cone (I checked). It didn't do anything, though. It just sat there.[86] I let it be because it was pretty boring, plus I got distracted when my human brought our meals to the upper room.

After dinner, I got onto the table near the computer and spent some time looking out the tall window. Then I made my way over to the cat tree, climbed up to the V-shaped bench, and took a bath.

Later in the evening, I was sitting on the table in the upper room when my human picked up one of my new mouse toys and placed it on the table. I looked at him, then at the mouse, and batted it off the table. I guessed that's what he wanted me to do.

Day 303, Saturday, August 24, 2019:
This morning, I waited in the basement for my human. After I enjoyed lap time, I stayed in the basement while my human went upstairs. He returned a few minutes later with that thing that has a really long tail and that he sometimes pushes along the floor. I watched as he unwound the tail and shoved the tip of it into the wall. When the thing started to growl, I decided it was time to leave and quickly exited up the stairs.

When the noise stopped, I returned to the basement. I saw that my human had opened the curtain that covered the door and my bench. I walked over to him as he sat down on the bench. I got onto his lap to receive a back massage, happy that the growling stick thing was moved back to its own little room. We spent a lot of time together on the bench. I enjoyed my back rub until I got distracted by a bird I saw fly high above the house.

After our session on the bench, my human got up and went to the cold floor room. The door closed behind him. That normally meant loud noises would start coming from that room, and today was no different. In fact, he spent most of the day in that room. We spent some time together halfway through the day when we had a meal and then again later in the afternoon for another meal. While he was in that room being tortured by the loud sounds, I spent most of the day in the upper room, stretched out and napping.

Late in the evening, I climbed onto my human's arms and received a neck massage while he sat at the computer.

---

[86] A small desk lamp without a bulb at the time she investigated it.

Day 304, Sunday, August 25, 2019:
I played with my new purple fish toy this morning while my human
worked at the shelter. When he returned, I noticed he had several ban-
dages on his paws.[87] He seemed okay, but maybe a bit stressed. I
rubbed my head on his paws not to help heal his wounds but because
human paws are supposed to pet cats like me.

My human fixed our meals. I took a nap on the short cat tree
after I ate. My human took a brief nap on the floor nearby.

Later in the afternoon, my human went out to the car room. I
heard the big door open, but it didn't close for a long time. I didn't try
to sneak out there this time. Instead, I went to the storage room and
hopped onto the box that let me look out the window. After a while, I
saw the car leave. It returned a short time later, and my human soon
came back into the house.

This evening, I relaxed and just stretched out on the floor of the
upper room.

Day 305, Monday, August 26, 2019:
Things were a bit out of order this morning. I waited for my human in
the basement, but when he arrived, instead of scooping my pan, he just
looked at it and then sat on the floor for me. While I got my back
scratched on his lap, I was mildly entertained watching him fling my
pom-pom balls across the room. One landed on a shelf. Another got
stuck just below that shelf. I kind of wanted to chase them, but I was
perfectly content on my human's lap.

After I got up, I noticed my human return to my litter pan, but
this time with the scoop.[88] He cleaned it out. Then I decided it was lap
time again. After all, I always got lap time after he scooped my pan.
But he didn't sit back down for me, despite how much I tried to convince him.

I relaxed around the house while he was away at work. I spent
some time looking out the basement window. The buff cat wasn't
there. It was quiet most of the day, but for a few minutes it got really
loud and a bunch of water fell from the sky.

When my human arrived home this evening, I jumped onto the
scratching post in the front room. He walked over to me and scratched
the sides of my head. I was so excited to see him, I didn't even mind

---

[87]Scratches from a kitten that got scared when a nearby vacuum cleaner was
turned on.
[88]It looked unused, but it was checked with the scoop to be sure.

when he leaned over and kissed the top of my head. I stayed on the post and patiently waited while he prepared our meals.

After dinner, I followed my human back to the front room. There, he opened a cabinet in the wall and removed one of my toys from a container. It was a ball with a feather thingy. He held it close to me. It smelled of catnip! I followed closely behind as he carried it at cat-nose level to the upper room. As soon as he set it on the floor, I started to lick and bite it. I grabbed it with my front paws and kicked it with my hind paws. (I seem to do that frequently with catnip-laced toys.) He left the room and returned a few minutes later with a pom-pom ball that was equally enticing. I had a really good time with both of those toys.

This evening, I followed my human to the basement. I like to follow him as much as possible to make sure he stays out of trouble. He entered the cold floor room. I went in there, too, and walked over to the area where I keep my cobwebs. Unfortunately there weren't many there.[89]

I didn't stay in the cold floor room very long. I heard my human walking all over the house, moving some things around. I soon recognized the sounds. This was the day he puts the small plastic bags into the larger bag and takes it all to the car room. Might I be able to slip out there? I made my way to the car room door, but he stopped me as soon as he came back into the house.

A while later, I followed my human to the bedroom. He was busy folding his clothing and putting it in the drawers. With him occupied, I started a walking tour of the room. I stopped to rest when I found myself under the front of the bed. I stretched out on the floor and leaned against the wall. As soon as I heard my human leave the room, I hopped up and followed him to the upper room.

While in the upper room, I sat on the cat tree and played with my human and one of my new toy mice. He tossed it to me, and I batted it down. We did that several times until I decided to just hold onto the mouse. When I did that, my human reached up and scratched the sides of my neck. He also stroked the top of my head.

No evening would be complete without time on my human's arms or lap. I took care of that tonight while he was at the computer.

Day 306, Tuesday, August 27, 2019:
I made my way upstairs this morning and passed my human just as he

---

[89]A lot of vacuuming happened during Saturday's woodworking session.

started down the staircase. I almost missed lap time! I turned around and quickly followed him to the basement. As soon as he finished scooping my pan, I insisted that he sit down for me. He did, because I've trained him well. Also, I may have been a bit more insistent since he had denied my second lap session yesterday morning.

After lap time, my human went to look out the window. I followed him over there but received a surprise. He picked me up! It was kind of unusual, but I enjoyed spending more time with him before he left for work.

I sat on my post this afternoon while I waited for my human to fix dinner. Well, I sat there until I got distracted by movement outside my window. I jumped over to the bench for a better look. I saw a dog walking his human on the sidewalk in front of my house.

I left the dog and his human when my own human carried my dinner through the room. I followed him to the upper room and ran to the top of the table. My human put my food on the floor, but I was more interested in his food, which was on the table in front of me. Then he did something strange. He moved my plate to the table. That was the first time we'd both eaten at the table. I ate part of my food and then took a break. When my human was done eating, he put his plate up and moved mine to the floor. A few minutes later, I went back and finished my meal.

Later in the evening, I rested in the upper room. I was in the position that my human thinks is funny: I had my chin on the floor and my front legs stuck out from my sides with my front paws tucked under them. I was so relaxed that I ignored my human as he left the room. Soon, though, I heard a strange sound from the other side of the house. I went to investigate it. I found my human standing next to the big glass door in the kitchen with the curtain pulled back and letting a lot of light into the room. When I walked over to him, he picked me up and held me high enough that I could look over the wall of the deck. The buff cat was there! He was down on the grass, far away from the window. It looked like he was having dinner. I don't normally like being held when I get picked up, but this was different. I secured myself in my human's arms and watched the buff guy for a long time.

After that excitement, I freed myself from my human's hold. He pulled the curtain back over the big door and went to the basement. I followed him. He peered out the window briefly before he turned his attention back to me. I was interested in some lap time, so I convinced my human to sit down on the floor. He leaned back and lay down on the floor. I put my front paws on him as he stroked my head. He continued to massage my head and back, even as I got up, walked in front of him a few times, and then lay down near him. I reached out with my front paws and touched his legs while he reached over and massaged my belly. We spent a lot of time on the floor together. I may have even dozed off briefly. We didn't always have to throw mousies around for fun. Just being together was nice.

Day 307, Wednesday, August 28, 2019:
Well, this evening, things were a little strange. When my human arrived home, he didn't prepare our meals right away. Instead, he went upstairs and changed clothing. I waited in the front room and expected to see him go past me on his way to the kitchen. Instead, he went back to the car room. A few minutes later, I heard that growling machine start up. I went to the basement and watched him from my window bench. He pushed that thing all over the yard. When he was done, he found that other not-so-loud stick machine and walked along the edges of the grass with it. After he spent time with both of them, he finally came inside. I thought that would mean meal time, but no! He took his dirty clothing to the cold floor room and then went to that little room where he stands under falling water.

Starving from the lack of my evening meal, I stayed in the cold floor room to find some cobwebs. I checked my normal spot, but there weren't many there. Everything seemed cleaner than usual. It took a while, but I eventually found a big stash of them. I'm not going to say where. It's a secret.

After my human emerged from the water room, I heard him go to the kitchen and start fixing dinner. I went to the kitchen and made him aware of my displeasure about the delay. He acted like he was going to put my food on the floor, but then he didn't. Instead, he grabbed me! I tried to get away, but he overpowered me, no doubt low on energy because of a lack of food. He got down on his knees, wedged me between his legs, and wiped my whiskers clean of my cobweb leftovers. Well, I guess that was okay. Right after that, he put my food on the floor. I took a sniff but didn't eat anything. If he thought he could wait that long to feed me, then I didn't want it. I returned to the front room and looked out the window. I didn't stay mad at him very long, though. I waited for him to take our meals to the upper room so we could eat together. Today, my dinner was back on the floor instead of the table.

After dinner, I told my human I wanted onto his lap. As soon as he put the blanket across his legs, I jumped onto it, turned around, and stepped onto the arm of the chair and onto the table. Just passing through. Keep 'em guessing, and never take the most direct route. It's a cat thing. Although, later in the evening, as he had his hind paws up on the chair, I climbed back onto his arms and snuggled for a while.

I needed some exercise today, so before going to bed, I played with my orange fishy and also chased one of my new mousies around the upper room.

Day 308, Thursday, August 29, 2019:
I received plenty of lap time this morning before my human left for work. He came down a few minutes earlier than normal.[90]

I played with my black string today. I also spent some time at the basement window looking for the buff cat or anyone else who happened to walk into my territory.

My human was home slightly late today, but at least when he arrived the first thing he did (after patting the top of my head) was prepare our meals. After dinner, I got onto the table in the upper room so I could get closer to him. I groomed some of the fur on the top of his head.

I went down to the basement this evening. While there, I heard some commotion upstairs, so I went to check it out. As I made my way down the hallway, I met my human, but I couldn't see his face because he was carrying a large basket full of his clothing. It startled me, so my tail involuntarily puffed up. As soon as I saw that he saw me and wasn't going to drop the basket on me, I was able to relax.

I followed him to the basement. He put the basket down on the table. That was odd because he would normally take it to the cold floor room. He turned his attention to something else in his paws. It was a tiny plastic container. I didn't know what it was. He slowly reached toward me and grabbed me. He restrained me between his legs and massaged my shoulders with his front paws. He then parted the fur on the back of my neck. Soon I felt something drip onto the area where he had parted my fur.[91] Right after that, he praised me and

---

[90]The alarm was set 10 minutes earlier to ensure she received enough lap time before leaving for work.
[91]A dose of topical flea treatment required for her upcoming vacation.

released his grip. He reached toward me again, but I wasn't sure what to make of it, so I took off. We eventually met up again in the upper room. I could still feel that stuff, whatever it was, on the back of my neck. I cleaned myself as best I could. Eventually, the weird feeling went away.

After that strange encounter, I stretched out on the floor with my front paws extended in front of me.

Before going to bed, I played with one of my new mousies.

Day 309, Friday, August 30, 2019:
Things got kind of scary last night when my human and I went to bed. There were some loud sounds and bright flashes of light outside the window. I lay on the bed near my human and looked toward the window. I asked my human about the bright lights. We talked about the lights and sounds for quite some time. He didn't seem too con-cerned, and that made me feel better. Still, it was kind of mesmerizing.

I was napping on the top of the tall cat tree today when I heard something that didn't sound right. It sounded like my human was home, but it was much too early in the day for that. I sat up and looked across the room. I tried to figure out what was going on. Sure enough, my human soon appeared. That was strange.

I followed my human around the house as he moved various things around. One was a large, soft-sided, rectangular box with a handle. He pulled it out of the tiny room with all the shelves accessible from the hallway. He put some of his clothing in it.

He also had a box in the upper room that he put some things in. I played with a ball while he filled his box.

I heard him go to the car room a couple of times. While I was in the basement, I heard him walk down the steps and open the door to the car room, so I thought I'd see if I could sneak out there. As I emerged from the basement, I was horrified! He had my short cat tree from the upper room and was taking it to the car room! I went upstairs to confirm, and sure enough, there was an empty spot on the floor where my tree once stood. I started to get worried. That was just too strange.

I paid close attention to my human from that point on. I fol-lowed him to the basement. He closed the door behind him, but that didn't concern me at the time. I saw him go into the cold floor room. When he emerged a moment later, he was carrying a large plastic box that looked familiar. It was the box I was in when I came to live with him, and also the box I was in when I went to the doctor. My travel pod! Uh-oh.

He set the travel pod on the floor and opened its door. I sniffed it a couple of times but refused to enter it. He reached for me, so I took off. I ran to go upstairs but had forgotten the door was closed. I was trapped! He put the box on the table and then sat on the floor and talked to me. I had a few words for him, too. He came over and picked me up. I tried to stop him from pushing me into the box, but it was futile. He couldn't shut me up, though, so I let him know I didn't care for any of this. At least my travel pod has plenty of headroom.

Once in the travel pod, we went to the car room and got into the car. The big door went up, and we left the house. I complained and complained because there wasn't much else I could do.

A few minutes later, we arrived at the doctor's office. Was it time for my checkup already? We went into the building. My human set my travel pod down and left me there. He returned soon with my tree and one of my scratching posts, which I hadn't seen him load into the car. This was too different from my normal routine and was rather upsetting.

Soon, we were moving again. My human and another human came over and took me and my things down a hallway and into a large room. As soon as the door to my box was opened, I took off and hid under a bench. I looked around the room and saw my cat tree and scratching post.

I walked around the space under the bench as my human and the other human talked. Once the other human left, I came out to see my human. We talked for a bit, and he stroked my back. He also picked me up and set me on top of the cat tree. It was next to a tall window. I could see a plant on the other side of the window. We stood there and looked out the window for a bit.

My human told me he would be back after four sunrises, and then he left. I went back to hiding under the bench. This was too big of a change.

Soon, a human came in. I was told later her name was Allyson. I was kind of scared of her. She left but came back a bit later, and this time she had dinner for me. I decided she was okay, so I came out and brushed the top of my head against her. She gently stroked my back for a while. After I ate, I thought about my human and wondered what was going on. I went back under the bench to contemplate things.

From under the bench, I saw some familiar toys in the middle of the room, including one of my new fishies and one of my new mousies.

Day 310, Saturday, August 31, 2019:
After a night of rest, I felt more comfortable. There was a lot of activity at the office, at least in the morning, but I spent the day in my own room.

When Allyson brought my food to me, I was so excited to have someone to socialize with that I didn't eat my dinner right away. Instead, I spent time being affectionate with Allyson. We talked quite a bit, too. She's a nice human. I cuddled with her for a while and then followed her around the room while she cleaned my temporary living space.

Day 311, Sunday, September 1, 2019:
Things at the doctor's office were pretty quiet today. There wasn't the rush of activity like there was yesterday morning. I spent most of the day lounging in the various perches around this room, including my own familiar cat tree. It was nice that the humans placed it where I could look out the window.

On my cat tree.

Along one wall of the room was another type of cat tree, unlike any that I had at home. It was very tall and had many levels. Each level had a rectangular platform. On the very top platform, I found some clothing that belonged to my human. I wondered why he left it there. I enjoyed having a reminder of him, though.

A different human came by to see me today. I was later told her name was Natalie. She tried to get me to play with the toys from home, but I wasn't very interested. She also brought a different toy. I was told it belonged to Ophelia, a cat who lives here at the doctor's office. It was a long ribbon with many bright colors. I hid behind a leg of the bench and grabbed the ribbon when Natalie moved it close to me. It was great fun!

It was nice to once again have someone to talk with today. Natalie and I socialized quite a bit. I showed my appreciation for her attention by brushing myself against her legs.

Ophelia let me play with one of her toys.

It was fun!

Oh, today they also picked me up and set me on a flat tray. They let go of me but kept me from getting off the tray for several seconds. They took some notes and told me I had lost some weight. When I lived at the shelter, I couldn't get much exercise since I was confined to a relatively small space. Ever since I moved into my own house with many levels and rooms, I have been able to run around and get plenty of exercise. It has given me a sleek and slender figure.

Day 312, Monday, September 2, 2019:
Allyson came back to visit me again today. She stayed with me after dinner for a while. We cuddled for some time. I also rubbed myself against her legs. While she cleaned the room, I relaxed on my cat tree and supervised.

I missed my human and all the extra room at my house, but things here at the doctor's office really aren't that bad. In fact, I've gotten quite comfortable here and have enjoyed the company of some new humans.

Day 313, Tuesday, September 3, 2019:
When I heard some activity in the building this morning, I jumped to the top of my scratching post. From there, I could get a better look out the window of the door. That's when I heard a tap at the outside window across the room. I turned and saw my human outside! I didn't know why he was out there.[92] I was so confused about the situation that I just sat on my post and stared at him. He soon disappeared from view. I wondered if he would come inside.

Soon after that, one of the humans from the doctor's office came into my room and put me in my travel pod. I really didn't like that and complained about it. Rather loudly, I might add. Then my human walked into the room! He came over to see me, but I was still so annoyed about being put in my travel pod that I didn't pay much attention to him. He picked up my tree and post and left the room. The other human carried me in my travel pod. She took me all the way outside and put me in the car. My human and I then went back home. It was a short trip, but I complained the whole time.

When we got home, I walked into every room of the house to check out the situation. Everything was nearly like I remembered. My human brought my cat tree in from the car room and put it back in the upper room. My scratching post also reappeared in the living room. I

---

[92]I had arrived early and wanted to see her.

followed my human around and talked to him a lot. I frequently talk to him, but today, I had even more to say.

As soon as my human sat on his chair in the upper room, I climbed onto his arms. We talked some more. After that, I got down and took a bath on the upper room floor while my human worked on the computer.

Later in the morning, I went to investigate when I heard my human in the basement. I found him scooping out my litter pan. I talked to him some more, and as soon as he was done scooping, I climbed onto his lap, just like I do every morning.

My human went to work after he spent the morning with me. When I heard him come home, I went to the car room door and greeted him. I called for him before he entered the house. I was happy to see him again.

I waited on the bench in the front room and looked out the window while he prepared my dinner. He was a bit slow, so I went to the kitchen and asked him about it. He put my food on the floor, and I began to eat while he was still fixing his own food. When he finally took both of our plates to the upper room, I ate some more of my food and then climbed onto his arms. He had his dinner on the table, but I didn't care; I wanted to sit on his arms. His dinner would just have to wait.

Later in the evening, I followed my human to the hallway. He went to the bedroom, but I stayed in the hallway because something grabbed my attention. There was a skinny bug crawling across the floor. My human came out of the bedroom and walked right past both me and the bug. I left the bug and followed him to the basement.[93]

My human went to the cold floor room. I followed right behind him and explored the room while he busied himself at the workbench. A few minutes later, he rolled that short, fat, red-and-black tub with the thick tail across the floor. He pushed something onto that thing's tail and then poked the tub. It began to roar! That's when I left the room. The sound stopped soon after I departed, but I didn't risk going back in there. Right after that, the door to the cold floor room closed, so I couldn't have gotten back in there even if I wanted to.

I normally went upstairs when my human is in the cold floor room with the loud sounds, but since we had recently been apart for several days, I didn't want to let him out of my sight, at least as best I could. Even though I couldn't see him with the door closed, I knew

---

[93] The bug was found by her human a few minutes later.

there was no other way out of that room. I tucked all four paws under myself and waited on the floor about two cat lengths away from the door.

When the door opened sometime later, he said he was going up-stairs. I stayed close behind him. He stopped briefly to clean his front paws and then went to the upper room. As soon as he sat down, I was in his arms. I made several trips into his arms tonight.

During one of my brief periods between my arm sessions, I sat on the floor near his chair and found another bug. That one was much smaller. My human took care of it.

Oh, I almost forgot. Tonight, my human put a small plate of catnip out for me. It was a delightful diversion after all the chaos of the last several days.

Day 314, Wednesday, September 4, 2019:
I spent nearly the whole night lying next to my human. I missed him the last several days, so I wanted to spend as much time with him as I could. I stretched out with my hind legs around one of his arms and my chest next to one of his paws. He gave me a pleasant belly rub as he drifted off to sleep.

My right eye started doing that weird thing again. It's a bit un-comfortable. I ended up not doing much today because of it. I just rested and kept wishing it would go back to normal. Part of the after-noon, I took a nap on the upper room floor.

The eye bothered me so much, I didn't even get up to greet my human when he arrived home. When he did, he came upstairs and talked with me. I finally got up when he said he would go get some food for me. I followed him downstairs and sat on my scratching post while he fixed our meals.

After dinner, I took a bath on top of the short cat tree in the upper room. I followed that up with another nap.

Day 315, Thursday, September 5, 2019:
My eye still ached, so I took things easy today. I groomed my human a bit while he was having dinner. I waited for him to eat most of his food before I climbed onto his arm for a snuggle session.

I spent some time looking out the basement window. I didn't see the buff guy today. I wondered if he ever took a vacation, like the one I had at my doctor's office.

This evening, I rested on the floor of the upper room. Before going to bed, I climbed onto my human's arms again.

Day 316, Friday, September 6, 2019:
I groomed my human again this evening. I also spent a lot of time on my human's arms. Lately, that has been my favorite way to spend time with him.

My time on his arms was cut short, though, because something caught my attention. I leaped from his arms and ran over to the sliding doors that hide the shelves on the other side of the room. There was a bug up there! It was flying and was too high for me to reach. It landed on the door. My human got up and followed me to the door. Then he grabbed a device from one of the high shelves. I hadn't seen it before. The part near his paw was narrow, but the other end was wide. It had a bunch of thin bars in it. My human swung the wide part with the bars toward the bug, and then I heard a loud *ZAP!* The noise surprised me so much, I jumped back and looked at him from across the room. I wasn't sure what to make of the situation, so I just stayed attentive and watched my human. He picked up the bug that had fallen to the floor and disposed of it.

So that was kind of scary. But there was some good news today —my eye was getting better.

Day 317, Saturday, September 7, 2019:
Today was a great day. I was happy because my eye was mostly back to normal. What made me even more happy was the long, two-pawed neck massage I received this morning from my human while we sat on the basement floor. And even better than that: my human stayed home with me all day! I received plenty of lap time and snuggle sessions on his arms.

After my neck massage, I followed my human into the cold floor room. It was nice to get in there because that door had been closed nearly the entire time since I returned home. I went on the hunt for cobwebs, but there weren't very many. I had to reach behind a tall floor-to-ceiling black tube and some boards to find any.

While I was in there, minding my own business, my human started making some noise. He was preoccupied with some things on a table. What caught my attention was a rattle sound. My human was holding a metal can and was rapidly shaking it. He moved the can toward some things on the table, and then the can started to hiss. I don't like other cats hissing at me, and I don't like non-cats hissing at me, either, so I got out of there.

Around lunchtime, I waited on the bench in the front room for my human to prepare our food. After I ate, I was just sitting on the floor in the upper room, once again minding my own business, when my human put my purple fishy in front of me. I guessed he wanted me to play with it, but I wasn't in the mood.

This afternoon, I followed my human into the storage room. I saw him open the door on the other side of the room—the one that leads to a tiny room with shelves I like to explore. I didn't get a chance to go in there, though, because he picked me up! He put me on a tray similar to the one that the human at my doctor's office did several days ago. And just like they did, he let go of me but blocked me from jumping off the tray for several seconds. Once I found the opportunity, I jumped down to the floor. I decided exploring the small room was no longer important and got out of there as quickly as I could.

I took a nap on the big tree in the living room later in the afternoon. After a while, my human came into the room. I got down to greet him. We lay down on the floor for a bit. We were close to the three-level ball toy that Grandma and Grandpa gave me, so I played with it. I kept my paw on one level and hit the ball back and forth to myself. My human joined in the fun, too, whenever a ball stopped outside of my reach. We also played with some pom-pom balls.

Late in the afternoon, I lay on the bench in the front room and looked outside. I saw the dirt lady get into her car and drive away from her house. About that time, my human came over and gave me a back massage.

This evening, my human and I lay on the upper room floor. First, he gave me a belly rub. Then, we played with one of my new toy mousies.

I also spent some time this evening on my human's arms before we went to bed.

Day 318, Sunday, September 8, 2019:
I received another two-pawed neck massage this morning, but it wasn't as long as the one yesterday. After that, my human left for the shelter. It must have been a hard day because he was there longer than usual. While he was away, I went to the living room and took a nap on top of the tall cat tree.

I made many trips onto my human's arms today, mostly while he was at the computer or watching television. I also spent some time looking out the tall window by the computer. There wasn't much exciting out there today.

Day 319, Monday, September 9, 2019:
My human hunted today. When he came home, I watched him as he brought bags of food into the house. I had to wait for him to sort everything before he prepared our meals. While he did that, I played with my sparkly blue mouse.

Tonight, I also played with one of my new mousies in the upper room. After playing and eating, I lay down and stretch out on one of the tables. My human was on his chair nearby and reached out to pet me. I rested my head on his paw.

Later in the evening, I walked onto my human's lap while he sat at the computer. I made my way onto his arms and stretched out again, resting my chin against his upper arm.

Day 320, Tuesday, September 10, 2019:
I got up before my human today, but instead of going to the basement, I stayed in the front room. I sat on the bench (more specifically, the cat bed I never sleep in) and looked up at the curtain. There was something there that I didn't expect. When my human walked in, he asked me about it, but I turned my attention to him, hoping he would give me some affection. He patted my head and then went to the kitchen to fix my water and dry food dishes. I returned my attention to the curtain. I sat on the floor and looked up at it. When my human was done in the kitchen, he walked back into the room and asked me what I was looking at, but I didn't tell him. Couldn't he see it?[94]

I followed my human to the basement and waited for him to take care of my litter pan. Once that was done, I spent several minutes on his lap since I knew he would soon leave.

I went back upstairs to my bench and watched my human drive away in the car. After he left, things got interesting. I returned to the basement and was minding my own business, looking out the window, when I saw Benny, the big black-and-white cat, stroll by. He stopped near the bushes and looked at me. I stared him down, not knowing what he might do. He left soon after that. I checked the window frequently throughout the day to see if he would come back. He didn't, at least not at that window.

---

[94]She was intently focused on something, but I couldn't see it. She never told me what it was.

This evening, when I heard my human arrive home, he didn't come into the house right away. I went to the front room and looked out the window. There, I saw him talking to Benny's human. Is Benny back? At first, I just saw the two humans, but after searching some more, I saw Benny walk by the other side of the flowers and past my human. He got onto the steps and went toward the car room.

After what seemed like too long of a time, my human finally came into the house and prepared our food. I played with one of my new mousies while I waited for him to serve dinner.

This evening, I spent some time looking out the tall window by the computer. Then I walked over to see what my human was doing. He had picked up a small, thin stick from a nearby shelf. I didn't know what it was. Right after that, a small red dot appeared on the floor near his hind paws. The dot moved around on the floor and into the closet. I watched as it came back out, moved around on the floor near my human, and once again went into the closet. I went to the other end of the table for a closer look, but I didn't see it reemerge. I got down from the table and made my way over to the closet. Despite a thorough check of the floor and one of the shelves, I couldn't find the red dot.

Later in the evening, I went to the storage room. I got onto the table and poked around in some cardboard boxes. I must have made too much noise because my human came into the room to see what I was doing. Just exploring. Nothing to see here.

This evening, my human and I enjoyed some snacks. I'm not sure what he had, but I had some of my T/D dental treats. They're good for my teeth, and they taste great. I usually have to hunt for them because my human mixes them with my regular dry food, so getting some without having to hunt for them is great. Plus, I always enjoy eating any time my human does.

Day 321, Wednesday, September 11, 2019:
I don't think my human felt well last night. He went to bed early and then got up in the middle of the night. When he returned to bed, he brought extra pillows and slept with his head much higher than normal. Several times throughout the night, he woke up and wiggled around. I did what I could and stayed close to him. I snuggled between his side and his arm until it was time to go on my early morning prowl.

I spent a good part of the day resting after a long night taking care of my human. I also checked the windows to see if Benny or the buff cat came by outside. I didn't see either of them.

I was so excited when my human came home that I ran all over the house. I followed him for a while and also ran to the basement. He put my food on the kitchen floor before he fixed his own food. I sniffed it but then took off out to the front room. When he was done fixing his meal, he picked my plate up and started toward me. I bolted down the stairs to the basement, but he didn't follow me. Several min-utes later, he came down to check on me to see what was going on. He looked out the window, but there wasn't anything exciting happening out there, so he asked if I wanted some food. I followed him when he went upstairs. I passed him on the staircase because he's so slow. When I got to the upper room, I discovered that he had already brought my plate up there.

After dinner and all of my running, I relaxed in my human's arms.

Day 322, Thursday, September 12, 2019:
I didn't spend much time with my human last night. I saw him off to bed but then left. I went across the hall to the upper room and slept there. It was too warm in the bedroom, plus there was a device on the floor making gurgling noises and filling the room with steam. That de-vice normally isn't there.

I didn't run around the house, like I did yesterday. Instead, for my exercise today, I chased some balls around the living room.

This evening, I received a bit of a surprise. I was lying on the floor in the upper room when my human came in. Instead of going over to his chair, he lay down on the floor near me.

Day 323, Friday, September 13, 2019:
I went to bed with my human last night, but like the previous night, I didn't stay very long. I stretched out next to him until he made a sudden movement and a loud sound.[95] When that happened, I left the room. Plus, it was still rather warm in there, and that gurgling, steam-spitting thing was still there. I returned briefly to check up on him in the middle of the night.

Today, I spent some time in the basement, keeping an eye on my territory from the bench by the window. I also played with one of

---

[95]A cough.

my new mousies in the upper room. It almost got stuck under the pet steps near my water dish, but I recovered it by myself.

Tonight, I sat on my human's lap while he worked on the computer. I also checked out the cabinet under the bathroom sink while my human was in there. (He was in the bathroom, but not under the sink.) He opened the door and removed the jug that was always in my way so I could walk deeper into the cabinet.

Oh, tonight I also played with my black string in the upper room.

Day 324, Saturday, September 14, 2019:
The steam-spewing machine was still in the bedroom last night, but it wasn't doing anything. I also noticed the room was slightly cooler than it had been the previous couple of days. That made the room more comfortable, so I spent the whole night with my human. Well, until I got up to go on my morning prowl.

As always, I waited in the basement for my human. After taking care of my litter pan, he sat down and gave me his lap. He proceeded to also give me a long two-pawed neck massage. It was a great way to start the day!

When I'd had my fill, I got up and returned to the window. My human left the room but returned a few minutes later. He opened the curtain and then sat down near the bench. He gave me a back massage followed by a belly rub. I was enjoying that when my attention got diverted by movement in the distance. The buff cat was back! He was moving in and out of the plants at the edge of the lawn. I watched intently as he slowly made his way to the neighbor's yard. Soon, he was out of my sight.

I resumed my interrupted belly rub. After a bit, I stood up and rubbed the side of my head against my human several times. I was enjoying another back massage when I saw the buff cat again. His tail was tucked low, and he was really moving! He shot across the yard and disappeared into the bushes at the edge of the dirt lady's yard. Why didn't he come over to see me? He looked like he was on the hunt for something.

As soon as the buff cat disappeared, my human went upstairs. I stayed in the basement in case the buff cat came back.

Later in the morning, my human returned to the basement with a long springy thing. He got down on all four paws and looked under the shelves between the bench and the staircase door. I saw him stick the springy thing under the shelf. When he pulled it back out, my yellow mouse was at the other end! He put the springy stick under the shelf several more times and recovered all of my toys that had gotten stuck under there, including plastic springs and several mice.

One of the toys that was recovered was an orange plastic ring. It's thin but is big enough I can put my paw through it. It's fun to play with because it kind of bounces randomly when I push it around. I played with it, even after my human went back upstairs. When I was done playing with it for the day, I left it in one of his shoes near the door to the car room.

This afternoon, I rested on top of the tall cat tree in the living room while my human worked outside. When he came back into the house, there was some extra commotion. I went to investigate. From the top of the steps, I looked toward the car room door and saw my human. The dirt lady was there, too, but there was also one more tiny human I didn't recognize.

The little human was about as tall as me when I stretch and reach as high as I can. She was loud! And very busy! That was a lot more activity in my house than I was used to. I tried to stay low and slink away, but all three of them followed me. In the living room, my human caught up to me and picked me up. He put me on his leg as he knelt and moved toward the little human. It was a bit terrifying, but I felt safe in my human's paws.

Fortunately, the little human only seemed interested in my toys and not me. As soon as my human released his grip on me, I hopped from his leg. I quickly made my way past the little human and across the room. I climbed to the safety of the top shelf of my tall cat tree. I was happy to share my toys with the little human as long as she kept her chaotic energy far away from me.

All of the humans got up and went to the front room. That was when I saw my escape route. While their attention was diverted, I got down from the cat tree and made my way across the room. Then, I slipped through the front room behind them and darted up the steps.

Things quieted down significantly once the two extra humans left my house. After that wild afternoon, I needed a nap. I took care of that on the small cat tree in the upper room.

My nap was interrupted when my human walked into the room. He asked if I was ready for dinner. Of course I was! I went to the front room and waited while he fixed our meals. We ate in the upper room.

After eating, I relaxed on my human's arms for a while and then stretched out on the floor.

This evening, my human and I enjoyed some quiet time together. We played with an old toy mouse near the pet steps in the upper room (the ones near the table). Right after that, we played with one of the new toy mice on the cat tree. We threw the poor mouse to each other while I sat at the top of the tree. It got a little crazy at one point. While going after the mouse, I flipped around on the tree and almost fell off! Well, I guess I actually did fall, but with my cat-like reflexes, I grabbed the V-shaped shelf and tried to pull myself up. My human, who was normally rather slow, had some unusually quick reflexes tonight because he caught my backside and helped me back to the shelf.

After I nearly fell to the floor, we continued to play with the mouse until I decided it was time for a bath. That was good timing because my favorite place to clean myself is on top of my small cat tree, and I was already there.

Once my bath was over, I stretched out on the upper room floor and relaxed while my human played with his metal discs on the table.

Relaxing in the upper room.

Day 325, Sunday, September 15, 2019:
This morning, I took a nap on the large cat tree while my human worked at the shelter. When he came home, we had lunch. Then I took

a nap on the small cat tree in the upper room. I rested most of the day after all the excitement from yesterday.

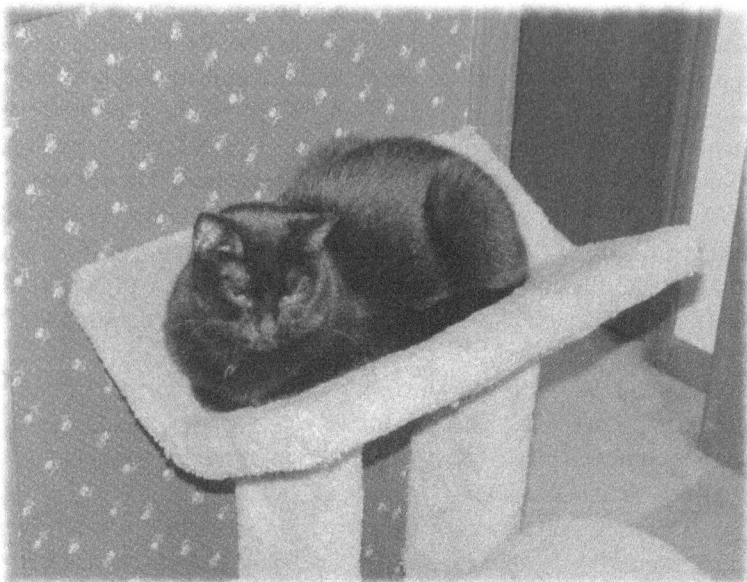

Enjoying my small cat tree

This afternoon, my human made several trips to the cold floor room and used the big white machines in there.[96] He left the door to the room open, so I was able to go play with some cobwebs. Once I was done with the cobwebs, I returned to the soft floor basement room and played with my orange ring. Upon returning upstairs, my human cleaned my whiskers for me.

This evening, I followed my human to the living room. He lay down on the sofa, so I hopped up next to him and curled up behind his legs. It was kind of warm, so I didn't stay there long.

Before going to bed, my human and I went back to the upper room. I sat on his arms for a bit.

Day 326, Monday, September 16, 2019:
I waited on the bench while my human prepared our meals tonight. After dinner, I sat on his arms. Later in the evening, I tried to sneak into the car room. My human wouldn't let me go out there, though.

Tonight, I played in the living room with the three-ball toy from Grandma and Grandpa. I stopped when my human entered the room

---

[96] A clothes washer and dryer.

and sat on the sofa. I walked over and joined him. I talked to him for a while and then lay down near him. He put a paw near me and gave me a gentle belly rub. It was so relaxing, I almost fell asleep. After that, I got up and went back to the three-ball toy. I also played with my white-and-red dot pom-pom ball.

After that, I followed my human to the upper room. I rested on the floor while he worked on the computer.

Day 327, Tuesday, September 17, 2019:
Before sunrise this morning, I sat at the front window and surveyed my territory. When I heard my human get up, I made my way to the basement and waited for him. My pan was clean this morning, so he didn't need to scoop it. That meant I didn't have to wait for lap time! When I got up from my morning lap session, I saw my human do something kind of strange. He took all of my toys that were in the room and set them out in a straight line.[97] I kept them there all day, except for the orange ring, which I batted around the room.

This afternoon, I was asleep on the big cat tree when I was awoken by the sounds of my human. He was home early. He came to the cat tree and greeted me before he went to the basement. I followed him and saw him scoop my litter pan. Right after that, he went to the car room while I went to the front room.

Not long after that, I heard more commotion. My human was back in the house, but there was another human with him.[98] I didn't recognize him. The humans went to the basement, but I stayed in the front room. Soon, my human came upstairs. He reached for me, but I slipped away and ran to the big cat tree. My human went back to the car room. After a couple of minutes, I decided to investigate. I quietly made my way down the stairs and to the basement. Suddenly, I saw the other human walking through the room! I ducked out of the way as he went past me. I heard my human return from the car room about the same time. The other human went up the steps. I heard him go out to the car room. I went back upstairs and found my human. He picked me up and took me to the upper room. He left the room and closed the door on his way out. After several more minutes, I could hear the humans talking, and then there was silence. The door to the upper room opened. I went down to the basement to inspect things and discovered that the other human had left.

---

[97]They were moved out of the way in preparation for a visitor later in the day.
[98]An HVAC technician to perform a tune-up of the furnace.

My human left soon after that, too, but he returned a short time later with some bags of supplies. I knew my human would go to the basement, so I waited for him there, on top of the table. It took a few minutes, but sure enough, he came down to the basement. I watched him put some supplies away. Then I went over to the bench and looked out the window.

I lost track of time and didn't realize that my human was preparing our meals until he called me from the front room. I came up from the basement and met him near the front door. I followed him to the upper room and made my way up the pet steps to the table. I found his plate of food, but not mine. Once he made it to the room (he's kind of slow), he pointed out my plate on the floor. I hopped down and enjoyed my tasty meal.

What to do after dinner but to stretch out and relax on the upper room floor?

Day 328, Wednesday, September 18, 2019:
I was in the front room looking out the window this morning when my human got up. I hopped down from the bench and used my scratching post. Then I made my way to the basement and waited for lap time.

My eye starting doing its weird things again today. This time, it's the left eye. So far, it hasn't bothered me too much.

This evening, I played with one of my new mousies in the upper room. After that, I followed my human around the house as he took care of various chores. Once he was done, I led him back to the upper room and convinced him to sit on the floor. I climbed aboard and enjoyed his lap.

Day 329, Thursday, September 19, 2019:
I performed a surprise inspection of my human this morning. I returned to the bedroom after my morning prowl. As my human got out of the bed, I hopped up onto the small pet steps and watched him straighten out the sheet and blanket. Once I confirmed he had successfully made the bed, I returned to the basement and waited for him. Naturally, when he finally showed up, I enjoyed my morning lap time with him.

Despite a good start this morning, things were kind of rough today. My eye was getting worse, and it kind of annoyed me. Also, embarrassingly, I had one, um, "clump" that missed my litter pan. I tried to cover it up using the absorbent pad that sticks out from underneath my pan, but that didn't work too well. I tried using the pad to pull the clump up into the pan so I could cover it with tiny rocks, but I couldn't get it in there. I had to settle for just covering it with the pad.

Things got much better later in the afternoon when my human arrived home. I stood at the end of the hallway near the steps while he put his things away and cleaned up. As he approached me, he sat down at the top step and made a lap for me. I climbed onto his legs and snuggled with him for a long time. We'd never sat together at that location. It was nice to do something different, but mostly I just enjoyed getting a neck massage and a full back rub. He suggested we get some food, but that didn't interest me—all I wanted was his attention. I purred contentedly and just took it all in.

My human prepared our meals after I eventually got up. Instead of waiting in the front room, I went to the basement. I didn't even realize that dinner was served until my human came down and informed me about it. After he did that, I ran upstairs and found my meal waiting for me on the floor of the upper room.

After dinner, I looked out the tall window near the computer and then went to the basement and looked out that window, with a stop on my human's arms for a snuggle session between the two. After that, I returned to the upper room for more snuggling on my human's lap using the blanket.

Day 330, Friday, September 20, 2019:
I felt much better today because my eye was mostly back to normal. In fact, I felt good enough that I played with my white string for a while.

Today, I saw the dirt lady riding all over the grass on that loud growling thing. She even came into my territory.

That wasn't the only weird thing that happened today. My human was home a bit late, and even when he got near the house, he didn't come inside. I heard him in the car room and went to look for him. I could see him from the front window. He was carrying that long stick thing that sometimes makes a growling noise. He walked all the way around the house with it. I lost sight of him for a while but eventually saw him again at the front window. The dirt lady also came over. I think she saw me because she tapped one of her claws on the window. I just looked at her and wondered when my human would come inside and fix dinner.

I didn't have to wait much longer, as he soon came into the house. I followed closely behind him. As soon as he fixed our meals, I gobbled mine up. After dinner, I curled up on the floor of the upper room.

Day 331, Saturday, September 21, 2019:
This was a bit of a strange morning. First, while snuggling with my human on the bed a bit before the sun came up, a slight buzzing sound broke the silence. A few minutes later, it happened again.[99] Both times I looked across the room to where I thought the sounds had come from, but I didn't see anything.

I got up at my normal time and left my human on the bed, just as I always do, but when he didn't show up in the basement at the appropriate time, I went upstairs to investigate. I found him in the upper room, typing on the computer. We talked for a bit and then went to the kitchen, where I supervised him as he cleaned and filled my dishes.

We sat on the bench in the front room for a few minutes before we went to the basement. I felt more comfortable because things seemed like they were getting back to normal. He cleaned my litter pan and then sat on the floor so I could use his lap. He also gave me a back rub.

A well-deserved nap.

My human brushed me today while I sat on the table between him and the computer. I didn't need to be brushed because I take such

---

[99]Text messages from my sister informing me that my great-niece, Serenity, had been born the night before.

good care of my coat, but I liked the attention from my human. Also, the brush just felt really good on my back.

After my brushing, I sat on my human's lap. Then I moved to the small cat tree and took a nap while he played with his metal discs.

This evening, we played with some toy mice. I sat at the top of the pet steps near my scratching post and batted at the mice that my human tossed onto or set on the platform atop the post. Sometimes, I'd immediately swing at a mouse as it came flying up toward me. Other times, when the mouse was set on the platform, I had to stare it down and get angry with it first before I whacked it. The best part, though, was playing this game with my human.

A backlit photo of me on top of my scratching post.

Day 332, Sunday, September 22, 2019:
My human surprised me today when he got up quite a bit earlier than normal. I hadn't even gotten out of the bed for my morning prowl. When he went to the small room with the human litter device, I hastily made my way to the basement. At least I got to enjoy plenty of lap time with him before he left for the shelter.

He was also home from the shelter much later than I expected. I met him at the door when he arrived. I followed him as he made his way around the house. First, we went to the bedroom. Then, we went to the basement. He opened the door to the cold floor room. He went to go work with the big white machines while I went on the hunt for some cobwebs. I found some on a few boards near my prime cobweb spot.

I stayed in the basement when he went upstairs. He must have prepared our meals (it was almost dinnertime) while I was in the basement. Once he told me food was available, I quickly ran upstairs. I went around the corner near the front door so fast I almost missed the steps to go to the upper floor. I waited for my human to catch up and enter the hallway before I shot past him and beat him to the upper room. He was right! A plate of my food was waiting for me.

After dinner, I spent a little time on my human's arms while he worked at the computer. Then I went over and sat on top of the scratching post. I told my human I wanted to play the whack-a-mouse game again, and he obliged. Sometimes, I'd hit the mouse back to him, and he'd catch it. Other times, it would land on the blanket chair. There were even times it landed far enough away that he had to get up to recover it. I figured it's good for my human to get some exercise.

Later in the evening, I chased a green pom-pom ball around the upper room. I stopped briefly when it ended up near one of my human's hind paws, but when he kicked it closer to me, I took off chasing it again.

This evening, I followed my human into the storage room, where he worked for a bit. He picked me up and put me on the long white tray, just like he did a couple of weeks ago. After he had his fun with that, he put me back on the perch near the window. What's the deal with that white tray, anyway?[100]

Day 333, Monday, September 23, 2019:
I got up before my human today. As usual, I waited in the basement for lap time. My human was a bit late to the basement. I still got to enjoy some lap time, but not as much as I'd have liked. When I made the mistake of stepping off his lap to reposition myself, he got up and left for work.

I enjoyed a snack this evening. My human took it to the upper room, along with a snack for himself. He put mine on the mat near his

---

[100]During her recent vacation at the vet's office while I was out of town, they noticed that her weight was down nearly two pounds since her prior visit. I continued to monitor her weight at home to make sure nothing was wrong. I attributed her weight loss to exercise since she now has her own house to run around, rather than being confined to a small condo at the shelter.

chair, just like he does with my regular meals. It was crunchy and tasty.

I spent a lot of time on my human's lap and arms tonight. I also stretched out on the floor of the upper room. I didn't play much, but rather just relaxed near my human.

I got excited later in the evening because I saw my human go through his weekly routine of picking up the small plastic bags and stuffing them into a bigger bag. I stayed close to him because I knew he would go to the car room. I tried really hard to get out there, but just like the last several attempts, I couldn't get past him.

Before I went to bed, I found my human in the small room with his litter box contraption. I asked him to open the cabinet under the sink for me since it had been a while since I'd looked in there. He did. I poked my head in but couldn't get very far until he removed the big jug that always sits in there. With that out of the way, I was able to walk farther in for my inspection. Everything checked out, so I stepped back out and left him alone.

Day 334, Tuesday, September 24, 2019:
After I enjoyed my morning lap time with my human, I went up to the front room to watch him leave for work. I sat on my bench at the front window and saw him push those two big plastic bins down the driveway and put them by the road. I saw him drag them again when he got home, but that time, he moved them back to the car room.

Before he came into the house, my human walked over to the window I was sitting at and put his paw up near me. Why was he still outside? The flowers are gone, so he didn't need to water them. He walked toward the car room. When I heard him come into the house, I ran over to the top of the steps and greeted him.

I followed my human to the basement, where he cleaned my litter pan. I kind of wanted him to sit down so I could use his lap, but he said we should get some food. I ran upstairs and went all the way to the upper room, but there wasn't any food. Then I realized my human had gone to the kitchen. I ran back to the front room, got on top of my scratching post, and waited for my dinner.

After I ate, I spent a little time with my human and then went to the basement. Later in the evening, I went back to the upper room and was sitting on top of my scratching post when I heard something strange. There was a deep, repetitive thumping sound that started off quietly but became louder and louder and then so loud the house started to vibrate.[101] It kind of freaked me out. Fortunately, as quickly as it came, it faded away until the house stopped shaking and I could no longer hear it. My human just sat at the computer and didn't seem bothered by it. Didn't he hear that thing?

With things back to normal, I hopped down to the floor near some of my toys. My human came over and started to play with the stick toy that has three long puffy tails. He flicked it around over my head. I sat back on my hind legs and tried to grab it. It was entertaining for a while.

After playing with the stick toy, I walked over to my human, who was sitting on the floor. I rubbed the top of my head against him a few times and then lay down on my side near his legs. He gave me a wonderful belly rub as I reached for the pet steps with my front paws. I scooted along the steps on my side as my human continued the belly rub. After my belly rub, I was just lying there for a while, thinking about how great the belly rub was, when suddenly my human touched the bottom of one of my hind paws. I quickly pulled it closer to me. Then he touched it again. And again. That was annoying. I gave him a look that let him know my feelings without saying a word.

Day 335, Wednesday, September 25, 2019:
I played with my small yellow mouse today. Not the white-and-yellow one that my human fixed, but one that is all yellow. I played with it in the basement and on the steps.

I was excited to see my human when he came home. He was late for some reason, which meant my dinner was also late. I checked up on him as he worked in the kitchen. I brushed myself against his legs to remind him that dinner was late. I think he knew because he took my meal to the upper room and served it to me before his was even ready.

After dinner, I stretched out on the table in the upper room and socialized with my human.

My human made snacks for us tonight. I waited excitedly on the post in the front room while he worked on them. As he came through the room, I jumped down and ran alongside him up the stairs. As usual, I passed him in the hallway since he was so slow. His snack was some cold thing in a cup.[102] I sniffed it but didn't try any. My snack was much better. It was some of my yummy, crunchy dental treats.

---

[101]A helicopter.
[102]Ice cream.

After our snacks, we went to the basement. My human opened the door to the cold floor room. I shot in there before he even got one paw into the room. I went to my favorite cobweb place but didn't find much.

Day 336, Thursday, September 26, 2019:
When I went to the basement this morning, I saw that my human had left the door to the cold floor room open. A-ha! More cobwebs! I figured I should go in there and hunt for them before he came down and closed it. I'm glad I did because, just as I predicted, he closed the door as soon as he came down to take care of my litter pan. He also cleaned my whiskers for me.

Today, I played with my lopsided purple ball in the front room until I got bored with it. I left it by the front door.

This afternoon, I sat on the post in the front room while I waited for my slow human to fix my dinner. After dinner, I lay down on my human's paws and rested my head on his left arm.

After I spent some time with my human, I left him at the computer and went across the room to play. I chased a pom-pom ball and a mouse around the small cat tree, including into the tube at the bottom of the tree.

I guess my human wanted to play, too, because he tossed the green pom-pom to me. I chased it into the hallway and then back into the upper room. We also played with both the tan ball that has the floppy bits hanging off it and one of the crinkly sparkle balls.

After all of that exercise, I rested on the floor of the upper room while my human sat close by.

We had some snacks before we went to bed. My snacks were my crunchy, tasty dental treats. They seem to be the only snack my human ever gets for me. I don't know what my human had, but it didn't smell nearly as good as my treats.

Day 337, Friday, September 27, 2019:
As usual, I got up for my morning prowl while my human was still in bed. Instead of waiting for him in the basement, I went back upstairs and got on the bed with him after I finished my cat stuff. He gave me a nice belly rub until he finally got out of the bed. As soon as he did, I ran downstairs and waited for him. I didn't get any lap time this morning, though. I guess he thought staying in bed and giving me a belly rub was enough to replace lap time. Perhaps tomorrow I should be more insistent.

I spent the day keeping an eye on my territory, except when I slept. I took a nap on top of the big cat tree.

When my human arrived home, he didn't come into the house right away. I went to the front window to look for him. I saw him walking all over the driveway with a big stick. The stick had a long, flat, bushy piece on the end.[103] I watched him push the bushy piece all over the driveway. I wondered why he played with that stick instead of coming inside and preparing my meal.

Fortunately, he didn't play with the stick for very long, and as soon as he finished with the stick, he came inside. That's when I discovered he had gone hunting for me today. He brought lots of my food into the house. Both kinds! There was a big bag that had the dry, crunchy kind and a tray with many cans of the wet kind. He put my food in the small room near the kitchen and immediately started making our dinners.

Soon after our meals, we had some snacks. Like last time, I had yummy, crunchy treats.

Before we went to bed, we stopped by the big window in the front room and looked outside. There was a lot of water falling from the sky. There were also a lot of loud sounds and bright flashes. It was kind of mesmerizing, but a little scary.

Day 338, Saturday, September 28, 2019:
My human slept in today. I was in the basement, expecting him to show up, but he never did. I went back upstairs and found him still on the bed, long after he should have been in the basement providing a lap for me. I sat at the top of the pet steps and stared at him. That got him up.

With him now moving around, I decided to try again. I went to the basement and waited for him. This time, he showed up and made a lap for me. I enjoyed a nice long back massage. After my back rub, I stayed in the basement while my human went upstairs, only to return a few minutes later. He brought that loud stick with the really long tail. When I saw him shove its tail into the wall, I knew what would happen next. Sure enough, the thing started to growl. I watched for a little bit but then left the room. I waited upstairs, away from the noise.

While in the upper room, I played with a pom-pom and a mouse on the cat tree. After my human finished wrestling with that long-tailed beast, he came to the upper room, too. I saw him put the blanket

---

[103] A broom.

on his lap, so I went over and took advantage of it. I lay down on his lap and rested on one of his front paws. I have found lying on his paws to be very comfortable.

After our snuggle session, I hopped down to the floor and took a bath. Then I went to the front room and sat on the bench. Looking out the window, I was entertained by some squirrels that were climbing on the tree near the road. It looked like one of them was having a snack.

Back upstairs, I played with some of my toys on the cat tree while my human worked on the other side of the room. He got up and started to come toward me. That startled me, so I ran out of the room.

This afternoon, I took some naps on the big cat tree. That was exhausting, so after that, I decided to sleep for a while on the small cat tree in the upper room. Between some of my naps, I went to the front room and watched more water fall from the sky.

During the evening, I stretched out on the floor of the upper room while my human played with his metal discs. I also looked out the window in the storage room. I did that while my human tortured himself in the small room where water fell on him. Being in the storage room let me be close to him (just across the hall) without having to be in the same room to witness his suffering.

Day 339, Sunday, September 29, 2019:
This was a pretty chill day. I spent some time on my human's lap before he left to work at the shelter. When he returned, he slept on the sofa. That was a bit unusual for him, so I did something unusual, too. I went upstairs and rested on the floor of the bedroom.

Later in the afternoon, I found my human sitting up on the sofa. I talked to him briefly, then curled up near him. He gave me an occasional belly rub as I stretched out near his right arm.

Early in the evening, I left my human on the sofa and went to the basement. I didn't hear him get up. A bit later, I went back upstairs, but he wasn't there. I went up farther and found him in the upper room. Even better, I found my dinner there! Why didn't he come get me when he made dinner? It didn't matter. I was just happy to have a tasty meal.

Later in the evening, we had some snacks. I followed that up with a nap on the upper room floor.

Day 340, Monday, September 30, 2019:
I saw something strange today. As I observed my territory from the basement, some movement caught my attention. It was big! It was . . .

a car? Why was there a car in the backyard? The car was between my
territory and the dirt lady's territory. I hunkered down and watched it
intently. Then I saw the dirt lady get out of it. She went to the back of
the car and removed many bags from it. She put the bags on the
ground. After that, she got back into the car and disappeared out of
sight along with the car. Moments later, my human appeared in that
same part of the yard. He was carrying some sticks. He dropped the
sticks on a pile of other sticks and then came over to the door and
talked with me. I couldn't quite hear him through the door. I talked
back to him, but I'm not sure he heard me.[104] Then he disappeared
around the other side of the house. I next heard him in the car room, so
I ran up the steps and met him at the door.

Checking out some catnip.

I got to look in the cabinet under the bathroom sink again today,
but this time, my human opened both of the doors for me. There are
still a bunch of those rolls of white paper in there.

This evening, I sat on the floor of the upper room and stared at
the doorway, watching things my human couldn't see. He got up and

---

[104]When I arrived home, I picked up some sticks that had fallen on the lawn and
moved them to a pile in the back just after my neighbor finished unloading
gardening supplies. When I made my way to the backyard, I saw that Blackie had
been watching her.

left the room. He came back a minute later with a small plate and set it on the floor in front of me. Catnip! I knelt down and sampled it. Then I lifted my head up and swung it about. The good stuff! I licked up some more and also rubbed the sides of my head on the plate. It had been a while since I had last partaken in some catnip, so I really enjoyed it.

The catnip was excellent.

After getting zonked out from catnip, I needed to rest. I stretched out under the table for quite some time. I didn't get up until my human left the room. I followed him as he went to the kitchen, but I stopped in the front room. There, I found my yellow mouse from the basement. I had left it near the door to the car room several days ago. How did it get here? I tossed it around the room and chased it for a bit. I got startled and ran up the steps to the hallway when my human came back through the room. My human tossed the mouse up to the landing. I couldn't help but pounce on it. When he started to walk up the steps, I left the mouse and took off for the upper room. He followed me and apparently had picked the mouse up on his way there because the next thing I knew, it was flying over my head. I chased it a bit longer before I climbed up to the table and looked out the tall window.

I ended the evening resting on the table while my human typed away at the computer.

Day 341, Tuesday, October 1, 2019:
I spent some time on my human's lap using the blanket today. I used to use the blanket on the chair a lot, but now I only use it when my human puts it on his lap.

I wasn't very active this evening. I just wanted to be near my human while he worked on the computer. I lay down on the floor near him for a while. I also stretched out under the table. There used to be some plastic containers under the table. They had been there as long as I'd lived here, but a few days ago, my human moved them into the closet. Ever since then, I've tried to make good use of the floor space under that table.

After stretching out on my side, I got back on my paws and shrank to the "hover cat" pose, with all of my paws tucked under me.

Day 342, Wednesday, October 2, 2019:
This was a great day! I had snacks twice! The first one happened right after dinner. When I saw my human go to the kitchen and heard him fix a snack for himself, I ran after him and made sure he fixed one for me, too. He did! We went back to the upper room to enjoy our snacks. Later in the evening, he went back to the kitchen and got another snack. Had he forgotten that we already had snacks? No matter, I got to enjoy a second snack.

After our snacks, we played the mouse game on the scratching post for a little bit. I sat on the platform atop the post and batted the mouse down to him when he tossed it up to me.

We didn't play very long because I just wasn't feeling it. Instead, I hopped down and brushed myself against my human. I flopped down onto my side for a massage. My human alternated between rubbing my back and my belly. That's what I really wanted. He lay down on the floor near me and stroked my fur from head to tail. He also massaged my neck and chin. It was a full-body massage. I stretched out and scooted across the carpet on my side, excited to be receiving so much attention.

Later in the evening, I went to the basement and got my orange plastic ring toy. I took it to the main level of the house and played with it on the hard floor near the front door. I liked playing with it there because it slides easily along that floor. Before I went to bed, I put the ring near my human's shoes.

Day 343, Thursday, October 3, 2019:
This morning, I waited in the basement for my human, but he took his

own sweet time for some reason. I heard him making noises at the top of the steps, but he didn't come down for me. Figuring I should investigate, I got up and walked across the room. When I poked my head around the corner, I saw him start to make his way down the stairs. I turned around and ran back into the room to wait for him. I hadn't used my litter pan since it was last scooped the night before. That meant there was nothing for him to do but sit and make a lap for me. Naturally, I climbed aboard as soon as possible.

That wasn't the only strange thing he did today. When he arrived home, he spent too much time in the car room before he came inside. I've learned that when that happens, I can often see him from the front window. I went there, and sure enough, I saw him outside. He came over to the window and waved a paw at me. Then he disappeared back into the car room and finally came into the house. I think my human might be a little strange.

This evening, I sat with my human on the floor of the upper room. He wanted to play, but I didn't. Instead, I just wanted to snuggle. As soon as he folded his legs and sat on the floor, I crawled onto his lap and lay down for some attention. His paws stroked my fur for a long time.

After I had my fill of attention (for the time being), I got down from his lap and took a bath. That was, until my human got up and went to the kitchen. I followed him but stopped in the front room and climbed atop my scratching post. I figured he was getting us some snacks. I was right! When he walked back through the front room, I could tell he had snacks in his paw, so I leaped from the post and ran past him on the steps. I walked to the mat near his chair, where he always sets my dinner and snacks. He put three crunchy dental treats on the mat for me.

After I enjoyed my treats, I went to my water dish for a drink. The water was fresh because my human had just cleaned and filled it.

With tasty treats in my belly and some fresh water, I was ready to play. I grabbed one of my new mouse toys and gave it a toss. I chased it all over the upper room, into the hallway, back to the upper room, near my cat tree, and even near my paper bag. I had a good time. I also played with a few other toys that I keep on the floor of that room.

After my exercise, I resumed my bath. Once I was clean, I rested in the spot I like under the table.

Before we went to bed, I talked with my human. He was at the computer and didn't seem to be paying much attention to me. I sat on the table behind him and stared at him. He finally turned to me and said he'd get cleaned up and then we'd go to bed. I trilled in agreement.

We didn't go to bed right away, though. I lay on the upper room floor, minding my own business, when I heard something that made me perk up. A door opened! I bolted from the room and ran to the storage room just as my human was closing the door to the tiny room near the window. I stopped and looked disappointedly at the closed door, but not for long. My human opened the door again, so I slipped in there and explored. It was a fun way to end a great day.

Day 344, Friday, October 4, 2019:

It was a bit colder last night than it had been previously. To help stay warm, I spent almost the whole night snuggled next to my human. It was still relatively cool during the day, too, so to warm up, I got some exercise by chasing my bright-yellow mouse. It was the one my human had brought to the upper room a few days ago. I played with it in the upper room, chased it down the hallway, and down the steps to the front room. I also played with my black string everywhere from the upper room to the kitchen.

I was in the basement, looking out the window, when my human came home. He was earlier than normal. I didn't expect that and got a bit spooked when I heard someone coming down the steps. I turned with my tail puffed out, but then I saw that it was my human. I relaxed and unpuffed my tail. After we talked for a bit, he suggested we go upstairs for some food. I followed him and made my way to the scratching post in the front room, where I waited patiently. Fortunately, it didn't take him long to prepare our meals this evening. On his way through the room, he stopped briefly so I could sniff my plate of food. I jumped down, passed him on the steps, and got to the upper room long before he did. I ate half of my meal, saving the rest for later, and returned to window watching in the basement.

I talked with my human when he came down to the basement and took care of my litter pan. I wanted to sit on his lap when he finished, but I didn't have the chance, at least not at first, because he picked me up. He held me close to his chest. I was annoyed and pushed away, but I was stuck because he had a good grip on me. He sat down and rolled onto his back with me still on his chest. He finally let me go. I walked across his stomach many times and brushed the side of my body against his legs. I hopped down after several minutes. As soon as he sat up, I climbed aboard his lap and lay down. He gave me a back rub and also massaged my chin and neck.

After I received my fill of affection, I walked off his lap. He went back upstairs. I stayed in the basement for a bit longer but soon followed him to the upper room. I finished my meal and then played with one of my new mousies. I had a lot of fun tossing it in the air and chasing it all over the upper room until it got stuck. One of its airborne journeys ended with it landing in a plastic bag that was inside a rectangular bin. It was one of those plastic bags that my human picked up every so often and put into a bigger plastic bag. I hoped I could get my mousie free from there before that happened. Thankfully, my human noticed my predicament and fetched the mouse for me. He gave it a toss, and I resumed the chase. I also played with the bright-green mouse before bedtime.

Day 345, Saturday, October 5, 2019:
Days like this, where my human is home all day, are really nice. I made several trips onto his lap today. While we were in the upper room this morning, I got on top of the scratching post. My human came over and sat on the floor near me. He tossed a toy mouse up to me. I guess he wanted to play, but I just wanted his lap. I hopped down and crawled onto his legs.

My human surprised me soon after we had lunch. I was sitting on the table in the upper room when he got up and went to the kitchen. When he returned, he had a snack for me. Instead of placing it on the floor, he put it on the table right in front of me. After snack time, I stretched out under the table and kept an eye on my human as he worked nearby.

This afternoon, I followed my human to the living room. I wasn't sure what he was doing, but I was determined to get more lap time. I convinced him to sit on the floor for me. I enjoyed a back rub while I lay on his lap.

We had some fun today, too. I ran around the front room a little bit, and I guess my human wanted to do the same. He chased me up the stairs and down the hall. I'm a lot faster than him, so I made it to the upper room before him, although he was surprisingly close behind me. Once in the upper room, I turned to the side and puffed my tail out. He stopped chasing me, laughed, and knelt down near me. I un-puffed my tail and received another back massage.

This evening, I enjoyed a plate of catnip, after which I relaxed on the floor. I was just lying there, resting up before bedtime, when I heard my name on the radio again. I perked up. How did the lady on the radio know my name?

Day 346, Sunday, October 6, 2019:
After my morning lap time in the basement, my human left for the shelter. It was somewhat cool, so after a while, I returned to the bed-room. I took a nap on the bed because the bed was warmer than other parts of the house. I didn't get up until my human returned. He was later than normal, so I had a nice long nap.

Once he returned home, my human prepared lunch for us. After I ate, I made a couple of trips onto my human's arms while he was at the computer. I also curled up on his legs a few times when he had his legs stretched out with his hind paws up on my blanket chair.

Late in the afternoon, I sat on the bench by the front window. I saw the dirt lady riding in circles on her loud machine. She slowly made her way from the grass in front of her house to the grass in front of mine. I also saw my human go outside with his loud stick that he likes to drag along the edges of the grass. These humans were enter-taining.

Day 347, Monday, October 7, 2019:
It was kind of cold again last night, so when we went to bed, I slept on one of my human's front paws. His paw was warm, plus I just liked being close to him. I got up in the middle of the night for a while but returned and snuggled next to him for most of the night. I got up as the sun rose and went to wait for him in the basement.

My human had left the door to the cold floor room open all night. During one of my nighttime prowls, I found a bug.[105] I caught it and ate it but left one of the legs because there wasn't much meat on it.

That wasn't the only bug I found today. This morning, I got onto the table near the computer and looked out the tall window. I saw a tiny bug on the window. I tried to get it, but it was on the other side.

My human stayed home today. I spent some time near him in the upper room. I also asked him to sit on the floor so I could use his lap. I will sit on his lap anywhere, but my current favorite place is

---

[105] A cricket.

when he sits on the floor. This morning, he sat on the floor in the upper room and leaned against the sliding doors. I enjoyed a long session on his lap.

There were some entertaining things outside today. First, I saw a truck and a human in front of the dirt lady's house. Later, I saw a squirrel in my yard close to the driveway.

My human left the house briefly this afternoon. While he was gone, I returned to the warm bed for a nap. When he came home, we had dinner. After that, I sat on his lap until I heard some strange sounds coming from above. It sounded like something was walking on the roof.[106] I got up from my human's lap and went over to the tall window, but I couldn't see what it was. The sound stopped, so I wasn't too concerned.

My human got up and left the room while I was at the window. When he returned, he had something for me—a snack! He set it on the table near the computer, and I gobbled it up. After that, I retreated to the blanket chair to relax.

Later in the evening, I followed my human to the living room. It looked like he was going to sit on the sofa, so I thought I would join him. He walked around a bit and moved the blanket and some pillows, but he didn't sit down. He just kept moving back and forth and tried to move the blanket I was walking on. He didn't lie down until I hopped up to the shelf behind the sofa. Once he was settled under the blanket, I got back on the sofa and curled up behind his legs. I think he fell asleep. I got off the sofa but stayed in the room and kept watch over him. After a while, he rolled onto his back. I jumped back onto the blanket and curled up on his chest.

Day 348, Tuesday, October 8, 2019:
I spent some time in the basement today, looking out the window to see if any of my friends would stop by. I also surveyed my territory from the front room. Benny and his human stopped by briefly and left something at the front door.

---

[106]Possibly a squirrel.

The package I received from Benny.

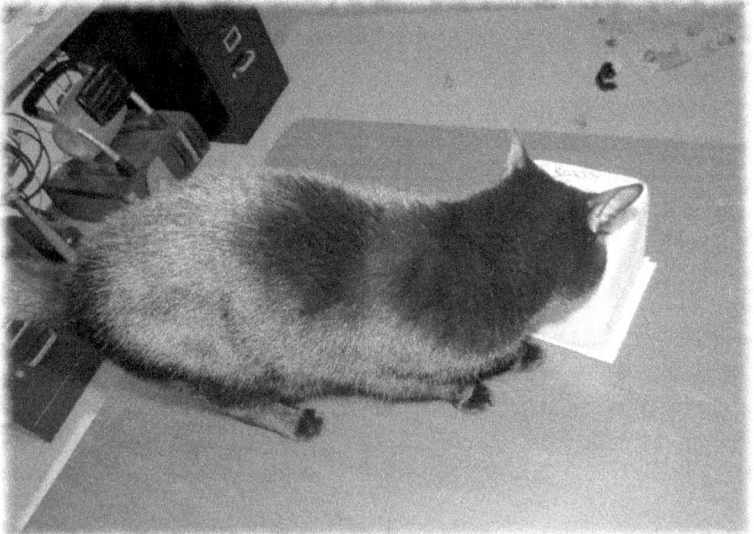

Carefully inspecting the package from Benny.

It's a cup.

I WORK HARD SO MY CATS CAN LIVE A BETTER LIFE

Benny's gift is a nice reminder for my human.

This evening, I wanted my dinner, but it was delayed because my human came home later than normal. When he finally got here, he had a white box grasped between his paws. I followed him upstairs, where he set the box down on the table. He said it was a gift for me from Benny. For a while, I forgot all about my late meal. My human helped me open the box. It was a cup similar in shape to others that my human uses. This one has some cats on the side and a reminder in human words about his purpose in life. What a great thing for my human to see every day! Thanks, Benny! Maybe you're okay after all.

Back to my missing meal. I followed my human to the other side of the house. I stayed in the front room while he worked in the kitchen. That was, until I heard the sound of a small can open. Then I ran into the kitchen and asked for my meal right away. He set my plate on the floor. I ate half of my meal in the kitchen and then waited for him to take both of our plates to the upper room before I finished the rest.

When I got done eating, I played in the front room for a while. After that, I went to go see my human but decided not to climb onto his lap or arms. Instead, I went to the blanket chair. I had to share the blanket with my human's hind paws. That was all right with me since his paws were near the edge of the chair and out of my way.

I tried to doze off, but a bell sound caught my attention. It sounded a lot like what I hear before humans appear at the front door. I sat up and looked toward the television.[107] My human still had his paws up on my chair and didn't seem to react to the sound. That was weird. I lay back down on the blanket and resumed my nap.

Day 349, Wednesday, October 9, 2019:
I met my human at the car room door today. He was home a bit later than usual, and I was hungry. I followed him to the kitchen and made sure he fixed dinner.

It was still a bit cool, so after I ate, I rested on the blanket chair. The blanket helped me stay warm. Not long after that, I noticed my human left the room. It sounded like he went to the kitchen. Maybe for a snack? I got up and quickly made my way to the other side of the house. He certainly was in the kitchen, and it looked like he was getting something for himself. I asked for a snack, too, so he got a few of my dental treats out of the tiny room. We went back upstairs and ate our snacks.

---

[107]It was the sound of a doorbell on the television.

Later, my human left the room but quickly returned. When he did, he sat down on the floor and tossed a mousie to me. I watched and took a couple of steps toward it but didn't chase after it. He then picked up that stick that has three soft string things and swung it about the room. It was entertaining watching him play with my toys.

He also picked up one of my fishies and wiggled it toward me. I walked over to him and sniffed it. I guess he was done playing because he got up and went over to his chair. I played with the fish by myself. I tossed it into the air and chased it around the room. I also found the other fish and played with it, too.

After I got my exercise, I went back to the blanket chair and rested. Later in the evening, I hopped down and walked a few steps over to my human. I jumped onto his lap and got him to position one of his arms for me to lie on. I spent over an hour on his arm.

Day 350, Thursday, October 10, 2019:
During the night, my human rolled over. He does that a lot. Sometimes when it happens, I'll lean up against him, but this time I moved to the other side of the bed. He eventually rolled over again and gave me his paw. Unfortunately, I didn't get very much time on his paw because he got up earlier than normal.

I spent a lot of time looking outside today. It was rather dark out there. Water fell from the sky. I was happy when my human returned home so I could sit on his arms and just be near him.

I followed my human to the basement this evening. While there, he scooped my litter pan. I kept an eye on him but also played with a green pom-pom ball. I tossed it into the air near the curtain by my window. It was fun until I got a claw stuck on the curtain. It took a bit of work to free it. Once I did, my human tossed the green ball across the room. I chased it.

While in the basement, I watched as my human recovered some toys that had gotten stuck under a wall of books. There were several balls and one of those springy things.

Day 351, Friday, October 11, 2019:
Last night, I slept on my blanket chair for a while. I saw my human off to bed, but as soon as he was settled in, I hopped down and went to my blanket chair. I stayed there for half the night until my human got up and came into the room. He talked to me and stroked my head and back. Then he went back to the bedroom. I got up and followed him. I snuggled between his body and one of his front paws.

Today, I got a lot of exercise. For a while, I played with my bright-yellow mouse on the staircase near the car room. I also played with my white string all over the house. While I was in the basement, I batted around one of the multicolored pom-poms.

My human arrived home a little earlier than I expected. I went to greet him, but he was already upstairs. I found him in the bedroom. He said we should get some food, so we left and went to the kitchen. We even had some snacks after our regular meal.

I played in the upper room this evening while my human worked on the computer. I chased one of my older mouse toys around the room.

After playing, I went to the basement and looked out the window for a while. I returned to the upper room later so I could be near my human. I took a bath on the blanket chair and then settled in for a nap.

Settling in on my blanket chair.

Day 352, Saturday, October 12, 2019:
It was a good thing I sat on my human's lap for a long time this morning because he left the house and was gone much longer than normal. Once he returned, I made sure I received more lap time. I also spent a lot of time on the blanket chair because it keeps me warm on these cool days.

My human tried to play with me today while I sat atop the scratching post in the upper room, but it was just a trick by me. I thought if I sat there and acted like I wanted to play, he'd get some toys, sit on the floor, and toss them up to me. That's exactly what he did. Humans are so predictable. I wasn't interested in playing, though. Instead, I just wanted him to sit on the floor so I could enjoy his lap.

We snuggled for a while, but we ended up playing after all. I got back on top of the post and batted at the mice that he tossed up to me.

When I was done playing, I went back to the blanket chair for a nap.

Day 353, Sunday, October 13, 2019:
My human was gone again today. While he was away, I played with my black string. I also looked out the basement window and watched for Benny and the buff tabby.

When my human returned, he went to the basement and opened the door to the cold floor room. I shot in there before he could do anything about it. While he worked with the big white boxes, I went on the prowl for some cobwebs. I found some, too!

Back upstairs, my human attempted to clean my whiskers. I resisted at first but eventually relented. Soon after that, I got to enjoy a snack. We hadn't even had dinner yet!

While my human sat on his chair in the upper room, I sat on the table near him and looked out the tall window. There was a good show today. There were many birds in the tree.

Later in the evening, I got onto my human's lap while he worked on the computer. After that, I hopped down and took a bath near his hind paws. Then I went to the blanket chair for a brief nap before bedtime.

Day 354, Monday, October 14, 2019:
This morning, I not only lay on my human's lap for a while, but I also climbed onto his arms and snuggled close to him before he left for work. That was fun! I really enjoyed the extra time I was able to spend with him.

After he went to work, I stayed in the basement. I looked out the window and played with some pom-pom balls.

When my human arrived home, he spent a little time outside before he came into the house. I watched him from the front window. He picked up some sticks and took them around to the side of the house out of my view. He returned empty pawed a moment later.

We had dinner in the upper room once he came inside. After I finished dinner, I noticed he was still sitting on his chair but had his legs stretched out and his hind paws up on my blanket chair. I hopped onto his legs and stretched out for a while.

Later in the evening, I curled up on the blanket chair for a nap, but I got up when I heard my human go to the kitchen. When he returned, he had a snack for me. I gobbled it up and returned to the blanket chair to resume my nap.

Day 355, Tuesday, October 15, 2019:
It sure can be hard to get in bed with my human sometimes. Last night, I waited on the bed as he put on his nighttime clothing. I wanted to be as close to him as possible, so I walked over to him. He walked to the other side of the bed, so naturally, I followed him. He took the long way around because he walked on the floor. I took the more direct route straight across the bed. Then he walked back to where he started, and of course I did likewise. I looked up at him and wondered why he wouldn't just get into the bed already. He walked toward the end with the pet steps, and I followed him some more, but then he quickly moved back, pulled the blankets down, and got between the sheets and partially under the blankets. His paws weren't petting me, so I went over to him, lowered my head, and brushed it against his paws. He petted me briefly but then reached for the blankets. I climbed up the blankets to get my head closer to one of his paws again. And again, he stroked the top of my head briefly before he grabbed the blankets. Why couldn't he just leave the blankets alone and pet me already? It can be so annoying and challenging sharing a bed with a human.

He eventually got settled in and stopped moving the blankets. Finally, he extended one of his arms and gave me a front paw to snuggle. I really wanted to snuggle with one of his paws because it was one of those rather cool nights.

The morning was a bit cold, too, while I sat at the basement window and surveyed my territory. It warmed up throughout the day. That made my window observation time more pleasant.

My human came home late today. Fortunately, he immediately came into the house and prepared our meals. He even put my plate on the kitchen floor so I could start eating while he finished fixing his own food. Once his meal was ready, he took both of our plates to the upper room.

This evening, I spent a lot of time in my human's arms. I spent time on his legs when he stretched them out and rested his hind paws on my blanket chair.

Between snuggle sessions, my human and I had some snacks.

Day 356, Wednesday, October 16, 2019:
This morning, I snuggled in my human's arms in the basement. When I did that, he scooted over and leaned against a bookcase. He held me closely and stretched his legs out. I normally sit on his lap in the morning, but sitting in his arms was fun, too. We spent more time together this morning than we normally do. Maybe I should climb into his arms more often.

As usual, I spent some time today keeping an eye on things from my various windows. Unlike yesterday, it didn't warm up much.

After dinner, I went to the tall window to get an overview of things in the backyard. Then I went down to the basement for a closer look. When I returned to the upper room, I used my scratching post and then sat near its base. My human came over and sat near me. He played with a couple of my little toy mice, including one that makes a neat sound whenever it moves. It was entertaining watching him play with them. Once he was done, I went over to him and sat on his lap.

Later in the evening, I found my human in the kitchen. He had a cabinet door open near the sink. I hadn't seen that door open in quite some time, so I had to climb in there and check it out. There were boxes and containers in there, but there was enough room for me to crawl all the way in. There wasn't much interesting in there, but it was my job to check it out as part of the continual survey of my territory.

Day 357, Thursday, October 17, 2019:
I did something a bit different this morning. Instead of lying across my human's lap when he came to the basement, I lay on his lap and arm while curled up into a ball. The tip of my tail rested against my nose. It was cozy and *very* comfortable. I stayed on his lap much longer than normal.

I spent the day resting on the blanket chair and occasionally looking out the basement window. When my human came home, I played with my plastic ring near the front door while he prepared some food. After dinner, I rested on the blanket chair while my human worked on the computer. I got up from the blanket chair when my human brought a snack to the upper room for me.

Something out of the ordinary happened this evening, too. After my human got out of that small room where water falls on him, instead of going to bed, he returned to the upper room. He sat on his chair and put his hind paws up on my blanket chair. I took the opportunity to jump onto his lap and climb into his arms. We snuggled for a long time before we went to bed.

Day 358, Friday, October 18, 2019:
Like yesterday, my morning basement time with my human was a little unusual. Only this time, after I was on his lap for a while, he kicked his hind paws out from under him and rolled onto his back. At that point, I walked back and forth across his stomach.

Things got interesting this evening, too. When my human came home, he prepared our meals and took them to the upper room. After I finished mine, I caught a whiff of an enchanting fishy aroma. I got onto the table to check it out. I could smell it, but I couldn't find the source. I went back to the floor and sniffed around. The odor was stronger at that bin with the plastic bag that my human takes to the car room every so often.[108] At that point, my human removed the bag from the plastic bin and proceeded to do just that. I also saw him move a small container from the table and place it high up on a shelf in the closet.[109] I got on top of my scratching post and could still smell it. The odor faded away with time.

With that pleasant aroma gone, I turned my attention to getting some exercise. I played with a big puffy white mouse in the front room.

Day 359, Saturday, October 19, 2019:
This morning, I spent some time in the basement, but when my human didn't show up when I expected, I went searching for him. I found him in the bedroom. At least he was up. I got onto the bed and asked him to sit so I could use his lap for a bit. He did, but I didn't stay there very long.

I followed him to the kitchen and looked around the room while he cleaned and filled the bowls for my water and dry food. He was still working on those when I went to the front room to play with a multicolored pom-pom.

This afternoon, I took a bath and then a nap on the blanket chair. I also sat at the top of the pet steps near my scratching post and waited

[108]The bag contained the paper seal from a container of Omega-3 fish oil capsules.
[109]Moving the container of capsules outside of her reach.

for my human to play. He put various mousies on top of the scratching post, and I'd bat them down. I had a good time, but then I realized my human was sitting on the floor without me on his lap. I walked across the post, hopped down to the floor near him, and got onto his lap.

Later in the afternoon, I followed him to the living room and asked him to sit there, too. He did, and we enjoyed several minutes together until he made a sudden movement and a loud noise.[110] That startled me enough that I jumped from his lap and got away from him.

Something really fun happened this evening. My human and I were in the upper room, doing our own things, when some movement in the small, mostly dark room near my water dish caught my attention. I went over there and found a bug. It was thin but long. It was next to a weird-looking wall that I had never really paid close attention to. The wall was kind of clear but very wavy. There was metal on all sides of the wall, and some in the middle.[111] It looked like there might be another room on the other side of it, but I couldn't tell. I poked at the bug a few times. Eventually, my human came over, turned the light on, and asked me what I was doing. I didn't say anything but kept my attention in the corner near that strange wall. Then the wall moved! Half of it slid behind the other half and revealed a tiny room with a small metal circle in the middle of the floor. With the wall out of the way, the bug had nowhere to hide. I chased it into that little room. I whacked at it a few times, but it kept moving. My human left but came back a moment later with something in his paw. He entered the tiny room with me and went after the bug. He must have gotten it because I didn't see it again after that.

I kept a close watch on that tiny room the rest of the evening, just in case that bug (or another one) showed up.

Day 360, Sunday, October 20, 2019:
I got up early today because my human got up early. In fact, I was still on the bed when he got up. I followed him around the house as he performed his morning routine. That, of course, included going to the basement to take care of my litter pan. Once he was done with that, he sat down for me. I climbed aboard his lap and enjoyed his gentle caressing until I got distracted by something else: another bug. It was a tiny one, and it was crawling along the floor near the edge of the pads that my litter pan rests on. I got up and checked it out. My human got

---

[110]A sneeze.

[111]A translucent sliding shower door.

up, too. I lost track of the bug but then saw my human get it and eliminate it.

My human said he had to go to the shelter. While he was gone, I
looked out the basement window and also watched for more bugs.

When my human came home, he fixed our meals. After I ate, I
returned to the basement because the door to the cold floor room was
open and I wanted to explore in there some more. There weren't many
cobwebs this time.

Later in the afternoon, I went back to the upper room and spent
some time on the blanket chair. I also looked out the tall window. I got
really excited when I saw a bug near it. I couldn't get to it because it
was on the other side of the glass, but I put my paws on the window to
let that bug know it wasn't welcome here.

I played with the white mouse again today. I also played with
the orange plastic ring. I had a good time chasing it all the way down
the stairs and into the basement.

As the evening wound down, I rested on the floor of the upper
room and kept an eye on my human. He was busy at the computer, so
I went to the blanket chair for a bath and a nap.

Day 361, Monday, October 21, 2019:
It was sort of cool today, so after surveying my territory from the
basement window, I returned upstairs. I spent a good part of the day
resting on the warm bed.

My human didn't come into the house right away when he came
home, so naturally I went to the front window to investigate. I saw
him walking all over the driveway, pushing that stick again.[112] Once he
finished, the driveway appeared cleaner.

I followed him upstairs when he came inside. He said he'd get
some food for me and left the room. I followed him but stopped in the
front room. After our meals were ready, we went to the upper room to
eat.

I rested on the blanket chair tonight. I also climbed onto my human's arms and snuggled with him before I went back to the front
room to play.

I followed my human to the basement later in the evening. I had
a hunch that he would open the door to the cold floor room again, so I
stayed close behind him. Sure enough, after he cleaned my litter pan,
he opened that door. I shot into the cold floor room before he even got

---

[112]Sweeping acorns off the driveway.

one paw past the threshold. He's so slow. I turned right and went on the prowl for cobwebs, while he turned left toward those big white boxes he likes to put his clothing in. I hung out in that room for a while even after he left.

Day 362, Tuesday, October 22, 2019:
My human stayed home today, which seemed out of the ordinary. I was happy to have him here.

This morning, I spent some time looking out the front window. There wasn't much activity today. I didn't even see any squirrels.

I went to the upper room, where my human was working with some paper.[113] He gave me a couple of long, thin strips to play with. They had a bunch of holes, which made them easy to grab. It was different and fun to play with something that was normally one of his toys. I played with the paper for a while and then took a nap on the blanket chair.

I was still sleeping on the blanket chair when some commotion woke me up. I noticed my human left the room and closed the door on his way out. That was odd. I sat up on the blanket and tried to figure out what was going on. Soon, he returned. When he opened the door, he was holding my travel pod! I leaped from the blanket chair and hid under the table. He put my travel pod on the table and then got down on all four paws. He picked up one of my mousies and played with it for a bit. He offered it to me. I was intrigued, but didn't fall for it. I let my guard down briefly, and then he grabbed me! I tried to avoid entering the travel pod, but he overpowered me. I made it very clear to him that I didn't want this.

He took me to the car room and then put me in the car. We only drove for a few minutes, but I told him off nearly the whole ride. Then I noticed we had arrived at my doctor's office. The last time I was there, my human brought a bag with my supplies and one of my short cat trees, but I didn't see him take anything from the house except me, so I hoped I wouldn't have to stay there very long.

I waited patiently in the big room of the doctor's office. I kept an eye on the humans behind the counter and another human who came into the building. Then the doctor's assistant appeared in the big room and called my name. My human picked up my travel pod, and we were once again on the move.

---

[113]Removing the tractor-feed strips from fanfold printer paper.

We went to a small room. I remembered briefly visiting a room similar to it soon after I went to live with my human. The door to my travel pod opened. I got out and briefly explored the space. I saw my human sitting on a bench, so I decided to hide under that bench.

A couple of minutes later, my human stood up. The bench moved, and the lady picked me up. I didn't complain because she was very gentle with me. She put me on a platform similar to the one my human occasionally has me stand on. She seemed happy and didn't complain when I stepped off the platform and onto the table. After a few minutes, she left the room. I jumped down from the table and went back to the safe space under the bench. My human got off the bench and sat on the floor near me. I walked over and sat on his lap. I only stayed there a short time and then retreated back under the bench.

Soon, that same lady was back, but she brought the doctor, too. They put me back on the table. There was a towel on the table, which was much nicer to lie on than the bare table. As I lay there, she gave me a full manicure and pedicure. She was also really fast at it. Why couldn't my human be that efficient about it?

They proceeded to take my temperature in a rather rude way. I didn't say a word about it. I wasn't going to give them the satisfaction of yelling. I also didn't say anything when they poked me—twice. After that, they said everything looked good and that I was free to go. I hopped down and went over to my human, who had returned to the bench. I got onto the bench and lay down next to him.

Soon after that, we went back home. Except for getting up to have dinner, I spent the remainder of the day resting on the blanket chair.

Day 363, Wednesday, October 23, 2019:
It was rather cool this morning, so I stayed on the bed near my human. In fact, I didn't get up until he did. Once I saw that he wasn't going to come back to bed, I got up and made my way to the basement. I looked out the window while I waited for him to arrive. I performed my normal morning routine of climbing onto his lap for a back rub before he left for work. Once he left, I went back upstairs and slept on the big warm bed.

Today, I played with a multicolored pom-pom in the front room and kitchen while my human fixed our meals. During the evening, I chased one of my mousies around the upper room. I also played with that piece of paper from yesterday. After I spent a few minutes on my human's lap, followed by a trip to the basement, I returned to the upper room and settled in for a nap on the blanket chair.

Day 364, Thursday, October 24, 2019:
This morning, I followed my human around after he got out of bed. He went to the kitchen, but I stopped in the front room to grab a multi-colored pom-pom. I hit it into the kitchen, then chased it into the living room. With a burst of energy, I ran all the way through the living room, into the front room, and back into the kitchen. There, I found one of the doors below the sink had been opened. I hadn't gotten to look under the sink in a long time, so I stopped my run and approached the opening. There was a lot of stuff in there, so I didn't venture into it.

In addition to the pom-pom, I played with my orange plastic ring. I also batted a ball that had a bell in it. It made a neat noise every time I hit it.

This evening was very relaxing. While my human worked on the computer, I took a nap on the blanket chair. After my nap, I gave myself a bath.

Day 365, Friday, October 25, 2019:
This morning, I came up from the basement to find my human. I saw him in the small room off the hallway that has the human litter device. I left him there and went to survey some more of my territory.

When he went to the kitchen, I followed him. After a good night of resting, I had all sorts of energy, just like I had yesterday. I ran the circuit through the kitchen, living room, and front room. I also played with my white string.

This afternoon, I sat on the bench at the front window and watched my human pick up sticks from the yard. Soon after that, he came inside and prepared a meal for me.

I got double snacks tonight! One was right after my meal, and the second one was later in the evening.

This evening, I relaxed in my human's arms a couple of times. Between trips to his arms, I took a nap on the blanket chair. Before I went to bed, I took a bath near my human's hind paws while he sat on his chair by the computer.

Aftermeow

My human says we've made one full trip around the sun since I moved in with him. Really? I feel like I've barely left the house. I think he meant the sun has made one complete trip around me.

Still, a lot of things have happened in that time. Things were good for me at the shelter, but I'm really glad to have my own house now and my own human. It's great to have so much room to run around and explore. I've even lost some weight and now have a fantastic kitty figure. At the shelter, I had put on a few extra ounces because there wasn't much room for me to exercise.

My house has a lot of vertical spaces for me to explore. That is great because life can be a bit boring when your eyes are only a foot off the ground. Those vertical spaces also provide safe places for me to retreat to when strangers are in my house or when something scary happens.

I love that there are a variety of windows for me to look through, many of which have conveniently placed perches that permit comfortable long-term viewing and surveillance of my territory. There are also many scratching posts that not only let me take care of my claws but also provide additional vertical space for me. I like to sit atop them so I can be closer to my human. And the toys! There are so many things to play with here that a kitty can really wear herself out.

It's also quiet here. There are no young kittens keeping me up all night, nor are there any toms trying to chase me down, not counting the few who might stop by my basement window occasionally. They know better than to come inside. I've made sure of that.

Best of all, it's been wonderful having my very own human. He listens to me when I ask for his lap or for a snack. He never has a meal or snack himself without also providing one for me. He makes sure I always have a supply of fresh water, dry food, and treats that help keep my teeth clean. He has provided many places throughout the house for me to explore, to nap, and to observe. If I want to look inside a cabinet, he'll open the door for me. I also appreciate that he shares his big warm bed with me. I really like snuggling next to him, especially when I can lie down on one of his front paws. He gives me the most fantastic massages and belly rubs. I'm glad that I don't have to share him with any other cats.

My human has also made sure I receive regular checkups from my doctor, even though I don't particularly enjoy those. I think I see my doctor more often than he sees his.

Blackie's Acknowledgments

Many things have happened in my life that have brought me to this point. I'd like to take the time to thank some humans who have helped me along the way.

I'd like to thank the volunteers at Purrfect Pets who treated me so well during my stay there, including (in no particular order) Elaine, Debbie, Devin, Rachel, Jen, Paula, Kymberli, Cody, Mike, Vivian, Margie, Amy, Chelsea, and many others. My apologies if I forgot to list your name.

I'd especially like to thank Elaine for not giving up on me when I had some medical problems and for sharing her home with me while I recovered from surgery. Elaine was very patient with me and good at understanding my needs.

It was always a joy when Devin came to take care of me at the shelter. I loved jumping onto her lap as soon as she opened the door. I had fun with Rachel, too, who would always provide a lap and lots of affection.

Finally, I'd like to thank my human for sharing his home with me. It's a great place for a cat. There are plenty of big windows that provide great outdoor scenes, including trees, birds, squirrels, chipmunks, people, people with dogs, cars, trucks, and interesting things that fall out of the sky. The big tree in the front yard provides hours of entertainment, especially in the autumn when the leaves fall and fly around everywhere.

I also want to thank him for helping me put this journal together. He translated my feline words into human words. The footnotes were added by him to clarify some things.

Jerome's Acknowledgments

Many people have either worked directly on *Blackie's Diary* or have had an impact on Blackie's life in some way that has led to this project. I would like to offer my sincere thanks to:

Elaine Doran, the founder and president of Purrfect Pets Cat Adoptions, the 501(c)(3) nonprofit humane organization that originally cared for Blackie. Elaine understands cats better than anyone I know and makes sure all cats that come to the shelter get the best care possible before they go to their fur-ever homes. She takes the time to make sure each and every cat is matched up with a human who will continue to provide wonderful care.

Devin Araujo, a Purrfect Pets volunteer, whose lap was one of Blackie's favorites when she was at the shelter. Devin was commissioned to create the drawing of Blackie for the cover. Devin also created the drawing that appears on page 5.

Debbie Gafford and Rachel Swezy, who, along with Devin, I have the pleasure of working with as one of the cleaning teams at Purrfect Pets. They were very supportive when I disclosed the development of *Blackie's Diary*.

Jen Zaman, another Purrfect Pets volunteer, who agreed to suffer through an early draft of this work and provided a lot of missing commas. Knowing what she went through for *Buttercup*, I couldn't believe she was willing to do it again for *Blackie's Diary*.

Meg Dendler, an award-winning author, editor, and speaker, who provided advice and editing services, including another large helping of commas.

Sue Tonneson and Lora Cox, for reviews before publishing.

Dr. Natasha "Tash" Taylor, the vet technicians, and the other employees of the Cat Clinic of Johnson County, for providing compassionate care during checkups and boarding. Special thanks go out to Allyson Rollins and Natalie Patton for helping Blackie with her diary entries for the days she was boarded at the clinic while I was out of town. Without their efforts, this collection would have been incomplete.

Thanks, also, to the rest of the folks at Purrfect Pets Cat Adoptions for their fantastic care of Blackie during her time there.

You can help!

There are many fine humane organizations throughout the country that could use your support to help the lives of cats and other domestic animals. Below are two fantastic nonprofit rescue organizations for your consideration.

Purrfect Pets Cat Adoptions, www.purrfectpets.org

Mailing Address:
PO Box 3813
Shawnee Mission, KS 66203

Physical Address:
11425 West 95th Street
Overland Park, KS 66214
Space #50-A

Safe Haven of Iowa County, www.wesavepets.com

Mailing Address:
PO Box 444
Williamsburg, IA 52361

Physical Address:
2783 Highway 6 Trail
South Amana, IA 52334

About the Authors

Blackie is a domestic short-haired cat who grew up in a cat shelter with her sister. She moved around the Kansas City area before making her home in Lenexa, Kansas. She enjoys massages, bird-watching, human-watching, strings, belly rubs, catnip, and chasing balls, toy mice, and toy fishes. She shares her home with a human, whom she has trained to give belly rubs on command.

Jerome Tonneson has spent over twenty-six years in the aviation industry as an electrical and software engineer. He has worked on satellite communication systems, transponders, traffic awareness systems, navigation radios, multi-function instruments, and flight controls. Outside of work, his time is occupied with recreational cycling, numismatics, and technical hobbies involving amateur radio, electronics, high-power rocketry, or any mix thereof. He also spends time metalworking, woodworking, maintaining his acreage, and designing and building cat furniture. Since 2009, he has volunteered at a nonprofit, no-kill, all-volunteer, all-cat animal shelter.

www.ingramcontent.com/pod-product-compliance
Lightning Source LLC
Chambersburg PA
CBHW031829090426
42741CB00005B/176